LORD NELSON.

LOVE LETTERS OF GREAT MEN & WOMEN

FROM THE EIGHTEENTH CENTURY TO THE PRESENT DAY

BY

C. H. CHARLES, Ph.D.

WITH FIFTY-FOUR ILLUSTRATIONS IN HALF-TONE

Martino Publishing
Mansfield Centre, CT
2010

Martino Publishing
P.O. Box 373,
Mansfield Centre, CT 06250 USA

www.martinopublishing.com

ISBN 1-57898-882-9

Cover design by T. Matarazzo

Printed in the United States of America On 100% Acid-Free Paper

LOVE LETTERS OF
GREAT MEN & WOMEN

FROM THE EIGHTEENTH CENTURY
TO THE PRESENT DAY

BY

C. H. CHARLES, Ph.D.

WITH FIFTY-FOUR ILLUSTRATIONS IN HALF-TONE

NEW YORK
BRENTANO'S
1924

Printed in Great Britain

First published in 1924

CONTENTS

GALLANTRY OF THE GREAT IN POLITE SOCIETY.

ENGLAND: STILTED EPISTOLARY ART

LADIES OF THE EIGHTEENTH-CENTURY FRENCH SALONS AND THEIR ADMIRERS.

AIRY MARIVAUDAGE

CONTENTS 5

THE PHILOSOPHERS AND THEIR LADY ADMIRERS

AGE OF CLASSIC ROMANTICISM IN GERMANY

THE FRENCH REVOLUTION

MADAME RÉCAMIER AND HER ADMIRERS

CONTENTS

THE NAPOLEONIC ERA

NAPOLEONIC INFLUENCES

THE ROMANTIC REVIVAL IN ENGLAND

THE ROMANTICS IN FRANCE AND ON THE CONTINENT GENERALLY

THE VICTORIAN ERA

A SYMPOSIUM OF POETS AND MUSICIANS

LIST OF ILLUSTRATIONS

1* 9

LOVE LETTERS OF
GREAT MEN AND WOMEN

THE LOST ART OF LETTER WRITING

THE ultimate end of all social intercourse, says Emerson, is a little high conversation. But the universal solvent of high conversation, that which turns " into shining ether the solid angularity of facts," is the gracious presence of high-bred and charming women who preside as the queens of the tourney over the clash of opinions and safeguard the lists for rule of knightly manners and the laws of courtesy and fair play. For, without their gentle precept and example, men will argue, their opponents wrangle, women gossip, tub-thumpers brawl, Yankees brag, the clergy and schoolmasters dogmatise, children and ill-bred people interrupt and contradict, while the masses, childlike, inquisitive, familiar, sway from cuffs to caresses, " will stand a pint one minute, and black your eye the next."

The Ideal Love-letter.—Letter writing, in its ideal form, is really nothing else but indirect conversation, and love-letter writing, conversation of affection between man and woman. But what is affection ? A love-letter can still be a love-letter, although it does not discourse about love. I have dealt with the " ideal love-letter," as such, in a separate chapter (q.v.), and analysed the difference between young people's letters, those of the middle-aged, and old people's letters, and I maintain that there can be as much love in chops and tomatoes as in a whole cartload of Maréchal Niel roses.

Other Times, Other Love-letters.—So every country, every epoch, every woman, has the love-letters that she deserves. Style is the man, even in effusions of the heart.

Our young people of to-day, flappers and hobblede-hoys, who are all of that stuff which Love is made of, no longer indulge, if at all, in the rambling, rumbling style of the stage-coach era, for the hurry and scurry of modern life, with its switchbacks in kinema, aeroplane, and motor-car, have killed the leisurely habit of dreaming and putting one's dreams on paper. Our modern young people deal in chewing-gum phrases and expectorated word-parings, like United States screen captions : old bean—topping—top hole —priceless—I don't think—gadgets—the wind up— fed up—and then some. A clever continuation writer for the film could manufacture a five-reel love-story out of that.

Thus we are still a tongue-tied nation, in spite of the fountain-pen ; and yet—Love holds its own as the universal topic. What books are read, what plays succeed, what daily happenings interest, but those of the eternal passion, unrequited, thwarted, or rewarded with or without marriage bells ?

Prize for the Best Love-letter.—Which of our young people of to-day can write a love-letter worth keeping ? Cupid's quiver no longer contains those divine missiles which transfixed the heart. To-day people aim at the pocket. " I loves Annie ; Annie loves me ; give us a share in the business."

If I had my way, I would have classes in all the schools to teach our adolescents " in love with loving," not only how to love, but how to say so ; because, in the words of the worldly-wise old French saw, " Il faut non seulement s'aimer, mais il faut aussi se le dire —et bien souvent."

Every Love-letter Writer a Poet—for the Time Being. —To every man, says Emerson, "(love) was the dawn of music, poetry, and art . . . when the moonlight was a pleasant fever, and the stars were letters, and

the flowers ciphers, and the air was coined into song.
. . . Does that other see the same star, the same
melting cloud, read the same book, feel the same
emotion that now delights me ? . . . They try and
weigh their affection, and adding up costly advantages, friends, opportunities, properties, exult in dis-
covering that wilfully, joyfully, they would give all
as a ransom for the beautiful, the beloved head, not
one hair of which shall be harmed."

The reader who has never written such letters,
never received such letters, is greatly to be pitied,
for without such generous altruism, life is but a
Barmecide's feast of empty dishes. Such divine
shamelessness, such passion for self-immolation, is
the essence of the love-letter. It is the subject-
matter of the poet's sonnet to his beloved. All the
best poetry in the world would never have been written
if the lover had obtained his wish and married his
inamorata without let or hindrance. It was the
thwarting of his desires that produced the thoughts
and language which have remained, long after the
charmers who caused them have discovered that the
more durable way to men's hearts is in cooking steak
and potatoes. Complacent, smug possession wet-
blankets the soul, struggling to emerge from its
swaddling-clothes. The nightingale sings no more,
once the eggs are in the nest. Petrarch's sonnets
would never have been written had he married Laura.

*Modern Love-letter Writing Unknown before the
Eighteenth century.*—Modern love-letter writing, such
as we are here concerned with, can hardly have arisen
before the eighteenth century ; for while the seven-
teenth-century salon of Madame de Rambouillet
freed social intercourse from the etiquette of kings
and courts, society was yet practically confined to
the aristocracy, and it was not till the dissemination
of enlightenment brought about by the Encyclopædists with Diderot, and the new air blowing through
the advent of Voltaire, and Rousseau, with his " Return
to Nature," that women were emancipated from their

position as household drudges and conceded equal intelligence and social rights with men.

In England, the Puritans of the seventeenth century had never given their womenkind much scope for intellectual attainments (Milton said, " One tongue enough for a woman "), while the men and women of the Restoration frittered away their time in brainless amusements, orgies of sensuous love or of the table. Beau Nash, in 1703, the arbiter of fashion at Bath, said that all the morning was passed in saying " How d'ye do ? " and all the afternoon in asking " What's trumps ? "

The separation from France during the war after William of Orange's accession led to an increase of boorishness ; nor had the Stuart grace of manner been transmitted to Mary or Anne, or any of the great ladies of the period. It was not till the eighteenth century that the Novel, the new form of fiction, introduced by Richardson and Fielding, held the mirror up to women, and gained its lasting popularity by its presentation and analysis of female individuality. Clarissa, the " Eve of fiction, the prototype of the modern heroine," set the example to the women of her time, with equal rights of independence—of choice, volition, and action—to man. The epistolary vows and virtues of Amelia and her sisters led the way to the literary outpourings of the eighteenth-century women, and especially to their love-letters.

The Age of Good Sense

Pope, 1688–1744 ; Swift, 1667–1745 ; Steele, 1672–1729 ; Sterne, 1713–68.

Of the earliest English love-letters that we quote, those of Pope, Swift, and Steele show hardly any signs of the coming female emancipation. Pope, smooth and ingenious versifier, puts on Homeric pompousness and patronising airs in his literary essays to the sisters Blount. His is the very essence of polish and good sense, but there is not a throb of passion in him.

Swift, savagely irritable and violent, in spite of his sardonic wit, contracts a secret marriage with a woman whom he never sees, except in the presence of witnesses. He treats "Vanessa" (Esther Van-homrigh), who humiliates herself before him, abominably, and is directly responsible for her untimely death. Dick Steele, the writer of frivolous comedies, who becomes a preacher of morality, writes flowery and well-turned compliments to Mrs. Scurlock. So far, the indications of female emancipation and equality are absent ; it is to Germany and France that we have to look for woman as man's equal. Sterne's writings already show deeper feeling, a subtle blending of laughter and pathos. His *grande passion* was Eliza Draper, the wife of a Bombay lawyer.

In Germany : Return to Naturalness

Luise Kulmus, 1700–66; Gotthold Ephraim Lessing, 1729–81.

Luise Kulmus, afterwards to become the celebrated wife of Gottsched, the critic, and arbiter of German literary taste at Leipzig in the early eighteenth century, writes a pattern letter, which can be held up even now as a model to headmistresses of schools for young ladies for use in their classes on good conduct and deportment. She disposes of her day in the most improving fashion, and descants, with the gravity befitting a fellow-citizeness of Kant, on her " philosophic Love."

Lessing, greatest of German critics, dilates to his fiancée, the intellectual and energetic Eva Koenig, on his bad health and hypochondria, and receives a description of her travels in return. It is the age of " Pure Reason."

Dr. Johnson and his Time (1709–84).

There had been something French about Pope and Swift and Steele. Their wit and fine writing, as Addison puts it, consisted "in giving things that are known an agreeable turn." But there was nothing French or agreeable about JOHNSON. With him, as with no one else, English writing, like English dress and the common way of life, became plainer and graver and thought stronger and deeper. Johnson did not make a school. There is no one to put in the same class with him. He stands alone, as an emblem of emancipation from foreign influence into pure Englishry. His attitude towards women is as typically English to-day as it was with him. It was that of good-humoured toleration, provided they ministered to his wants, and kept the ring, while he folded his legs and had his talk out. Stern critics will object that Dr. Johnson's letters to Mrs. Thrale are not love-letters. But neither are those that the average middle-aged Englishman writes to his wife. To him the finest scenery in the world is a well-laid dinner-table. Of course Johnson dignified every subject he touched. He might be plain, but he would never be commonplace, and he certainly carried conviction with him. He laid down the law, even to the ladies, which is exactly what every Englishman longs to do, provided he can carry it off with flying colours. One notices that Johnson, whatever he did at other times, was commonly inclined to put his wig on before he took up his pen. Indeed, as Goldsmith remarked to him once, when Dr. Johnson had laughed at the necessity of making little fishes (in a fable) talk like little fishes : "Why, Dr. Johnson, that is not so easy as you seem to think ; for, if *you* were to make little fishes talk, they would talk like whales." And indeed, when Dr. Johnson let himself go, you could almost see him spouting. For over twenty years he ruled literary London. But he was the very antithesis to the gallant letter writers in high society who, under the influence of Louis XV rococo, threaded their way through pointed phrase and epigram, with the stately obeisances and stilted gestures of a court minuet in the Salle de Glaces at Versailles.

GALLANTRY OF THE GREAT IN POLITE SOCIETY

JOHN CHURCHILL, FIRST DUKE OF MARLBOROUGH
  (1650–1722) ; LORD PETERBOROUGH (1658–1735) ;
  WILLIAM CONGREVE (1670–1729) ; LADY MARY
  WORTLEY MONTAGU (1689–1762) ; HORACE WAL-
  POLE (1717–97) ; GEORGE IV (PRINCE OF WALES,
  1762–1830) ; BEAU BRUMMELL (1778-1840).

A list of these names forms a procession into the realms of powder, paint, and patches, of the eighteenth-century alcove intrigues in the artificial court life of England, which, oblivious of the habits of Farmer George, with his boiled mutton and turnips, took its attitude from the court of Louis the Well-beloved. JOHN CHURCHILL, first Duke of Marlborough, with his magnificent periwig, really dates from the times of Louis XIV, but he heralds the new era, though his letters to his strong-willed wife, Sarah Jennings, show him to have been a very devoted husband to her who made his fortune. CHARLES MORDAUNT, first Earl of Monmouth and third Earl of Peterborough, was a celebrated maker of "*bons-mots* and idle verses," with which he sought to dazzle the beautiful Mrs. Howard (for many years the mistress of George II), while she, on her part, enlists the pen of the poet Gay in self-defence to such fine writing. WILLIAM CONGREVE, author of the magnificent eighteenth-century comedies of manners, who was celebrated for his *bonnes fortunes*, protests his love, amongst others, to Mrs. Arabella Hunt, a public singer. LADY MARY WORTLEY MONTAGU was the typical *précieuse ridicule* of the eighteenth century ; she discourses *de omnibus rebus et de quibusdam aliis* to her prospective husband, Mr. Wortley Montagu. HORACE WALPOLE, in ease, playful wit, racy description and anecdote, variety of topic, is the king of them all. He writes as an elderly gentleman to the charming Misses Berry. Every elderly gentleman (especially when single) needs to hang his heart upon something, and as he says himself, " espoused a couple of helpmeets, but being

2

less provident than the son of David, suffered both to ramble in the land of Goshen, when I most wanted their attendance."

The fitting crown in this atmosphere of irresponsible frivolity must of course be reserved for GEORGE IV, when First Gentleman in Europe, writing his amatory epistles to the beautiful Mrs. Fitzherbert, whom he married in secret in 1795. He hopes that "the haughty yet lovely Margaritta, . . . like the sun may draw some latent blossom from an expiring plant, that otherwise must sink into obscurity." His *fidus Achates*, BEAU BRUMMELL, last of the dandies, only had the organ of love faintly developed, although he had the habit of asking every woman he paid his addresses to to marry him.

But the persistent attentions of the Beau always resulted in failure. "What could I do, my dear fellow," he expostulated on one occasion, "but to cut the connection ? I discovered that Lady Mary actually ate cabbage ! "

This marivaudage was not confined to English high society; it was prevalent all over the Continent, and took its origin from the eighteenth-century rococo style of Louis Quinze. The difference, how- ever, from England was that in Paris female influence was paramount. The salons, *cuo l'on cause*, were always presided over by women of wit and intelligence, who attracted all the most cultured men of their time, and were instrumental in the spread of those new ideas which eventually overthrew the old régime. No other country could boast of such salons.

LADIES OF THE EIGHTEENTH CENTURY FRENCH SALONS
AND THEIR ADMIRERS

NINON DE L'ENCLOS (1616–1706)   MADAME DU BARRY
    (1741–93) ; MDLLE. DE L'ESPINASSE 1732–76) ;
    MADAME DU DEFFAND (1697–1780).

Even celebrated courtesans, in Paris, such as NINON DE L'ENCLOS, seem to have had the gift of holding salons and attracting eminent men. " Love is no more than a play of whim and vanity," declares Ninon to the Marquis de Sévigné. But these eighteenth-century French courtesans always carried on their intrigues in the grand manner.

Even MADAME DU BARRY, launching herself, without any scruples, on a life of pleasure, preserved a certain decorum, scatter-brained and spendthrift as she was. She threw in her lot with the *émigrés*, her intrigue with her last lover, the Duc de Brissac, bringing her to the guillotine.

MADEMOISELLE DE L'ESPINASSE attracted so much attention for her wit and originality at Madame du Deffand's salon, that the old lady, jealous of her younger rival, parted company with her, and Julie de l'Espinasse soon had a salon of her own. Her charming and pitiful letters to the Comte de Guibert, who had thrown her over callously, are considered a classic in French literature. Julie de l'Espinasse died from her un-requited love.

The MARQUISE DU DEFFAND'S salon had been cele-brated from 1740 onwards, as were her *petits soupers*. Her letters, like those of Walpole, to whom she wrote when old and blind, are not love-letters proper, but are witty and shrewd accounts of the happenings in great society of her day. They are valuable documents to the social historian.

PRINCE DE LIGNE (1735–1814).

The sparkling wit of French polite society is admir-ably illustrated in the letters of the PRINCE DE LIGNE, of whom Voltaire's criticism on Marivaux might apply that he knew all the bypaths of the human heart, but not the highways. Attached to the suite of Joseph II of Austria and of Catherine of Russia, he describes his august patrons wittily to his lady-love, the Marquise de Coigny.

CATHERINE II OF RUSSIA (1729–96).

We may here quote the influence of CATHERINE THE GREAT OF RUSSIA, who attracted many of the philosophers to her court, Grimm, Voltaire, Diderot; but this was only an interlude, after her senses had been appeased by her many amours of unbridled licence. We quote, as an example, a letter of the autocratic Empress to an unknown lover.

THE PHILOSOPHERS AND THEIR LADY ADMIRERS
VOLTAIRE (1694–1778); ROUSSEAU (1712–78); DIDEROT (1713–84).

VOLTAIRE is an outstanding figure in this, the wittiest and most cynical of French centuries. He changes his loves as he changes his clothes, and uses them as stepping-stones on his path to success. His most serious affair was, as youthful adorer, with Olympe Dunoyer, in The Hague, but a stern father orders him to return to Paris. The Marquise du Chatelet he loves with a fuller passion, but his letters to her have not been preserved.

ROUSSEAU's love-letters show ungovernable feeling and a return to simplicity. His lack of moral control causes him endless trouble. He became acquainted with the Countess d'Houdetot, and while on the estate of Madame d'Epinay, he wrote his *Héloïse*. To his distress, he realises that she does not love him, but the Marquis de Saint-Lambert. His intercourse with Thérèse Levasseur, a servant-girl, all of whose five children he allows her to send to the foundling hospital, is tragic and sordid.

DIDEROT's idyllic friendship with Sophie Voland strikes a deeper note. The Encyclopædist is concerned about the rising tide of democratic claims, ignored by the frivolous aristocrats, passing their time in rococo gallantry and alcove intrigue.

AGE OF CLASSIC ROMANTICISM IN GERMANY
PESTALOZZI (1746–1827); KLEIST (1777–1811); SCHILLER (1759–1805); GOETHE (1749–1832).

The Swiss reformer, PESTALOZZI, attempted to carry out Rousseau's teaching of a return to nature, educating his own child after the fashion of *Emile*. But Pestalozzi was too much of a sentimentalist; we see that in the correspondence between him and his bride, the seven-years-older Anna Schulthess, daughter of a well-to-do merchant in Zurich, whom he married in spite of her parents' opposition, in 1769.

To the era of Classical Romanticism in Germany belongs HEINRICH VON KLEIST, one of that little band of German Romantic poets around Goethe, and the one great German dramatist after Schiller's death, with his *Penthesilea* and *Kaetchen von Heilbronn*. His relations with Frau Henrietta Vogel, who was suffering from an incurable disease, led him to commit suicide in his thirty-fourth year.

SCHILLER, one of Germany's greatest poets and dramatists, is a most sympathetic figure in literature. Strikingly handsome, he—after liberating himself from the influence of Frau von Kalb—addressed rhapsodies to the two delightful daughters of Frau von Lengefeld, and married one of them, Lotte, in 1790.

GOETHE, in his long life, most of it passed in idyllic peace in the small Grand Duchy of Weimar, was a universal lover. His love-letters are legion, and did not diminish with increasing age, nor did the number of his fair admirers, of whom the best known are Charlotte Buff, Frau von Stein, and Christiane Vulpius.

THE FRENCH REVOLUTION.

From the frivolities of Louis XV period to the Revolution is but a step. Rousseau's *Rights of Man* and the French Encyclopædists had done the work which led to the claim of the proletariat for the Utopia of " Liberty—Fraternity—Equality."

MIRABEAU (1748–91); MADAME ROLAND (1754–93); CAMILLE DESMOULINS (1760–94).

In MIRABEAU's impassioned letters from prison to Sophie de Mounier, the wife of an old judge, with whom he had eloped, are signs of that fascination and personal magnetism by which, later on, he tries to guide the States-General and the unrulier elements of the French Revolution to a constitutional monarchy, and might possibly have succeeded had Louis XVI trusted him.

MADAME ROLAND, beautiful and brilliant hostess of the Girondists, the enthusiastic but visionary party of the early French Revolution, writes from prison, from whence she goes to perish by the guillotine together with the heads of her party, those she loves, Henri Bancal, a Parisian lawyer, and her final lover, the deputy Buzot.

CAMILLE DESMOULINS, revolutionary advocate and friend of Danton, is only thirty-four years old when he goes to the guillotine at the same time as the first of the triumvirate, destroyed by his associates Marat and Robespierre. Through the page of his farewell letter to his wife, Lucile, the portent of death stalks, hollow-eyed and grim. Even in his last words he cannot avoid rhetorical declamation. Like Cato, he would have fallen on his sword, had it not been for the guillotine forestalling him.

MADAME RÉCAMIER (1777–1849); LUCIEN BONAPARTE (1775–1840); BENJAMIN CONSTANT (1767–1830); CHATEAUBRIAND (1768–1848); MADAME DE STAËL (1766–1817).

The story of MADAME RÉCAMIER really constitutes a panorama of the leading people of the times, who frequented her salon and made love to her, always unsuccessfully. LUCIEN BONAPARTE, Napoleon's next brother, retired discomfited after a year's incessant courtship. To BENJAMIN CONSTANT, the French statesman, she was only one of his many affairs. CHATEAUBRIAND did not become assiduous till after the Restoration. Hs was always a favourite of the ladies of the *ancien régime*. MADAME DE STAËL also cultivated a passion for Benjamin Constant.

The Napoleonic Era

Napoleon (1769–1821); Joséphine (1763–1814); Luise of Prussia (1776–1810); Nelson (1758–1805); Bluecher (1742–1819); The Duc de Reichstadt (1811–32).

General Bonaparte, young and unknown artillery officer, writes amidst alarums and excursions love-letters to Joséphine, the charming Creole, to whom he owes his entrance into polite society, and his recommendation to Barras, who puts him in command. His later letters to the Empress take on a more re-proving note, in reply to his own elderly wife, jealous and complaining of her being neglected for other and more charming women. In 1810 the Empress Joséphine writes to him, after her divorce. In spite of his having cast her off, she humbles herself and wishes him all good fortune. Luise of Prussia, William III's beautiful queen, implores her vacillating husband not to give way to Napoleon. Nelson writes to his dear Lady Hamilton before his victory and death at Trafalgar. Field-Marshal Bluecher describes the battle of Leipzig to his wife. Old men's letters, statesmen's letters, or letters from those with a mission in life, express their love, not by the usual juvenile protestations, but by confiding their hopes and plans to the women who understand and sympathise. And finally, to close the era on a note of compassion, we have Napoleon's chained " eaglet," his son, the Duc de Reichstadt, guided and intentionally debauched by Metternich, crafty welder of the Holy Alliance. The younger dreamer confides his hopes of fame and power to his beloved, the Archduchess Sophie.

Napoleonic Influences

Alfieri (1749–1803); Foscolo (1778–1827); Metternich (1773–1859); Béranger (1780–1857).

We have two Italian patriots here, Alfieri and Foscolo, both of them inspired by republican ideals, as a consequence of the French Revolution. ALFIERI, poet of ancient tragedies, driven from France by the Revolution, is deeply attached to Louise von Stolberg, wife of " Bonnie Prince Charlie," the young Pretender. A letter of his to a fair unknown at Siena shows that poets are not distinguished by the fidelity of their affections.   FOSCOLO's republican ideals were quenched by his serving in a Napoleonic army, and eventually he had to fly to England.   He frittered away that fiery ardour of an Italian patriot in his frivolous love-affairs. METTERNICH, his life's work, as counterweight to Napoleon, finished, writes love-letters to the Princess Lieven, wife of the Russian Ambassador in London. BÉRANGER, the perpetuator of the Napoleonic legend in his poems, is a Bohemian in his loves.

THE ROMANTIC REVIVAL IN ENGLAND

BURNS (1759–96) ; HOGG (1770–1835) ; SCOTT (1771–
    1832) ; HAZLITT (1778–1830) ; LEIGH HUNT (1784–
    1859); KEATS (1795–1821); SHELLEY (1792–1822) ;
    BYRON (1788–1824).

" BOBBIE " BURNS, poet of Scotch vernacular, turns his rich and humorous wit to the charms of Mrs. MacLehose, his " Clarinda," for whom he masquerades as " Sylvander," while giving his homely pathos full scope in his outpourings to his dear Elli, the servant-girl.   HOGG, the Ettrick Shepherd, is now regarded as the legitimate heir to Burns ; after waiting ten years he married Margaret Phillips, an acknowledged belle of Edinburgh, who preferred the struggling poet to all others.   Of SCOTT we have really only his disjointed notes, but we quote the very level-headed letters from the young lady whom he married, Miss CHARLOTTE CARPENTER, who advises him not to give up the cavalry, as she loves anything that is " stylish." HAZLITT, the " critics' critic," fond of the ladies, separates from his wife, and falls in love with the tailor's daughter, Sally Walker, who jilts him for a former lodger.   LEIGH HUNT takes his place in English poetry as leader of the " Cockney " School. He writes boyish letters to his one and only love, Marianne Kent. KEATS, a Cockney dispenser of drugs, is hopelessly in love with Fanny Brawne till his collapse in health and death at Rome. SHELLEY, anarchist in literature, long since exonerated by posterity, writes to his wife Mary Godwin from Ravenna, a short year before he was drowned in the Gulf of Spezzia. BYRON, wayward, egotistical, and sensuous, corresponds with the beautiful Countess Guiccioli, who divorces her old husband for him.

THE ROMANTICS IN FRANCE AND ON THE CONTINENT GENERALLY

After Waterloo, Europe has breathing-space to repair the ravages of war. But for many years the arts lie dormant under the colourless kings of the Restoration. Europe became monotonous, respectable and commonplace. The ROMANTIC MOVEMENT IN FRANCE and on the Continent generally did not begin till about 1830.

PUSHKIN (1799–1837) ; VICTOR HUGO (1802–85) ;
     STENDHAL (1783–1842) ; BALZAC (1799–1850) ;
     FLAUBERT (1821–1880).

We may begin with PUSHKIN, who was the Byron of Russia. The violence of one of his love-passions brought about his death in a duel. VICTOR HUGO is the chief of the Romantics in France. His youthful love-letters are all aglow with passion for his future wife Adèle, although, as father of a family, his poet's heart belonged to the actress, Juliette Drouet.
    STENDHAL (whose real name was Beyle) author of that great novel *Le Rouge et le Noir*, stylist, satirist, and man of the world, writes predicting disenchantment to his lady loves. Forerunner of that charming novelist Merimée, he is of the same school as BALZAC, father of the French realistic school of fiction, who lives most of his life by expedients and make-shifts.

Many women pass through his life; he is faithful to none. He marries the Polish Countess Hanska, after a romantic correspondence of many years, and dies three months afterwards. FLAUBERT, greatest of novelists with MADAME BOVARY, is a recluse and writes cynical letters from Croisset to Louise Colet, the authoress, but she wishes to become more than his *amie*, and so the connection ends.

THE VICTORIAN ERA

PUECKLER-MUSKAU (1785–1871); SOUTHEY (1774–1843): MILLER (1802–56); HOOD (1799–1845); BROWNING (1812–89); ELIZABETH BARRETT (1806–61); CARLYLE (1795–1881); DICKENS (1812–70).

We place PRINCE PUECKLER-MUSKAU first; although a German, his easy wit and charming letters to his wife about early nineteenth-century high life in England make him an excellent chronicler of the times.

SOUTHEY, the English Poet Laureate, corresponds with Catherine Bowles, his second wife, more than twenty years before they were married. HUGH MILLER, Scotch geologist, was preferred by Lydia Fraser, though he was only a stonemason and ten years older than herself. HOOD, always to be remembered for his "Song of the Shirt," addresses sweet, tender letters to his wife when obliged, through pressure of debt, to live away from her on the Rhine. BROWNING rhapsodises to his dearest "Ba," whose replies show far more lucidity than do the involved missives of the author of "Sordello." CARLYLE dilates upon his hopes and fears to Jane Welsh, and is answered in a similar discursive strain by her. There exist two thick volumes of their correspondence for those who like that sort of thing. DICKENS's letters to his dear Kate as a struggling reporter are full of his chances for the publication of his forthcoming work, the immortal *Pickwick*.

Symposium of Poets and Musicians

Lenau (1802–50); Mozart (1756–91); Beethoven (1770–1827); Weber (1786–1825); Schumann (1810–56); Wagner (1813–83).

The Hungarian poet Lenau, author of lyrical poems, may herald the musicians. His overwhelming passion for the wife of his friend Loewenthal undermined his short life. Mozart, boy-genius and creator of sparkling melodies, overflows in his love-letters with quaint conceits and high spirits to his young wife, Constanze Weber. The wildest of pathetic sound-symphonies come to us from the three love-letters of Beethoven's to his "Immortal Beloved." They never appear to have been sent off. Weber relates to his wife the triumphant reception in London of *Oberon*. Schumann, romantic and intellectual musician, had to combat the opposition of his wife's family; he married her against their will. Wagner, fettered in an unworthy marriage with Frau Minna, finds spiritual relief in Mathilde Wesendonk's charming home at Zurich. Not till 1870 did he marry his second wife, Cosima, daughter of the composer, Liszt.

Modern Politicians and Great Men

Ludwig I of Bavaria (1786–1868); Heine (1797–1856); Lassalle (1825–64); Napoleon III (1803–73); Garibaldi (1807–82); Moltke (1800–91); Bismarck (1815–98); Benedek (1804–81); Gambetta (1838–82); Musset (1810–57); George Sand (1804–76); Maupassant (1850–93); Nietzsche (1844–1900); Multatuli (1820–87); Bjoernson (1832–1910); Ibsen (1828–1906); Tolstoi (1828–1910); Segantini (1858–99).

King Ludwig of Bavaria, who abdicated in 1848, was not half so interesting as his mistress, the dancer and adventuress Lola Montez, who may well have cost him his crown. Heine, Germany's greatest lyrical poet, was chained to a " mattress-grave " through a paralytic stroke, the last years of his life being cheered by the lady to whom he wrote as " Mouche " or his " beautiful angel of death." LASSALLE, co-founder with Karl Marx of the Social Democratic Party in Germany, dies in a duel for Helene Doenniges, the beautiful but erratic daughter of a diplomat. NAPO- LEON III's occasional love-letters and love-affairs were perfectly well-known to the Empress, to whom he always faithfully returned after his escapades. MOLTKE, " the great silent one," writes fatherly instructions to his young fiancée and cousin, Marie Burt. BIS- MARCK, though of robust appetites, never strayed very far from his admirable wife Johanna, to whom he writes lucid disquisitions upon the moving events of his time. GAMBETTA wrote romantic letters of passion to Léonie Léon. MUSSET, the *fin-de-siècle* decadent child of the century, makes love to George Sand, who, after his death, makes literary capital out of it in *Elle et Lui*. MAUPASSANT philanders with Marie Bashkirtseff in a delightful battle of Gallic wit. NIETZSCHE offers marriage to and is refused by a pretty Dutch girl, whom he meets on a stroll in Switzerland. BJOERNSON, impulsive dramatist, travel- ling, protests to his wife that he has ever been faithful to her. IBSEN pays his addresses to Emilie Bardach, a young Viennese girl, whom he incorporates as " Hilda Wangel " in his *Solness*. TOLSTOI's mystical schemes for the world's regeneration find no sympathy from his wife, whom he loves and hates in turn. And finally we have SEGANTINI, the painter, writing charming letters of heartfelt sympathy to his wife, on the ever-old and ever-young theme " When I am dead "—and so we come to a fitting close of our Love-letters.

THE IDEAL LOVE-LETTER

WHEN one takes a survey of these selected love-letters, chosen after exhaustive analysis and careful consideration from the vast storehouse of the world's amatory correspondence, one is inclined to sit back and ask oneself the question : WHAT ARE THE ESSENTIALS OF THE IDEAL LOVE-LETTER ? For, quite apart from the arrangement we have adopted of grouping the writers into chronological periods, one must recognise that the love-letter in itself, of no matter what period, displays so much intrinsic and perennial truth, that the same sentiments and passions sway Antony and Cleopatra as they do Romeo and Juliet ; that there is as much eternal verity in the loves of Tom Bowling and Black-eyed Susan as in those of Abélard and Héloïse, of Petrarca and Laura. Time, as the lawyer would say, is not an essence of the contract. Plato's Symposium finds its counterpart in the coster's courtship in Whitechapel Road.

ALL LOVE-LETTERS A SUBSTITUTE

We all love the same way, fundamentally, and, divested of our frills, trappings, and other accidentals, we all say the same things, though we find different ways of saying and—in these letters—of writing them.

In any case, writing is only a poor substitute for the real love-making, or, as Jane Welsh puts it to Carlyle (who would have believed it of her ?), " But, indeed, dear, these kisses on paper are scarce worth keeping. You gave me one on my neck that night you were in good humour, and one on my lips on some forgotten occasion, that I would not part with for a hundred thousand paper ones. Perhaps some day or other, I shall get none of either sort—*sic transit gloria mundi.*" Poor woman! Hers was the tragedy of many marriages.

THE FARANDOLE OF LOVE

But here we have, under our eyes, a motley farandole of love from which to choose. Kings and queens, knaves, knights and jesters, all barking their shins over their own wit, beaux and belles with quip and epigram, joining hands with profound philosophers, threadbare poets, transcendental musicians, flighty dancers, precise blue-stockings, bashful ingénues, critics and tailors' daughters, painters and pro's, adventurers and courtesans, all of them alike in the ruling passion—Love.

> " For the Colonel's lady and Biddy O'Grady
> Are sisters under their skins."

MAN PROPOSES, BUT WOMAN HAS THE LAST WORD

In these accents of pleading and passion, whose pulses still throb, long after the writers and their beloved have crumbled into dust, there is something that never dies, through which Man speaks to Woman, alluring and repelling, protesting and retracting, complaining and pardoning, regretting and hoping, praying and cursing, weeping and laughing, all in the same breath, with the irresistible, all-conquering voice of Love.

Biologists tell us that the Male forms the Variety, the Female the Species. The Wave advances, the Ocean remains constant. This principle, applied to our love-letters, goes to explain the fact that it is the man who writes the first letter, and the woman who answers him. Indeed, it is rare to find the woman initiating the correspondence, but she reserves to herself the right to have the last word.

So Man proposes, and the Woman says " No "—
meaning, when repeated often enough, " Yes ! "

> " I kissed her first, then asked her leave.
> She, swearing she would ne'er consent—consented ! "

YOUNG MEN'S LOVE-LETTERS

Thus lovers' letters proper devote themselves purely
and simply to the theme of Love. They are written
with the heart and not with the head. Love-letters,
as such, are young men's letters. They are personal
letters, they are foolish letters, they are indiscretions,
sweet intimate nothings, that do not read to advantage in a divorce court. They are strange, incoherent,
obscure, incomprehensible to all the world save the
anointed eye. As brilliant, boyish Mozart puts it,
in writing to his wife Constance, when he has invented
some new term of endearment for the portrait of
" Cossy " — Rogue — Rowdy-dowdy — Snub-nose —
Good-for-nothing, " Now, really, I believe I have
written down something quite too stupid (for the
world at least); but for us who love each other so
very dearly, it is not stupid at all."

And so are the letters which Victor Hugo writes
to his Adèle, Goethe to Lotte, Keats to Fanny,
Napoleon to Joséphine, in such accents of passion
and overweening desire, that sober people shake their
heads and smile when, in after-years, a faded packet
of these early protestations falls into their hands.
Are they the ideal love-letters ?

THE LOVE-LETTERS OF THE MIDDLE-AGED

But time passes. The impetuous desire for the
loved one has been satisfied by possession, or (*faute
de mieux*) has turned in another direction. The
struggle for existence has more imperious demands.
Responsibilities, each in their own sphere, have to be
shouldered.

Diderot confides his misgivings and his troubles to

Sophie Voland. The times are out of joint. Madame du Deffand, Horace Walpole, the Prince de Ligne, George Augustus, First Gentleman of Europe, and his *alter ego*, Beau Brummell, philander ; while, under the shadow of the guillotine, the rhetoric of Mirabeau, the beauty of Madame Roland, the advocacy of Camille Desmoulins, are extinguished. Goethe makes literary capital in *Werther* out of his passion for Lotte, as George Sand does from her love-episode with Alfred de Musset in *Elle et Lui*.

Every man in his humour and every shoemaker to his last. Dickens informs his Kate that the offer of fourteen pounds a month from Chapman & Hall to write the *Pickwick Papers* is too good to be refused ; Napoleon, after laying the trophies of his Italian victories at the feet of his elderly charmer, Joséphine, becomes more circumspect and reproves her for imprudent behaviour, unbefitting the wife of the First Consul. Beautiful Queen Luise of Prussia implores her easy-going husband not to knuckle under to Napoleon's demands ; Shelley maps out Mary Godwin's voyage to meet him in Italy. Nelson is full of his manœuvres to beat the French when writing from aboard ship to his dear Lady Hamilton ; Moltke, the great silent one, instructs his bride as to the social etiquette for officers' wives ; Bismarck relates the " storm and stress " of '48 revolutionary Berlin to his dear Johanna ; Carlyle talks of his plans on German literature with Jane Welsh ; and Browning, despiser of earthly dross (has he not lived on bread and potatoes for a couple of years ?), has even lent an ear to a sordid project of compiling a novel on Napoleon, in order to bring grist to the mill for his dearest " Ba," though, of course, one can live at Pisa for £100 a year.

WOMAN THE HELPMEET

Thus, in these letters, the woman has become the helpmeet, the confessor, the comforter, the sharer of joys and fears, the provider of creature comforts, no longer restricted to the sewing of buttons, the darning of socks, as in the confined scope of the German Hausfrau with her church, cookery, and children.

The Old Man's Letters

With the approach of age, the fierce struggle for daily bread and social advancement slackens off. The affections become blunted into melancholy resignation to the inevitable. The altruistic sentiments fade away. Life is full of narrowing horizons.

Luther's " Wine, Woman, and Song " have given way to regular gruel, warm slippers, and red flannel to wrap up the Little Mary. Even Goethe, the sempiternal lover, dwells on beds and mattresses and pillows in writing to his dear Christiane, is anxious for her to become a house-treasure, and sends baskets of liqueurs and confectionery for the store cupboards. Victor Hugo, flying from Paris after the coup d'état, longs for his home and pours out the vials of his wrath and scorn on Napoléon le petit. Bluecher, " Field-marshal Forwards," relates to his wife the great doings which led up to the battle of Waterloo. Poor Benedek, Austrian Field-marshal, under a cloud of obloquy, because he has been beaten by the Prussians at Sadowa, reproaches his wife for listening to idle tales against him. Bismarck, after his apogee at Sedan, feels bitterly the absence from his faithful and devoted wife, Johanna ; " it is as if all the world were dead, and I alone were left." Beethoven, stone deaf and prematurely aged through ill-health, longs for a quiet home and solitude with his " Immortal Beloved."

For the human heart is so constituted that as the end draws near, it yearns for peace and rest, and the presence of the loved ones.

" It is not Death itself which is so terrible," says poor Heine ; " it is the Dying of it, which is such a villainous business."

BEYOND GOOD AND EVIL

So Gaffer Darby, with his pipe and his dog and his glass (happy if Joan be within easy call), " beyond good and evil," writes no more love-letters, while Joan's heart is wrapped up in her grandchildren.

And when, one fine day, the old couple come across the faded packets of old love-letters, undo the ribbons, and decipher them one by one, they shake their heads with a smile of melancholy. Did they really write such nonsense ?

Which of these epistles can be considered the ideal love-letters ?   There is something of the Promethean spark in them all.

THE AGE OF GOOD SENSE

The Classic period in England : its urbanity, its love of good sense and moderation, its instinctive distrust of emotion, and its invincible good breeding.

ALEXANDER POPE

(1688–1744)

THE controversy whether Pope was a poet has long been laid to rest. His work is the most perfect expression in our literature of the " classical " theories of poetry. He is unexcelled in precision, terseness and epigrammatic sparkle. He is incomparably our most brilliant versifier, and his wit and fine writing consist in " giving things that are known an agreeable turn."

Amidst his poetical pursuits, Pope was never so entirely absorbed as not to cultivate a variety of friendships, some of which were with the female sex. Two ladies, Teresa and Martha Blount, daughters of a clergyman, attracted his particular attention, and they became his most intimate friends. To Teresa, the handsomer of the two, he seems to have been at first principally attached; but Martha afterwards became his intimate confidant and companion.

Pope writes to Teresa from Bath

September, 1714.

MADAM,—I write to you for two reasons, one is because you commanded it, which will be always a reason to me in anything; the other, because I sit

35

at home to take physic, and they tell me that I must do nothing that costs me great application or great pains, therefore I can neither say my prayers nor write verses.   I am ordered to think but slightly of anything, and I am practising, if I can think so of you, which, if I can bring about, I shall be above regarding anything in nature for the future; I may then think of the world as a hazel nut, the sun as a spangle, and the king's coronation as a puppet-show.   When my physic makes me remember those I love, may it not be said to work kindly ?

. . . You are to understand, madam, that my *violent* passion for your fair self and your sister has been divided, and with the most wonderful regularity in the world.   Even from my infancy I have been in love with one after the other of you week by week, and my journey to Bath fell out in the three hundred and seventy-sixth week of the reign of my sovereign lady Martha.   At the present writing hereof it is the three hundred and eighty-ninth week of the reign of your most serene majesty, in whose service I was listed some weeks before I beheld her.   This information will account for my writing to either of you hereafter, as she shall happen to be queen regent at that time.

I could tell you a most delightful story of Dr. Parnelle, but want room to display it in all its shining circumstances.   He had heard it was an ex-cellent cure for love, to kiss the aunt of the person beloved, who is generally of years and experienced enough to damp the fiercest flame.   He tried this course in his passion for you, and kissed Mrs. Engle-field at Mrs. Dancaster's [Duncastle—Ed.].   This recipe he hath left written in the style of a divine as follows :

" Whoso loveth Miss Blount shall kiss her aunt and be healed ; for he kisseth her not as her husband, who kisseth and is enslaved for ever as one of the foolish ones ; but as a passenger who passeth away and forgetteth the kiss of her mouth, even as the wind

(1)

(2)

(3)

(1) ALEXANDER POPE.   (2) LAURENCE STERNE.   (3) DEAN SWIFT.

saluteth a flower in his passage, and knoweth not the odour thereof."

(Pope, it must be remembered, was always an invalid, was at no time of his life more depressed than about the years 1719 and 1720, which accounts for the despondent tone of some of his letters.)

Pope to Teresa

August 7th, 1716.

MADAM,—I have so much esteem for you, and so much of the other thing, that, were I a handsome fellow, I should do you a vast deal of good ; but, as it is, all that I am good for, is to write a civil letter, or to make a fine speech. The truth is, that considering how often and how openly I have declared love to you, I am astonished (and a little affronted) that you have not forbid my correspondence and directly said, *See my face no more* ! . . . I am vain enough to conclude that (like most young fellows) a fine lady's silence is consent, and so I write on.—

But in order to be as innocent as possible in this epistle, I will tell you news. You have asked me news a thousand times, at the first word you spoke to me ; which some would interpret as if you expected nothing from my lips ; and truly it is not a sign two lovers are together, when they can be so impertinent as to inquire, what the world does. All I mean by this is that either you or I cannot be in love with the other ; I leave you to guess which of the two is that stupid and insensible creature, so blind to the other's excellences and charms. . . .

Pope to Martha Blount on her Birthday

June 15th, 1724

This is the day of wishes for you, and I hope you have long known that there is not one good one that I do not form in your behalf. Every year that passes I wish something more for my friends and something less for myself.   Yet, were I to tell you what I wish for you in particular, it would be only to repeat in prose what I told you last year in rhyme (so sincere is my poetry).

I can only add, that as I then wished you a friend, I now wish that friend were Mrs ——.

(The verses were—To Mrs. Blount on her birthday) :

> "O be thou blest with all that Heaven can send,
> Long health, long youth, long pleasures, and a friend."

Pope to Lady Mary Wortley Montagu

(Shortly after her marriage, Lady Wortley Montagu went with her husband on an embassy to Constantinople, during which time Pope's correspondence with her commenced.   On her return she settled at Twickenham, which afforded Pope constant opportunities of seeing her.   But ere long there was a misunderstanding ending in an open quarrel, in which they indulged in vituperations (as says Merydew) to say the least, intensely vulgar).

August 18th, 1716.

. . . I think I love you as well as King Herod could Herodias (though I never had so much as one dance with you) and would as freely give you my heart in a dish as he did another's head.

But since Jupiter will not have it so, I must be content to show my taste in life, as I do my taste in painting, by loving to have as little drapery as possible, " not that I think every body naked altogether so fine a sight as yourself and a few more would be " ; but because it is good to use people to what they must be acquainted with ; and there certainly will come some day of judgment to uncover every soul of us. We shall then see how the prudes of this world owed all their fine figures only to their being a little straiter-laced, and that they were naturally as arrant squabs as those that went more loose, nay as those that never girded their loins at all.

. . . You may easily imagine how desirous I must be of corresponding with a person who had taught me long ago that it was as possible to esteem at first sight, as to love; and who have since ruined me for all the conversation of one sex, and almost all the friendship of the other.

How often have I been quietly going to take possession of that tranquillity and indolence I had so long found in the country, when one evening of your conversation has spoiled me for a solitaire too. Books have lost their effect upon me, and I was convinced, since I saw you, that there is something more powerful than philosophy, and, since I heard you, that there is one alive wiser than all the sages. A plague of female wisdom! it makes a man ten times more uneasy than his own.

JONATHAN SWIFT
(1667–1745)

In virtue of so wide-reaching and philosophical a creation as the tale of *Gulliver's Travels*, we may class Swift as the greatest satirist of modern times. There is no doubt but there was some radical disorder in his system; brain disease clouded his intellect in his old age, and his last years were death in life; right through his life he was a savagely irritable, sardonic, dark and violent man, impatient of the slightest contradiction or thwarting, and given to explosive and instantaneous rage.

Three women figure in the unhappy story of Swift's life. In his early years he had a passing courtship with a Miss Waring ("Varina"). But his cold temper and unconfined humour ever militated against his putting his head into the matrimonial noose. Could she, he asks, manage their joint affairs with an income of less than £300 a year?

The real affection of his life was for Esther Johnson

—the "Stella" of his verse. For her he wrote the "Journal to Stella" descriptive of his life in London, and there is a strong probability that he was latterly privately married to her. A third woman, Esther Vanhomrigh ("Vanessa") loved Swift and received from him in return an ardent friendship easily mistaken for love. But when jealousy moved her to ask for an explanation of his relations with Stella, Swift was so enraged that he abruptly broke with her. Vanessa was so overcome that she died shortly afterwards (1723).

Swift to Stella

(whom he gives various pet names, as " M.D." in his letters, he himself being in the "little language" "P.D.F.R.", usually changed in print into Presto, a name given him by the Duchess of Shrewsbury.)

LONDON, *September 21st*, 1710.

Here I must begin another letter on a whole sheet for fear saucy little M.D. should be angry and think much that the paper is too little. I had your letter this night as I told you just and no more in my last ; for this must be taken up in answering yours, saucebox . . .

(*September 23rd.*) . . . Here is such a stir and bustle with this little M.D. of ours ; I must be writing every night ; I cannot go to bed without a word to them ; I cannot put out my candle till I have bid them good night. Oh Lord ! Oh Lord ! . . . Stella writes like an emperor ; I am afraid it hurts your eyes ; take care of that, pray, pray, Mrs. Stella ! Write constantly ! why, sirrah, do not I write every day, and sometimes twice a day to M.D. ?

LONDON, *December 9th*, 1710.

Stay, I will answer some of your letter this morning in bed ; let me see ; come and appear, little letter. Here I am, says he, and what say you to Mrs. D. this

morning, fresh and fasting? Oh, then, you keep
Presto's little birthday; would to God I had been
with you. I forgot it, as I told you before. Redicu-
lous, madam? I suppose you mean *ridiculous;* let
me have no more of that, it is the author of the
Atlantis's bad spelling. I have mended it in your
letter. And can Stella read this writing without
hurting her dear eyes? O faith, I am afraid not.
Have a care of those eyes, pray, pray, pretty Stella—
why do you not go down to Clogher, nauti, nauti,
nauti, dear girls. I dare not say nauti without dear.
O, faith, you govern me—you win eight shillings!
you win eight fiddlesticks. Faith, you say nothing of
what you lose.

(None of Stella's letters to Swift have been preserved.
If they were married, it was in 1716, under conditions
of strict secrecy and a separate life. She died in
1727.)

Amongst the families in London where Swift was
chiefly domesticated was that of a Mrs. Vanhomrigh
(pronounced "Vannumery"), a rich widow. Her
eldest daughter became the celebrated Vanessa. She
was a woman, says Dr. Johnson, in his Life of Swift,
made unhappy by her admiration of wit. Being
proud of the Dean's praise, she ended by becoming
fond of his person. There is nothing in all Swift's
love-letters to show that he had much feeling, and
his indulgence of Vanessa's hopes after his marriage
to Stella was the egotistic act of a man who, however
witty he may have been, could never have had much
feeling for others.

Swift's First Letter to Esther Vanhomrigh

OVER AGAINST PARK PLACE IN ST. JAMES'S STREET, LONDON,
1712.

I thought to have written to little Missessy by the
Colonel, but at last I did not approve of him as a
messenger. . . . I cannot imagine how you pass your
time in our absence, unless by lying abed till twelve,

and then having your followers about you till dinner
. . . what do you do all the afternoon ? I will steal
to town one of these days and catch you napping. I
desire you and Moll (his sister Mary) will walk as
often as you can in the Park, and do not sit moping
at home, you that can neither work, nor read, nor
play, nor care for company. I long to drink a dish
of coffee in the sluttery, and hear you dun me for
Secrete and " Drink your coffee, why don't you drink
your coffee ? " My humble service to your mother
and Moll, and the Colonel. Adieu !

(The letters of Vanessa are on a different plane.
They are those of a noble, kind, self-sacrificing, and
womanly nature, but their effect on him was little
or nothing ; no echo of responsive affection or decent
compassion is heard in any of his replies.)

Esther Vanhomrigh to Swift

DUBLIN, 1714.

Well ! now I plainly see how great a regard you
have for me. You bid me be easy and you'd see me
as often as you could ; you had better have said as
often as you could get the better of your inclinations
so much, or as often as you remembered there was such
a person in the world.

If you continue to treat me as you do, you will not
be made uneasy by me long. 'Tis impossible to describe what I have suffered since I saw you last. I
am sure I could have *born* [sic] the rack much better
than those killing, killing words of yours. Sometimes
I have resolved to die without seeing you more, but
these resolves to your misfortune did not last long ;
for there is something in human nature that prompts
one so to find relief in this world, I must give way to
it and beg you'd see me, and speak kindly to me, for
I am sure you would not condemn anyone to suffer
what I have done could you but know it.

The reason I write to you is because I cannot tell
it you should I see you, for when I begin to complain

then you are angry and there is something in your look so awful that it strikes me dumb.

Oh ! that you may but have so much regard for me left that this complaint may touch your soul with pity.

I say as little as ever I can. Did you but know what I thought I am sure it would move you.

Forgive me, and believe me I cannot help telling you this and live.

Swift's Last Letter to Vanessa

. . . I had your last with a splendid account of your law affairs . . . when you are melancholy, read diverting or amusing books ; it is my receipt and seldom fails. Health, good-humour, and fortune are all that is valuable in this life, and the last contributes to the two former. . . . I desire you will not venture to shake me by the hand, for I am in mortal fear of the itch, and have no hope left, but that some ugly vermin called ticks have got into my skin, of which I have pulled out some and must scratch out the rest [sic.] Is not this enough to give me the spleen ? for I doubt no Christian family will receive me ; and this is all a man gets by a northern journey. . . .Yesterday I rode twenty-nine miles without being weary, and I wish little *Heskinage* could do as much. . . . How do you wear away the time ? Is it among the fields and groves of your country seat, or among your cousins in town, or thinking in a train that will be sure to vex you, and then reasoning and forming teasing conclusions from mistaken thoughts ? The best company for you is a philosopher, whom you would regard as much as a sermon. . . . What a foolish thing is time, and how foolish is man, who would be as angry if time stop't, as if it pressed ! But I will not proceed at this rate ; for I am writing and thinking myself fast into a spleen, which is the only thing that I would not compliment you by imitating. So, adieu till the next place I fix in (if I fix at all) till I return, and that I leave to fortune and the weather.

SIR RICHARD STEELE

(1672-1729)

STEELE we know very intimately from his own writings and from Thackeray's portrait of him. He was an emotional, full-blooded kind of a man, reckless and dissipated and improvident, but fundamentally honest and good-hearted—a type very common in those days. What there is of pathos and sentiment and most of what there is of humour, in the *Tatler* and the *Spectator*, are his.

The correspondence of Dick Steele with his " dear Prue " embraces upwards of four hundred letters. They are " such masterpieces of ardour and respect, of tender passion and honest feeling, of good sense and earnestness as well as of playful sweetness " (as a critic has observed), " that the lady may be fairly forgiven for having so soon surrendered." The lady to whom they were addressed is Mary Scurlock, who was at first averse to all ideas of marriage, but quickly yielded after a month's wooing to a man who " was as agreeable and pleasant as any in England." Previous to her marriage, she is styled, according to the custom of the period, " Mrs.," though a single lady—she being about eight or nine and twenty at the time, and the term " Miss " being considered derogatory to persons (as honest Merydew says) of " mature age."

His letters were much admired by Coleridge, who regarded them as models.

Steele to Mary Scurlock

August 11th, 1707.

. . . I shall not trouble you with my sentiments till I know how they will be received ; and as I know no reason why the difference of sex should make our language to each other differ from the ordinary rules of right reason, I shall affect plainness and sincerity in my discourse to you, as much as other lovers do perplexity and rapture. Instead of saying " I shall

die for you," I profess I should be glad to lead my
life with you. You are as beautiful, as witty, as pru-
dent, and as good-humoured as any woman breathing;
but I must confess to you, I regard all these excellences
as you will be pleased to direct them for my happiness
or misery. . . .

And after meeting her, his letters become more
devoted, and are sent at lesser intervals, so anxious
is he to impress upon his lady-love his intense regard
for her.

MADAM,—With what language shall I address my
lovely fair to acquaint her with the sentiments of a
heart she delights to torture ? I have not a minute's
quiet out of your sight; and when I am with you,
you use me with such distance, that I am still in a
state of absence, heightened with a view of the charms
which I am denied to approach. In a word, you must
give me either a fan, a mask, or a glove you have worn,
or I cannot live; otherwise you must expect that I'll
kiss your hand, or, when I next sit by you, steal
your handkerchief. You yourself are too great a
bounty to be secured at once; therefore I must be
prepared by degrees, less the mighty gift distract me
with joy.

Dear Miss Scurlock, I am tired of calling you by
that name; therefore, say the day in which you will
take that of MADAM.

Your most obedient, most devoted, humble servant,
RICH. STEELE.

MADAM,—It is the hardest thing in the world to be
in love and yet attend to business. As for me, all who
speak to me find me out, and I must lock myself up
or other people will do it for me.

A gentleman asked me this morning, " What news
from Lisbon ? " and I answered, " She is exquisitely
handsome." Another desired to know when I had
been last at Hampton Court. I replied, " It will be
on Tuesday come se'nnight. Prythee, allow me

at least to kiss your hand before that day, that my mind may be in some composure. O love!—

> " A thousand torments dwell about me!
> Yet who would live to live without thee ? "

Methinks I could write a volume to you; but all the language on earth would fail in saying how much and with what disinterested passion I am ever yours,

Rich. Steele.

LAURENCE STERNE

(1713–68)

Sterne is one of the greatest of English humorists, the true secret of his power being the subtle blending of laughter and pathos. In some things he resembles Rabelais; in others, he anticipated Jean Paul (Richter). He is distinguished by three principal amours, in which he wrote love-letters; the first was with Elizabeth Lumley, who became his wife; the second with Catherine Formantel; third—his *grande passion*—with Elizabeth Draper.

Mrs. Sterne is commonly addressed as " My L." Sterne calls her his " contemplative girl "—" I would wish," he says in one of his first epistles, " to steal from the world and live in a little sun-gilt cottage on the side of a romantic hill." " Thou wilt hold me thine," says Laurence to Elizabeth, " while virtue and faith hold this world together "; and then he suddenly remembers some evening duty, for as he poetically puts it, " The vesper bell calls me from thee to my God."

So far, so good (says Merydew); but mark the change when the man is married. " For God's sake," writes the husband, " rise early and gallop away in the cool," and always " see that you have not forgot your baggage "; and then come careful directions about the manufacture of Scotch snuff. Then " Drink small Rhenish to keep you cool "—(he was not formerly so desirous of this coolness)—" God in Heaven prosper and go along with you."

In Sterne's first letters to Kitty Formantel, he begs the lady's acceptance of a few bottles of Calcavillo, which he has ordered his man to leave at her dore [sic]. In another he says : " If this billet catches you in bed, you are a lazy, sleepy little slut," tells her she is " sweeter than honey," that he " loves her to distraction and will love her to eternity."

Again he sends her sweetmeats and more honey, " neither of them half so sweet as herself," and if she grows " sour on this declaration " tells her he will " send her a pot of pickles."

This letter was signed by the Prebendary of the Church of York—with considerable humour to one who knows his story " Qui ne changera pas que en Mourant.—L.S." Yorick was ever proud of his French. On the whole, what with his " sweet lass," his " yours for ever and ever," his " dear enchanting slut, for a squeeze of whose hand he would give a guinea," there is more of the nature of ardent love in the letters than in any others written by Sterne.

Sterne's last Liaison with Elizabeth Draper

Eliza Draper was the wife of a Bombay lawyer, who from ill-health was sent to England. She came, saw, and conquered.

To Eliza

MY DEAREST ELIZA,—I have begun a new journal this morning; you shall see it; for if I live not till your return to England, I will leave it you as a legacy. 'Tis a sorrowful page; but I will write cheerful ones; and could I write letters to thee they should be cheerful ones, too. . . .

If I remember right, Eliza, you endeavoured to collect every charm of your person into your face, with more than common care, the day you sat for Mrs. James, your colour, too, brightened, and your eyes shone with more than usual brilliancy. I then requested you to come simple and unadorned, when you sat for me; knowing (as I see with unprejudiced eyes) that you would receive no addition from the silkworm's aid or jeweller's polish.

Let me now tell you a truth, which I believe I have uttered before. When I first saw you, I beheld you as an object of compassion, and as a very plain woman. The mode of your dress (tho' fashionable) disfigured you. But nothing would now render you such, but the being solicitous to make yourself admired as a handsome one. You are not handsome, Eliza, nor is yours a face that will please the tenth part of your beholders, but are something more; for I scruple not to tell you, I never saw so intelligent, so animated, so good a countenance; nor was there, nor ever will be, that man of sense, tenderness, and feeling, in your company three hours, that was not, or will not be, your admirer, or friend, in consequence of it; that is, if you assume, or assumed, no character foreign to your own, but appeared the artless being nature designed you for. A something in your eyes and voice you possess in a degree more persuasive than any woman I ever saw, read or heard of. But it is that bewitching sort of nameless excellence, that men of nice sensibility alone can be touched with.

Were your husband in England, I would freely give him five hundred pounds, if money could purchase the acquisition, to let you only sit by me two hours in a day, while I wrote my *Sentimental Journey.* I am sure the work would sell so much the better for it, that I should be re-imbursed more than seven times told. . . .

IN GERMANY: RETURN TO NATURALNESS.

(1713–62)

*A Pattern Letter from a Bride of the Eighteenth Century
to her Future Husband*

This letter was written by Fräulein Luise Adelgunde
Kulmus, the later Gottschedin, authoress, blue-stock-
ing, and translator of the *Spectator* and Pope's *Rape of
the Lock*, to her future husband the German philosopher and arbiter of literature, Gottsched.

DANZIG, *October 20th*, 1733.

HIGHLY HONOURABLE HERR,—The common-sense[1]
arrangement of your lessons has my entire approval.
The two translated speeches I have read with much
pleasure. Of the one, which is particularly of moment
to our good town Danzig, much good is already fore-
told.

My ode had deserved no better fate, than to be
passed over in silence. In the best of worlds, it had
to be so, in order not to bring about my downfall.
Who knows but what I might have become conceited.

. . . I, for my part, know how to employ profitably
every moment. Will you read the disposal of my
time ?

Immediately on the day's beginning, I occupy myself
with spiritual contemplation, which elevates my soul
to its Maker ; the soul, which is unable to fathom the
origin of its being, as little as its immortality, enjoys
in these holy sentiments a foretaste of the happiness
of hereafter, of the brightest hope.

[1] Common-sense = *Biedermann.* Gottsched had lectured on
Biedermann criticisms.

Thereupon my mind takes delight at the excellent works of Nature. The smallest thereof shows me the greatness of the Creator, new Beauties and new Wonders. This is the most pleasant occupation of all for me. I lose myself therein and exclaim full of admiration, What an agglomeration of riches! Finally my spirits droop, when I ponder on the brevity of my span of life, and how small a part of this science, so important to me, I shall discover.

When I wish to comfort my downcast mind, I sit down at the piano, and practise, to perfect myself in conformity with your desires expressed in 1729. Here I think with redoubled vigour of my friend and desire to obtain his approval, and that the days of our probation may be at an end, and that our patience be rewarded. The rest of the time I fill up in reading useful books. Now I am reading Labruyère and Horace, and envy a Dacier all the pleasure he has found at this work. [Dacier was a French Academician of the eighteenth century, who made indifferent translations of Horace, etc.—ED.] Thus do my days and hours pass, amongst which I hold those pre-eminently happy in which I converse with you, and repeat the assurance of my eternal devotion.

KULMUS.

Letter two, in which Fräulein Kulmus discurses learnedly about their philosophic love, while setting forth the most economical way of getting married.

DANZIG, March 1st, 1735.

BEST OF FRIENDS,—You are right in calling our love a philosophic love. It is different from those unions, only too frequent, although one has the habit of applying that appellation to them as well. Our hearts were united, and we had not paid attention to the outward sign of our engagement. For the sake of others we confirmed our unison in the usual way; but how often it occurs that even the most meticulous observance of the solemn ceremonies avails nought to prevent the rupture of many alliances ? How often does it not happen, that the latter, in spite of the former, are declared null and void by the spiritual and temporal courts ?

We are not liable to such an accident. Where two hearts have been created for each other, how could there be a possibility of separation ? Of you, my virtuous friend, I hope the best, and of myself I will stand surety for everything. I do not even wish to exercise myself in surmising the sad possibility of a change of mind. I await you with impatience. Will you approve of all my arrangements, made with a certain economy ? All superfluous display, which is only too often squandered at such festivals, I believe to be quite unnecessary.

To a well-ordered household there belongs necessarily a reasonable thrift, and one cannot begin soon enough to behave prudently. How many do not squander on such an occasion the income of a whole year in a few hours ? Our wedding shall not cost more than a hundred thalers [at that period about £15]. My outlay for things of real necessity does not amount to much more. We have to make a long journey and incur therein absolutely unavoidable expenses. We have to think of our furnishing in Leipzig, and these are necessary requirements, from which no deductions can be made. I have therefore tried to draw the line at the superfluous and fancied necessities. Not more than eighteen people shall be witnesses of our festival, but the whole town of our happiness.

In case your worthy parents cannot be present owing to their age and their weak health, please beseech them to bestow their blessing on us, which God will not refuse to his faithful servant for the welfare of his children. At least after long tedious waiting, there will come the happy moment, when I shall be able to embrace you with the purest tenderness, and can assure you with the greatest joy, that I know no other earthly happiness than to be entirely your own.

KULMUS.

GOTTHOLD EPHRAIM LESSING
(1729–81)

Lessing, greatest of German eighteenth-century critics, whose *Laocoon* on the limitations between painting and poetry is still the classical text-book on æsthetics, and makes him the greatest German writer since Luther, shows his sincerity and independence in his letters to the energetic and intellectual widow of a Hamburg merchant, Eva Koenig, to whom he had become engaged in 1771, and married, when his circumstances had become more settled, in 1776. Unfortunately the wife, for whom he had waited so long, died in childbirth two years after their marriage.

He writes to his fiancée from Wolfenbuettel, where he had accepted the post of librarian of the ducal library.

January 8th, 1773.

MEINE LIEBE,—You see now, that I am incorrigible in my evil habits. If it be not part of my good habits, that I really cannot write to people for whom I have some regard, when my head is full of whims and my heart is full of gall.

That I should herein make an exception towards my best friend, she will probably insist. But she will desire it from excessive kindness, which I would rather appear to ignore than to abuse. It is enough, that even then she will hear more of my discontent, than I may flatter myself is good for her own contentment.

Truly, my love, I would have caused you more sorrow, than I saved you from, had I written you before now. For now I am only just beginning to cheer up, and only eight days ago, every word would have betrayed to you the temper overclouding my mind. I can unfortunately no longer disguise the fact even to myself that I am more a victim to hypochrondria than I had ever believed possible. The only thing which still consoles me, is, as I know from experience, that my hypochrondria cannot yet be very deeply rooted. For as soon as I am out of the enchanted castle and again amongst human beings; for the time being, matters improve. And then I say to myself: why do you then continue to remain in this enchanted castle? Had I still been the old sparrow on the roof, I should have flitted off again a hundred times!

And since eight days, I have been obliged to mingle with others. At the New Year, I have been to Brunswick to the Court, and have done with others what is utterly useless when one does it, but still can be hurtful when one persists in not doing it. I have made obeisances, and opened and shut my jaws.

. . . My only wish, when I thought of something during this time was—But you know it too well, my love! Will there never more come a happy year for you and me? . . .

Still oftener I had this thought, when, several days later, on the 6th of this month, I was at Z[acharias]'s wedding. It took a long time before I became lively. But at last the example set carried me with it; and I was gay, because they all were. You know Z; but yet you could hardly imagine, what a pleasant and magnificent wedding it was in every respect. Nothing was wanting; and twenty things were there, of which no one would have dreamt. All those who were present, you can see from the sheet of verses, which I have wrapped round that-what-you-know, and have handed it over to the post-coach yesterday. We kept up the jollification till the next day; and nobody went to bed but the bride and bridegroom. Of course the wedding took place at the Way-house [Weghaus].

May you fare well, my love; for otherwise I hardly have room to say to you, what I really ought no more to say to you; that I love you above everything, and embrace you daily in my thoughts a thousand times. Yours for ever,

G. E. L.

DR. JOHNSON'S ERA: SOBRIETY AND STRAIGHTFORWARD DICTION

SAMUEL JOHNSON

(1709–84)

JOHNSON had the qualities of a typical Englishman, who considers himself a plain man, more honest and direct in word and deed than the rest of the world. He attained a position of almost unique authority amongst his fellow-countrymen, not as a lexicographer or by any other outstanding work, but by his signal possession of this hereditary gift of veracity, honesty, and good sense. Nor did he confine his friendships to men. He had a higher opinion of the intellectual capacities of women than most men of his time, and had from his early youth been susceptible to female charms. As a schoolboy he fell in love with a Quaker, called Olivia Lloyd, to whom he wrote poetry of no great merit. A certain Miss Hickman "playing on the spinet" and a lady on "receiving from her a sprig of myrtle" (says Merydew) were also the causes of feeble amatory effusions in verse. The celebrated "Tetty," a Mrs. Porter, who eventually became his wife, was double Johnson's age. "Poor dear Tetty" or "Tetsey"—a provincial contraction of Elizabeth— was, according to Garrick, very fat, but Johnson, who was shortsighted, saw in her the graces of the Queens-berrys and the Lepels. "Sir," said the Lexicographer, "it was a love marriage on both sides."

His intimate friendship with Mrs. Thrale, his own brilliant and witty Mrs. Thrale, who was not a professed "bluestocking," has long since become almost his-

torical. Johnson's introduction into Mr. Thrale's
family contributed much to the happiness of his
life. When this acquaintance commenced, Mrs. Thrale
was very pretty, about twenty-four or twenty-five
years old, clever and witty. He found here a constant
succession of what gave him the highest enjoyment,
the society of the learned, the witty, and the eminent
in every walk of life ; in whose company he could fold
his legs and have his talk out. Mrs. Thrale was always
willing to pour out unlimited cups of tea ; and to bear
with a cheerful and amiable good-nature those out-
bursts of ill-temper in which Dr. Johnson occasionally
indulged. The subjoined letter affords sufficient clear
indication of Dr. Johnson's feelings for Mrs. Thrale.

LICHFIELD, *October 27th*, 1777.

DEAREST MADAM,—You talk of writing and writing
as if you had all the writing to yourself. If our correspondence were printed, I am sure posterity—for
posterity is always the author's favourite—would say
that I am a good writer too. To sit down so often
with nothing to say,—to say something so often, almost
without consciousness of saying, and without any
remembrance of having said—is a power of which I
will not violate my modesty by boasting ; but I do
not believe everybody has it.

Some, when they write to their friends, are all
affection, some, wise and contentious, some strain
their powers for efforts of gaiety, some write news
and some write secrets ; but to make a letter without
affection, without wisdom, without gaiety, without
news, and without a secret, is, doubtless, the great
epistolic art.

In a man's letters, you know, madam, his soul lies
naked. His letters are only the mirror of his heart.
Whatever passes within him is there shown undis-
guised in its natural progress ; nothing is invented,
nothing distorted ; you see systems in their elements,
you discover actions in their motives.

Of this great truth, sounded by the knowing to

the ignorant, and so echoed by the ignorant to the knowing, what evidence have you now before you? Is not my soul laid open before you in these veracious pages? Do you not see me reduced to my first principles? This is the pleasure of corresponding with a friend, where doubt and distrust have no place, and everything is said as it is thought. These are the letters by which souls are united, and by which minds naturally in unison move each as they are moved themselves. I know, dearest lady, that in the perusal of this—such is the consanguinity of our intellects—you will be touched as I am touched. I have indeed concealed nothing from you, nor do I ever expect to repent of having thus opened my heart. I am, etc.,

SAMUEL JOHNSON.

But the death of Mr. Thrale made a very material alteration to Johnson's comfort and friendship with his lively widow, especially when she married the singer Gabriel Piozzi. Mrs. Thrale, it is true, sent him a letter, asking for his consent, but it was merely a matter of form. Dr. Johnson replied as follows:

LONDON, *July 8th*, 1784.

DEAR MADAM,—What you have done, however I may lament it, I have no pretence to resent, as it has not been injurious to me; I therefore breathe out one sigh more of tenderness, perhaps useless but at least sincere.

I wish that God may grant you every blessing, that you may be happy in this world for its short continuance, and eternally happy in a better state; and whatever I can contribute to your happiness I am ever ready to repay, for that kindness which soothed twenty years of a life radically wretched. Do not think slightly of the advice I now presume to offer. Prevail upon Mr. Piozzi to settle in England, you may live here with more dignity than in Italy, and with more security. Your rank will be higher, and

your fortune more under your own eye. I desire not
to detail all my reasons, but every argument of prudence, and interest, is for England, and only some
phantoms of imagination seduce you to Italy.

I am afraid, however, that my counsel is vain ; yet
I have eased my heart in giving it.

When Queen Mary took the resolution of sheltering
herself in England, the Archbishop of St. Andrews,
attempting to dissuade her, attended on her journey ;
and when they came to the irremeable stream that
separated the two kingdoms, walked by her side into
the water, in the middle of which he seized her bridle,
and with earnestness proportioned to her danger
and his own affection pressed her to return. The
Queen went forward. If the parallel reaches thus
far, may it go no farther. The tears stand in my
eyes.

I am going into Derbyshire, and hope to be followed
by your good wishes, for I am with great affection,
your, etc.,

Sam. Johnson.

GALLANTRY OF THE GREAT IN POLITE SOCIETY

England: Stilted Epistolary Art

JOHN CHURCHILL, FIRST DUKE OF MARL-BOROUGH

(1650–1722)

JOHN CHURCHILL, first Duke of Marlborough, was noted for his personal beauty and charm of manner. Unsurpassed in his time as a military tactician against France in such battles as those of Blenheim, Ramillies, and Oudenarde, he was besides the first diplomatist of his age, though the ignoble love of pelf was the most distinctive fault of his character. Largely through the influence of his wife, Sarah Jennings, the quick-tempered and strong-willed lady of the Bed-chamber to Queen Anne, he became Captain-General of the British Army. His courtship was carried on with difficulty, his parents being desirous that he should make a wealthier marriage, whereupon Sarah Jennings, his "dearest soul," threatened to break it off, which produced so effective a remonstrance from her lover that they were married early in 1678. From the letters quoted it will be seen that Churchill loved his wife very deeply, and the fear of displeasing her is occasionally mentioned in such passages as this: "I am never so happy as when I think you are kind."

Marlborough to his Wife

THE HAGUE, *April 20th*, 1703

I received this morning two of your dear letters, which I read with all the pleasure imaginable. They

(1)

(2)

(3)

(1) JOHN, DUKE OF MARLBOROUGH.　　　(2) WILLIAM CONGREVE.
(3) SARAH JENNINGS, DUCHESS OF MARLBOROUGH.

were so very kind that if it were possible, you are dearer
to me ten thousand times than you ever were. I am
so entirely yours, that if I might have all the world
given me, I could not be happy but in your love.

THE HAGUE, *April 23rd*, 1706.

I am very uneasy at not having heard from you
since my being in this country; and the wind continuing in the east, I am afraid I shall not have the satisfaction of receiving any letter from my dearest soul
before I leave this place. . . .

My dearest soul, my desire of being with you is
so great, that I am not able to express the impatience
I am in to have this campaign over. I pray God it
may so happen that there be no more occasion of
my coming, but that I may ever stay with you, my
dearest soul.

His prolonged absence seems to have caused him a
great deal of anxiety, as may be gathered from the
following extract :

. . . It is impossible for my dearest soul to imagine
the weary thoughts I have every day in thinking that
I have the curse, at my age, of being in a foreign
country from you, and at the same time very little
prospect of being able to do any considerable service
for my country or the common cause.

LORD PETERBOROUGH
(1658–1735)

CHARLES MORDAUNT, first Earl of Monmouth and
third Earl of Peterborough, identified himself with
the cause of William of Orange against James II, and
was well known for his romantic courage and adven-
ture. He has also been celebrated as (says Merydew)
one of those men of careless wit and negligent grace
who scatter a thousand *bons mots* and idle verse, " which
on inspection often appear little worthy of their repu-

tation." The subjoined extracts from letters between
the philandering earl and the beautiful Mrs. Howard
(for many years the mistress of George II) will serve
as specimens of the stilted but polished style of epistolary art then in vogue, where polish and fine writing
is applied so liberally that the true feelings are pinched
and pale under all this weight of fine clothes and
artificial flourishes.

Lord Peterborough writes thus :

. . . By my honour, by truth (which I love almost
as well as the author of my torments), I protest to
you there is a lady so terrible to me that the first
moments I approach her I can hardly speak; and I
feel myself the greatest fool in nature near the woman
in the world who has the most wit.

To what has a friend innocently exposed me ?
The brims of the cup were sweet, but the dose was
strong, and I drank it down with much greediness.
What I may obtain, I know not ; what I have lost,
I know—in a word, all satisfaction and my quiet ; and
I remain tasteless to all pleasures, and to all of your
sex but one.

It is supposed that Gay had a hand in Mrs. Howard's
replies, one of which is as follows :

I cannot much wonder that men are always so
liberal in making presents of their hearts, yet I cannot
help admiring the women who are so very fond of
these acquisitions. Let us consider the ingredients
that make up the heart of man. It is composed of
dissimulation, self-love, vanity, inconstancy, equivoca-
tion, and such fine qualities. Who then would make
that a present to a lady, when they have one of their
own so very like it ?

A man's heart never wants the outward appearance
of truth and sincerity. Every lover's heart is so finely
varnished with them, that it is almost impossible to
distinguish the true from the false ones. According

to my observations, the false ones have generally the finest gloss.

. . . Therefore, let everyone who expects an equivalent for his heart be provided with a false one, which is equally fit for the most professed lover. It will burn, flame, bleed, pant, sigh, and receive as many darts, and appear altogether as charming as the true one. Besides, it does not in the least embarrass the wearer, and I think your lordship was always a lover of liberty.

To which he replies :

By your letter you seem to insinuate mine might be like yours ; for you honestly confess a mighty resemblance between the male and female hearts ; I wish the likeness could be carried on throughout. I should almost be content (as you advise) to change a true one though for a false one, if at the same time I could receive as much beauty, wit, and youth.

Mrs. Howard's reply :

I think your lordship, in the last paragraph of your letter, is a little ungenerous. In a present which you tell me you have made to me, you expect the most exact return, which generosity generally leaves to the courtesy of the receiver. You quote Scripture to justify the reasonableness of your request, " An eye for an eye, a tooth for a tooth, a heart for a heart."

This seems to me to be rather a demand of revenge and resentment than love. But a man cannot give a heart for a heart that has none to give.

Consider, my lord, you have but one heart, and then consider whether you have a right to dispose of it. Is there not a lady in Paris who is convinced that nobody has it but herself ? Did you not bequeath it to another lady in Turin ? At Venice you disposed of it to six or seven, and you again parted with it at Naples and in Sicily. I am therefore obliged, my lord, to believe that one who disposes of his heart in so profuse a manner is like a juggler, who seems to fling away a piece of money, but still has it in his own keeping.

And Lord Peterborough protests as follows:

Before I complain, I give you thanks that in the several dispositions of my heart, you have had the grace not to bestow it on any German lady [this is a sneer at the taste of George I and, indeed (so it turns out afterwards) of George II too.—Merydew], but have you not too much confined my generosity, and forgot that some Blacks are very beautiful, and Indians very lively! . . .

But give me leave to tell you your intelligence is very imperfect and in many cases false. I was ever too good an Englishman to submit to a French enemy, and were I to offer anything to a lady at Paris, it should be three bottles of champagne, and not one heart.

At Turin I was so busied in making kings that I had no time to think of ladies, and was so far from making a conveyance that I know no person that ever had the slightest pretence to me or I to them. Venice, indeed, was an idle place and proper enough for an idle engagement; but alas! madam, hate does not differ more from love than a Venetian amusement from an English passion, such an one as I feel for you.

In truth you never had in any country, nor could have, but one rival; for in no place I ever found any to compare to you but one, and that was an English lady and a wife; so that after all this vagabond heart never went out of his own country, and the first and last and true and warm passions seized me in this cold climate and the deep and lasting wounds were given me at home. . . .

Oh, madam, may I not say, were there a possibility of some return, that I would prefer one kind thought to the mines of Peru and Mexico?

A heart for a heart is a natural though unreasonable demand. Oh, dearest lady, refuse not mine and do

with your own as you think fit, provide you keep it
to yourself; or keep it, at least, till you can find one
who deserves it.

WILLIAM CONGREVE
(1670–1729)

With the exception of Dryden, William Congreve
had no possible rival. He was by far the most distinguished writer of the school of Molière, as witness
his magnificent comedies of manners, *Love for Love*
and *The Way of the World.* At the age of twenty-seven
he found himself the most admired of living writers.

A thorough man of pleasure, moving in the best
society of wit and fashion, William Congreve warmed
both hands at the fire of life. He was celebrated, says
Leigh Hunt, for his *bonnes fortunes*, and was always
in tender connection with some reigning charmer.
At one time, says Merydew, it is Mrs. Arabella
Hunt, a public singer; at another, he is residing at
the same house with "Madame Beranger"; at
another and for a longer while, his relations with
Mrs. Bracegirdle, whose very name sounds like a
Venus, were, says Mr. Leslie Stephen, "ambiguous,
but in any case, very intimate." During the last
years of his life he was the cherished companion of
Henrietta, Duchess of Marlborough, to whom, says
Dr. Johnson, he left ten thousand pounds. The
famous description of the cathedral in *The Mourning
Bride* was always maintained by Johnson to be superior
to anything written by Shakespeare, and to contain
lines unequalled in English poetry.

Congreve to Mrs. Arabella Hunt

DEAR MADAM,—Not believe that I love you? You
cannot pretend to be so incredulous. If you do not
believe my tongue, consult my eyes, consult your own.
You will find by yours that they have charms; by
mine that I have a heart which feels them. Recall
[sic] to mind what happened last night. That at

least was a lover's kiss. Its eagerness, its fierceness, its warmth, expressed the God its parent. But oh! its sweetness and its melting softness expressed Him more. With trembling in my limbs and fevers in my soul I ravish'd it. Convulsions, pantings, murmurings, showed the mighty disorder within me; the mighty disorder increased by it. For those dear lips shot through my heart, and thro' my bleeding vitals, delicious poison, and an avoidless but yet a charming ruin. What cannot a day produce? The night before I thought myself a happy man, in want of nothing, and in fairest expectation of fortune; approved of by men of wit, and applauded by others. Pleased, nay, charmed with my friends, my then dearest friends, sensible of every delicate pleasure, and in their turns possessing all.

But Love, almighty Love, seems in a moment to have removed me to a prodigious distance from every object but you alone. In the midst of crowds I remain in solitude. Nothing but you can lay hold of my mind, and that can lay hold of nothing but you. I appear transported to some foreign desert with you (oh that I were really thus transported), where, abundantly supplied with everything, in thee, I might live out an age of uninterrupted extasy.

The scene of the world's great stage seems suddenly and sadly changed. Unlovely objects are all around me, excepting thee; the charms of all the world appear to be translated to thee. Thus in this said [sic: sad?] but oh, too pleasing state! my soul can fix upon nothing but thee; thee it contemplates, admires, adores, nay depends on, trusts on you alone.

If you and hope forsake it, despair and endless misery attend it.

LADY MARY WORTLEY MONTAGU
(1689-1762)

The eldest daughter of the Duke of Kingston, Lady Mary, at sixteen had translated the *Encheiridion* of

Epictetus. The letters describing her travels with her husband, Edward Wortley Montagu, who went as Ambassador to the Porte in 1716, had an immediate reputation for their liveliness, novelty, and wit. Of high intellectual faculties and somewhat chilly in her feelings, she may be considered as a typical *précieuse ridicule* of the eighteenth century, in fact a kind of a counterpart of Madame de Staël in France, and Gottsched's wife in Germany, whose love-letters we have quoted as Jungfer Kulmus. One remembers Lady Mary perhaps best for her leaning to abstruse conversation, such as " Ladies, let us now talk about the soul." If a literary *salon* had been possible in England, she would have been its founder.

Lady Mary discourses on Woman, Marriage, Travel, and so forth, to her Prospective Husband, Mr. Wortley Montagu

POSTMARK, *April 25th*, 1710.

I have this minute received your two letters. I know not how to direct you, whether to London or the country. 'Tis very likely you will never receive this. I hazard a great deal if it falls into other hands, and I write for all that.

I wish with all my soul I thought as you do ; I endeavour to convince myself by your arguments, and am sorry my reason is so obstinate, not to be deluded into an opinion, that 'tis impossible a man can esteem a woman. I suppose I should then be very easy at your thoughts of me ; I should thank you for the wit and beauty you give me, and not be angry at the follies and weaknesses ; but, to my infinite affliction, I can believe neither one nor t'other.

One part of my character is not so good, nor t'other as bad as you fancy it. Should we ever live together, you would be disappointed both ways ; you would find an easy equality of temper you do not expect, and a thousand faults you do not imagine.

You think, if you married me, I should be passionately fond of you one month, and of somebody else

5

the next. Neither would happen. I can esteem, I can be a friend, but I don't know whether I can love. Expect all that is complaisant and easy, but never what is fond, in me. You judge very wrong of my heart when you suppose me capable of views of interest, and that anything could oblige me to flatter anybody.

Was I the most indigent creature in the world, I should answer you as I do now, without adding or diminishing. I am incapable of art, and 'tis because I will not be capable of it. Could I deceive one minute, I should never regain my own good opinion, and who could bear to live with one they despised ?

If you can resolve to live with a companion that will have all the deference due to your superiority of good sense, and that your proposals can be agreeable to those on whom I depend, I have nothing to say against them. . . .

HORACE WALPOLE

(1717-97)

In ease, playful wit, racy description and anecdote, variety of topic, and lightness of touch, no letter writer—unless it be Madame de Sévigné, author of the famous *Letters*—has surpassed Walpole. In character he was affected, capricious and sometimes spiteful, but not incapable of generosity or friendship. It is in the deeper qualities of mind and heart that he is found wanting.

The happiness of his closing years was intimately interwoven with the graceful charms and captivating manners of the fair and accomplished sisters, Mary and Agnes Berry.

"They are of pleasing figures," writes Walpole, "Mary, the eldest, sweet, with fine dark eyes that are very lively when she speaks, with a symmetry of face that is the more interesting from being pale. Agnes, the younger, has an agreeable, sensible countenance, hardly to be called handsome, but almost. She is less animated than Mary, but seems, out of deference

(1)

(2)

(3)

(1) HORACE WALPOLE.   (2) H.R.H. GEORGE, PRINCE OF WALES.
              (3) GEORGE BRUMMELL.

to her sister, to speak seldomer, for they dote on each other, and Mary is always praising her sister's talents."

When towards the end of June 1789, the elder Miss Berry left London for Yorkshire, Horace Walpole is full of anxiety and alarm because the letter to be written on their journey had not been received; he writes—

Horace Walpole to the Misses Berry

I am not at all consoled for my double loss; my only comfort is that I flatter myself the journey and air will be of service to you both. Tonton [a dog of Miss Berry's left in Walpole's care.—ED.] does not miss you as much as I do, not having so good a taste; for he is grown very fond of *me*, and I return it for your sakes, though he deserves it too, for he is perfectly good-natured and tractable; but he is not beautiful, like his " god-dog " as Mr. Selwyn, who dined here on Saturday, called my poor late favourite, especially as I have had him clipped. . . . I passed so many evenings of the last fortnight with you that I almost preferred it to our two honeymoons, and consequently am the more sensible to the deprivation; and how dismal was Sunday evening, compared to those of last Autumn! If you both felt as I do, we might surpass any event in the Annals of Dunmore. Oh! what a prodigy it would be if a husband and two wives should present themselves and demand the flitch of bacon, on swearing that not one of the three in a year and a day had wished to be unmarried? For my part I know that my affection has done nothing but increase; though, were there but one of you, I should be ashamed of being so strongly attached at my age; being in love with both, I glory in my passion, and think it a proof of my sense.

Why should not two affirmatives make a negative, as well as the reverse!? and then a double love will be wisdom—for what is wisdom in reality but a negative?

. . . and then, having met with an accident . . .

I fell with my whole weight against the corner of
the marble altar on my side, and bruised the muscle
so badly that for ten days I could not move without
screaming. I am convinced that I should have broken
a rib, but I fell on the cavity whence two of my ribs
had been removed that are gone to Yorkshire. I am
much better both of my bruise and of my lameness,
and shall be ready to dance at my own wedding when
my wives return. . . . You are not the first Eurydice
that has sent her husband to the devil, as you have
kindly proposed to do; but I will not undertake the
jaunt; for if old Nicholas Pluto should enjoin me not
to look back to you, I should certainly forget the pro-
hibition, like my predecessor. Besides, I am a little
too old to take a journey twice, which I am so soon
to repeat, and shall be laughed at by the good folks
on the other side of the water, if I proposed coming
back for a twinkling only. No, I chuse as long as I can

> Still with my fav'rite Berrier to remain.

And the last of the old gentleman's witty, kindly,
and gossipy letters we shall quote follows. He was
in his seventy-second year, and he lived to see another
eight.

When an ancient gentleman marries, it is his best
excuse that he wants a nurse, which I suppose was
the motive of Solomon, who was the wisest of mortals,
and a most puissant and opulent monarch, for marrying
a thousand wives in his old age when, I conclude,
he was very gouty. I, in humble imitation of that
sapient king, and no mine of Ophir flowing into my
exchequer, espoused a couple of helpmates, but being
less provident than the son of David, suffered both
to ramble in the land of Goshen when I most wanted
their attendance.

I tell a great story; I did not want you; on the
contrary, I am delighted that you did not accept
my invitation. I should have been mortified to
the death to have had you in my house when I am

lying helplessly on my couch, or going to bed early from pain. . . . Be sure that I find you both looking remarkably well; not that I have any reason for wishing it, but as I am not able to nurse you. Adieu!

FREDERIC AUGUSTUS, GEORGE IV
(1762–1830)

The Prince of Wales, First Gentleman in Europe, the eldest son of George III, married in secret in 1795 Mrs. Fitzherbert, a widow, a beauty, and a rigid Catholic. His subsequent marriage with Caroline of Brunswick, on condition of payment of his debts of about £200,000, and how he tried to get a divorce from the unhappy queen on his accession in 1820, are matters of history. Amongst the many epistles of his ardent courtship of the beautiful widow we quote at hazard, less for their literary style than as an example of the affected and mincing fashion in vogue, under the influence of the French rococo, at the end of the eighteenth century.

Mrs. Fitzherbert writes from Brighton:

I was drawn to the Steine this evening by a party who drank tea with us and would not excuse me (though I was really too ill to go out) because it was generally believed that your —— —— [Royal Highness], in imitation of a ridiculous Frenchman, was to run a race backwards! Oh, that you had a mentor to guard you from those numerous perils that around you wait! The greatest of which are your present companions. As I beheld you the other day like another Harry:

> " Rise from the ground like feathered Mercury,
> and vaulted with such ease into your seat
> as if an angel dropt down from the clouds;
> to turn and wind a fiery Pegasus,
> and witch the world with noble horsemanship,"

I could not avoid continuing the comparison, and

wish that you would sometimes use that Prince's words :

> " Reply not to me with a fool-born jest,
>   for Heaven doth know, so shall the world perceive ;
>   That I have turned away my former self,
>   so will I those that kept me company."

Adieu ! If I am free to remember it is your own condescension that draws on you the remarks of

MARGARITTA.

And his reply :

If you wish me a Mentor, let me entreat you to assume the character yourself ; no one can be more capable or so agreeable to me ; and you know not the good effect this may have ; but I must at the same time desire you will not give credit to all the idle reports you may hear to my disadvantage, as was the ridiculous one you mentioned ; if my situation in life makes me many friends, it likewise makes me many enemies, and you will allow for this. Your reproof, so far from offending (which Margaritta could not do), convinces me of a kind interest you take in my future welfare, and flatters me extremely. I answer you from the same author :

> —Warwick speaks thus to Henry IV.—
> " My gracious Lord, you look beyond him quite
>   the Prince but studies his companions
>   like a strange tongue wherein to gain the language ;
>   'tis needful that the most unmodest word
>   be look'd upon and learn'd, which once attain'd
>   Your Highness knows comes to no further use,
>   but to be known and hated—so like gross terms,
>   the Prince will in the perfectness of time
>   cast off his followers, and their memory
>   shall as a pattern or a measure live
>   by which his Grace must meet the lives of others
>   turning past evils to advantages."

You admire Shakespeare, I perceive ! he is indeed an author that all people of taste must love to enthusiasm ; I have read this play with attention, and a time may come when I may likewise surprise my subjects, if my better genius, which shines forth in the sweet form of the haughty yet lovely Margaritta, will deign to add her influence; which like the sun may draw some latent blossom from an expiring plant, that otherwise would sink into obscurity.

My companions, you must allow, are mostly men of rank and family; and one that you use frequently with me, whose extraordinary history I had the pleasure of giving you one night at the ball, has the sanction of being the most adopted child of a —— I venerate, and who all the world agree in pronouncing the best, the most perfect of mortals; and with justice allow her those many virtues, which I see her daily exercise—till I adore her worth and wish to be deserving of such a parent. In my friendship to him, I pay a just compliment to this best of mothers; while I give a double pleasure to myself. Poor H——, I pity, and he has his merits. Lord —— has been an unkind brother to him—H—— too generous in return; he has a fund of humour that is always entertaining and a fine voice. S—— is young and giddy as myself.

J—— O—— amuses me; I can say nothing in his praise; he has nothing indeed to boast but his coachmanship; such characters are necessary in society.

But I have engaged you too long. Correct me with friendship and I will prove worthy of your esteem. The obliged——

BEAU BRUMMELL

(1778-1840)

The leader of fashion, George Bryan Brummell, was boon companion of George IV, when Prince Regent, who " began to blubber, when told that Brummell did not like the cut of his coat."

" The organ of love," says Captain Jessel, " in the cranium of Beau Brummell was only faintly developed." The temperament of the Beau (says Merydew), or the Buck, as he was called at Eton and Oriel, was

elephantial [sic]. Yet he never attained any degree
of intimacy with a pretty woman of rank without
making her an offer—not with any idea of being
accepted, but because he thought it a matter of compliment. As this custom was understood, his offer
was seldom taken seriously; but even when all things
were in readiness, the marriage was a failure. On one
of such occasions he was asked, Why. "What could
I do, my dear fellow," he replied, "but cut the connection? I discovered that Lady Mary actually ate
cabbage."

He could write hundreds of *billets-doux* by his
fireside, but he was not the man to shiver near his
lady's *porte-cochère* in expectation of a note before
May was out. His heart seldom thawed to this
extent before the middle of June.

As a sample of the affected and stilted style of the
eighteenth-century *cacoethes scribendi*, when flashy
wit masqueraded as intelligence and a posturing sentimentality replaced real feeling, the following may
serve:

DEAR MISS ——,—When I wrote to you a century
ago in plaintive strains, and with all "Hackman's
sorrows and all Werther's woes," you told me with
pen dipped in oblivion's ink from Lethe's stream that
I must desist from my vagaries, because I was tres-
passing on consecrated ground; but you offered me
instead your friendship as a relic—by way of a bone
to pick among all my refined and elegant sensibilities.

Well, I struggled hard to bring myself to this meagre
abnegation and my efforts promised to be propitious.
I kissed the rod, cherished the relic, and enveloped
myself in austerity and sack-cloth. I then, by way
of initiating myself to penance, inscribed you a missive
in appropriate terms of mortification, presuming, too,
that it was the privilege, if not the duty, of my vocation to mortify you also, as a votary with a little
congenial castigation.

I daresay I wrote to you in a most absurd and recriminating manner, for I was excited by the pious enthusiasm of my recent apostasy; and I was anxious to impress upon your more favourable opinion the exemplary and salutary progress I had made in my new school.

And so on, and so on, Beau Brummell pours out the high-falutin and inane verbiage of a Georgian buck, to mortify us, who are not votaries, as well.

LADIES OF THE EIGHTEENTH CENTURY FRENCH SALONS AND THEIR ADMIRERS

Airy Marivaudage

NINON DE L'ENCLOS

(1616–1706)

Every schoolboy knows the story (as Macaulay would have said) of the perennial beauty of Ninon de l'Enclos, wittiest and most beautiful of French courtesans, one of whose sons is said to have fallen in love with his own mother, and to have shot himself on learning the truth (an incident that Lesage makes use of in his *Gil Blas*). Even to-day beauty-specialists often claim to have found the secret cosmetic by which Ninon is supposed to have preserved the youthfulness of her charms, but it may be assumed that Ninon's wit and charm had as much to do with it as her physical attractions, especially for such men as Scarron, Molière, Fontenelle, and Larochefoucauld, who congregated in her salon. Past-mistress in the art of attracting men, the following letter shows her clear insight into the *ars amandi*.

Ninon de l'Enclos to the Marquis de Sévigné

Shall I tell you what renders love dangerous ? It is the sublime idea which one often appears to have about it. But in exact truth, Love, taken as a passion, is only a blind instinct which one must know how to value correctly ; an *appetite* which determines you for one object rather than for another, without being able to give any reason for one's preference ; considered as a link of friendship, when reason presides over it,

74

(1)

(2)

(3)

(1) CATHERINE THE GREAT.   (2) NINON DE L'ENCLOS.
(3) JULIETTE DROUET.

it is not a passion, it is no longer love, it is an affectionate
esteem, in truth, but peaceful, incapable of leading
you out of bounds; when, however, you walk in the
traces of our ancient heroes of romance, you go in
for the grand sentiments, you will see that this pre-
tended heroism only makes of love a deplorable and
often disastrous folly. It is a true fanaticism; but
if you strip it of all those virtues of hearsay, it will
soon minister to your happiness and to your pleasures.
Believe me, that if it were reason or enthusiasm which
governed affairs of the heart, love would become either
insipid or a delirium. The only way to avoid these
two extremes is to follow the path I indicate to you.
You have need of being amused and you will only find
what you require for that amongst the women I speak
of. Your heart needs occupation; they are made
to captivate it. . . .

Honesty in love, marquis! How can you think of
that! Ah, you are a good man gone wrong. I shall
take great care not to show your letter; you would be
dishonoured. You could not, you say, take on yourself to employ the manœuvre which I have counselled
you. Your frankness, your grandiose sentiments would
have made your fortune in the old days. Then one
used to treat love as a matter of honour; but to-day,
when the corruption of the century has changed
everything, Love is no more than a play of whim and
vanity. . . . How many occasions do you not find
where a lover gains as much by dissimulating the excess
of his passion, as he would in others, by displaying
greater passion than he feels ?

MADAME DU BARRY
(Countess, 1741–93)

The natural daughter of an excise officer, Vaubernier,
educated as an orphan in Paris, where she started life
as a modiste, her great beauty and piquant air singled
her out for a life of pleasure, when she was launched
by the notorious woman Gourdon as Mademoiselle

Lange. There is much in the life of the du Barry that resembles the changing fortunes of Emma, Lady Hamilton. Du Barry became the mistress of an aristocrat, Count Jean du Barry, with whom she went through the ceremony of marriage, to give her a position as the mistress of Louis XV. Scatter-brained and spendthrift, after Louis XV's death, in 1774, she was imprisoned in a convent. Set at liberty, she fled to England at the Revolution, but returning and being found guilty of conspiring with the emigrants, Robespierre had her guillotined.

Again, one can hardly call these superficial effusions, conceived on the spur of a momentary desire or whim, love-letters. But they may serve as valuable documents of the frivolous rococo times, in which the aristocrats passed their time in gallantry and gossip, and totally ignored the rights of man as foreshadowed by Rousseau, Diderot, and the Encyclopædists. The whole attitude was, " After us, the deluge."

Marianne Lançon (the later Countess du Barry) to one of her first admirers, Monsieur Duval.

April 6th, 1761.

Yes, my dear friend, I have told you, and repeat it : I love you dearly. You certainly said the same thing to me, but on your side it is only impetuousness ; directly after the first enjoyment, you would think of me no more. I begin to know the world. I will tell you what I suggest, now : pay attention. I don't want to remain a shop girl, but a little more my own mistress, and would therefore like to find someone to keep me. If I did not love you, I would try to get money from you ; I would say to you, You shall begin by renting a room for me and furnishing it ; only as you told me that you were not rich, you can take me to your own place. It will not cost you any more rent, not more for your table and the rest of your housekeeping. To keep me and my headdress will be the only expense, and for those give me one hundred livres[1] a month, and that will include every-thing. Thus we could both live happily, and you would never again have to complain about my refusal. If you love me, accept this proposal; but if you do not love me, then let each of us try his luck elsewhere. Good-bye, I embrace you heartily.

LANÇON.

King Louis XV to the Countess du Barry

May 1769.

Instead of waiting till to-morrow, come this evening. I have something to say to you, which will please you. Good-bye, believe me that I love you.

LOUIS.

The "something to say" was a château, which the King made her a present of.

Countess du Barry to the Duc de Brissac in 1789, when he was arrested.

A deadly fear seizes me. You have the tran-quillity of a clear conscience, but that does not set at rest my concern for you. I remain far from you, do not know what will become of you, and perhaps you do not even know yourself.

I am sending the Abbé ——, in order to find out what has happened. Why am I not with you? I should console you. I am certain that you have nothing to fear, if reason and justice should reign in the National Convention. Your behaviour, since you have been in the Tuileries, is so pure, that they can lay nothing to your charge.

Duc de Brissac to the Countess du Barry

This morning I received the amiable letter from her who for a long time has been dear to my heart. Yes, you will be my last thought. I sigh; why am I not with you in a desert?

P.S.—So far, quiet reigns in the town.

---

[1] The livre was superseded by the franc in 1795.

MLLE. DE L'ESPINASSE TO THE COMTE DE GUIBERT

(1732–76)

Julie Jeanne Eleonore de l'Espinasse, the natural daughter of the Comtesse d'Albon, being early left unprotected, went to reside with the Marquise du Deffand, where her brilliant wit and originality attracted universal attention, so that d'Alembert, Turgot, Marmontel, and others of the marquise's circle soon transferred their allegiance to Mlle. de l'Espinasse's salon. Her charming letters to her lover, the Comte de Guibert, are considered a classic in French literature. One may doubt whether the following sentiment, which pervades all the letters from Mlle. de l'Espinasse to the Comte de Guibert :

> "*In all the instants of my life*
> I suffer, I love you, and I await you,"

would meet with the approval of our modern young ladies, who can hardly conceive a woman humiliating herself so entirely as to implore the presence of a man whom she recognises as shallow and unworthy. Love of this overwhelming, all-engrossing type, from which Julie de l'Espinasse dies, is more than a passion. It is a disease, as rare and as incomprehensible in its origin as that of the *Bacillus botulinus*, with which out of six hundred pots of game-paste, only one is infected. But when one belongs, as obviously did poor Mlle. de l'Espinasse, to those who say with Heine :

> "And my race are those of Asra,
> Who die, when they love,"

there is no cure for the infection, and, indeed, Mlle. de l'Espinasse died from it.

Julie de l'Espinasse to Hippolyte de Guibert
November 13th, 1774.

Ah, my friend, you hurt me, and a great curse for you and for me is the feeling which animates me. You

were right in saying that you did not need to be loved
as I know how to love; no, that is not your measure;
you are so perfectly lovable, that you must be or
become the first object (of desire) of all these charming
ladies, who stick upon their heads all they had in it,
and who are so lovable that they love themselves by
preference above everything. You will give pleasure,
you will satisfy the vanity of nearly all women. By
what fatality have you held me to life, and you make
me die of anxiety and of pain? My friend, I do
not complain; but it distresses me that you pay no
heed to my repose; this thought chills and tears my
heart alternately. How can one have an instant's
tranquillity with a man whose head is as defective
as his coach, who counts for nothing the dangers,
who never foresees anything, who is incapable of
taking care, of exactitude, to whom it never happens
to do what he has projected; in a word, a man whom
everything attracts, and whom nothing can stay nor
give stability . . . Good night. My door has not
been opened once to-day, but what my heart palpi-
tated. There were moments when I feared to hear
your voice, and then I was disconsolate that it was not
your voice. So many contradictions, so many contrary
movements are true, and can be explained in three
words : *I love you.*

Julie de l'Espinasse to M. de Guibert
Saturday 4 o'clock, May 1776, *written shortly before death.*

My dear friend, you are too good, too amiable.
You would like to revive a heart, which finally breaks
down under the hard load of its misery. I appreciate
the full value of your desire, but I no longer deserve it.

Once there was a time when I would have had no
other wish *than to be loved by you.* Yes, in that love,
perhaps my regrets would have been extinguished.
At least their bitterness would have turned to delight.
Then I would have liked to live. Now my only desire
is to die. I have found nothing to put in its place,
no sweet consolation for what I have lost. . . .

My dear, that is the only bitter feeling which I find in my soul against you. It was an evil fatality which led you to me when it did. It has cost me tears and pains, and finally it has brought about my ruin.

I should like to know your future fate. I desire that—in accordance with your capacities—you may be happy. Your character and your manner of feeling will preserve you from ever being very unhappy. Your letter I received at one o'clock. A violent attack of fever had prostrated me. How much pains and time I took to read it, I cannot tell you. But I did not want to put it by. This laborious reading almost made me delirious. I hope for news from you this evening. Good-bye, my dear friend; if life be granted me once again, I should like to devote it anew to loving you. But it is finished.

MADAME DU DEFFAND TO HORACE WALPOLE

(1697–1780)

The Marquise du Deffand, French letter writer and *dame de salon*, early became distinguished for her wit and beauty, and forming her own establishment, from 1740 onwards gave celebrated *petits soupers* to her admirers. In 1753 she took as a companion an orphan girl, Mlle. de l'Espinasse, whom she later dismissed from jealousy as she had become a dangerous rival. Madame du Deffand's letters, like those of Walpole, are valuable documents of the social history of the times. They are not love-letters proper, but they are true expressions of that dalliance and philandering which did duty as love, when Louis the Well-beloved was king.

Wednesday, 1 o'clock in the morning, 1767.

Yesterday I announced to you a story. I thought it would only be necessary to copy it, meanwhile my letter was sent off, and I had to dictate it anew, which was very irksome to me. Meanwhile I permitted the Duke of Choiseul to tell it to others. I could relate it to you this afternoon, but I would rather wait, until the messenger has gone, for if he happens to bring me a letter from you, that will put me in a good temper, and you shall have my story. Is there no letter, you will have to do without it. Farewell. Best greetings.

4 o'clock.

No letter, here is my story. It is about eight days old. The king visited after supper Madame Victoire. He calls a valet, gives him a letter with the words : "Jacques, take this letter to the Duke of Choiseul. He is to hand it immediately to the Bishop of Orleans." Jacques goes to the Duke of Choiseul ; they tell him that he is at Monsieur de Penthièvre's. He goes thither. Monsieur de Choiseul takes the letter, finds Cadet, the first lackey of Madame de Choiseul by his side, and orders him to seek everywhere for the bishop and to let him know where he is. After an hour and a half Cadet returns, relates that he called first at Monseigneur's, that he knocked with all his might at the door without receiving an answer ; that he has run afterwards all over the town, without finding Monseigneur or getting news of him. The duke decides to go himself to the said bishop. He climbs up one hundred and twenty stairs and knocks at the door so fiercely, that one, two servants awake and come to open, in their shirts. "Where is the bishop ? " "He is in bed since ten o'clock last night." "Open the door." The bishop wakes up. "Who is there ? " "It is I ! I have a letter from the king." "A letter from the king ? Great God, how late is it ? " "Two o'clock." The bishop takes the letter. "I cannot read it without my spectacles. Where are the spectacles ? In my trousers." The minister goes to find the trousers and meanwhile they both ask themselves "What can be in the letter ? Has the Archbishop of Paris died ? Has a bishop hung himself ? " Both of them are somewhat anxious.

6

The bishop takes the letter anew, the minister is prepared to read it to him, but the bishop, from prudence, wishes to read it first. He has not quite finished it, when he hands it to the minister, who reads the following words : " Monseigneur the Bishop of Orleans ! my daughter would like to have some of your Cotignac pastry. It must be in quite small boxes. If you have none, I beg of you "—at this point of the letter a sedan-chair was drawn, and over the sedan-chair, it said further—" to procure it immediately from your episcopal residence. But do not forget that it must be in quite small boxes. With that, Monsieur l'Evêque d'Orléans, I recommend you to God's holy care.

" [Signed] Louis."

And then as postscriptum : " The sedan-chair has no particular meaning ; my daughters had drawn it on this sheet, which happened to be at hand."

You can picture to yourself the stupefaction of the two ministers. They immediately sent off a courier, and the Cotignac arrived on the next day, and nobody took any further notice of it. The king himself first put the story about, for the ministers did not wish to be the first to tell it. If our historians always told the truth, as my story does, they would be quite trustworthy.

PRINCE DE LIGNE TO THE MARQUISE DE COIGNY

(1735–1814)

The Prince de Ligne, an Austrian General, travelled much on diplomatic missions, and was a favourite with Catherine II of Russia as well as with his master Joseph II of Austria, whom he accompanied on his journeys. His witty letters on the leading men and things of Europe in his day form valuable historical material for his times.

BARTSCHISARAI, *June 1st, 1787.*

I had hoped to elevate my soul in Tauris through the great real or invented happenings of this country. My spirit was ready to turn to the heroic with Mithridates, to the fabulous with Iphigenia, to the military with the Romans, to the fine arts with the Greeks, to pillage with the Tartars, to trading with the Genoese. All these people are sufficiently well known to me. But there is something besides all this. They have all disappeared behind the Arabian Nights. I am writing from the harem of the last Khan of the Crimea. He did very wrong to strike his tent and to relinquish to the Russians four years ago the most beautiful land on earth. Fate has reserved for me the apartment of the most beautiful sultana, and for Ségur that of the first of her black eunuchs. My cursed imagination will not grow old; it is fresh, rosy, and round like the cheeks of madame la marquise. In our castle, which has something Moorish, Arabic, Chinese, and Turkish about it, there are fountains, little gardens wall paintings, gildings, and inscriptions everywhere. Amongst other things one reads in the very entertaining and very beautiful audience-chamber around the window-frames a golden inscription in Turkish of the words : " In defiance of all the jealous folk, let the whole world know herewith, that there are in Ispahan, Damascus, and Stambul no treasures like these." Starting from Cherson we always met with camps of tents, which were wonderful in their Asiatic splendour in the midst of the wilderness. I know no longer, where and in which times I live. When I see quite suddenly moving hills arise, I think I am in a dream. They are merely the loaded humps of dromedaries, which, when these animals arise upon their long legs, appear from a certain distance to be moving hills. Then I ask myself, " Are those not the goods and chattels of the three kings upon their celebrated journey to Bethlehem ? " I say to myself, " You are still dreaming." When I meet young princes of the Caucasus, almost covered in silver, upon their shining white horses—when I meet them thus, armed with bow and arrows, I fancy I am living in the times of the elder or younger Cyrus. Their adornment is sumptuous, but their arrows strike sharper and more gracefully. When I meet with troops of Circassians, as beautiful as the day, and see that their waists, laced up in stomachers, are smaller than that of Madame de L., when I see Murzas better dressed than the Duchess de Choiseul at the festivals of the queen, and Cossack officers who dress themselves with more taste than Mademoiselle Bertin, and furniture and clothing as harmonious in colouring as the paintings of Madame Lebrun, then I can hardly contain myself in admiration. From Staro Crimea, out of which they have made a castle for a single night only, I can see the finest scenes of both continents, and almost the Caspian Sea. I consider that outdoes the temptation by Satan, who could never show our Saviour such a wonderful world. When I leave my room, I see from one spot the sea of Azow, the Black Sea, the sea of Zabak and the Caucasus. The guilty one, who, as I understand, was here eternally devoured by a vulture, surely never stole as much fire as shines from your eyes and your imagination. Thus, at any rate, would speak your supple, hot-headed friar, the Abbé d'Espagnac.

I think I am still dreaming, when I find myself ensconced at the back of a six-seated carriage, a veritable car of triumph adorned with initials of brilliant pearls, between two persons against whose shoulders I often fall asleep in the heat, and that when I wake, one of my travelling companions speaks the words : " I have thirty millions of subjects, counting the men alone." " And I, two and twenty, all in all." " From Kamschatka to Riga I need an army of at least one hundred thousand men." " With half of that number," the other one says, " I have just as many as I need."

Ségur will tell you how pleased he was with this imperial companion. On the other hand, Ségur pleased the Emperor very much too. This monarch delights everybody who can see him. Freed from the cares of his Empire, he makes his friends happy with his company. A short while ago, he had, however, a mild attack of bad humour, when he received news of the revolt in the Netherlands. All the old land owners of the Crimea, as well as all the Murzas and those newly presented with estates by the Empress, amongst them myself, have sworn him the oath of fidelity. The Emperor came towards me, and taking hold of my chain of the Golden Fleece with the words, " You are the first knight of the order who has sworn his oath together with longbearded gentlemen." I answered to that, " It is better for your majesty and myself, to have to do with Tartaric great gentlemen, than with those of the Netherlands." In the carriage we let all the States and all high personalities pass before us. " Before I would have signed the surrender of thirteen provinces like my brother George," said Catherine softly, " I would rather have put a bullet through my brain." "And before I, like my brother and monsieur mon beaufrère, had called together the nation to abdicate—I don't know what I would have rather done," replied Joseph to that.

About the King of Sweden, whom they both did not love, they were of *one* opinion. The Emperor related that he got tired of him in Italy, where he used to run about in a silver-blue dressing-gown with a diamond plaque. But both of them admitted that he had energy, talent, and wit. " Certainly," I said then, to defend him, for the kindness he had often shown me and his large-hearted ways that I often saw him display forced me to this, " your majesty ought to suppress a horrid pamphlet, in which they dare to speak of such a good, charming, and highly talented prince as Don Quixote."

Their Imperial Majesties sometimes put out their feelers as to those poor devils the Turks. They looked at each other and hazarded a few remarks. As a lover of beautiful antiquity and of certain novelties, I advised that the Greeks should be reinstated. Catherine was of the opinion that Lycurgus and Solon might arise anew. I spoke of Alcibiades. But Joseph, who has more inclination to the future than the past, and for the practical than the fabulous, replied, " What the devil is to be done with Constantinople ? "

In this fashion, one conquers many islands and provinces, without moving an eyelid. I said to myself, " Your Majesties will conquer a piece of d——." " We treat him too well," the Emperor observed with regard to me ; " he has not enough respect for us. Do you know, madame, that he was in love with a mistress of my father's and that he prevented me being successful with a marquise as beautiful as an angel, who was the first passion of both of us ? "

One day the Empress asked us in the gallery, " How does one make verses ? Write it down for me, Monsieur le Comte de Ségur." He wrote out the rules for her with delightful examples and she set to work. She composed six verses with so many mistakes that we had all three to laugh about it. " I will teach you to make fun of me. You are at once to compose some verses in front of me, and then I will give up trying. I have had enough to last me for a lifetime." " Very well," then said Fitzherbert, " you should have stopped at your two lines on the burial of the lady dog :

> " ' Here rests the lady Anderson
> She bit the doctor Rogerson ! ' "

She thought of that again in Bartschisarai. " Now, messieurs," she said to us, " I shall lock myself in, then you will see." And she brought us the following lines, further than which she could not get :

> " On the khan's divan, on a silken bed,
> In the golden kiosk where cool waters shed . . ."

You can quite understand what reproaches we covered her with, that after reflecting for four hours, she could not proceed beyond such a beautiful theme, for when one is travelling, one has to entertain oneself the best one can.

This country is really a romantic country, but is not the country of romance ; for the women are shut in by dirty Mahommedans, who do not seem to know Ségur's poem upon the pleasure of being deceived by one's wife. The Duchess of L. would make me quite amorous, if she were here, and upon the Maréchale M. I would make a poem at Balaclava. Only you, dearest marquise, I can adore, even in the midst of Paris. That is the right word, for one has no time to love there. . . . Here there are several sects of dervishes ; some of them more entertaining than the others, the neck twisters and the howlers. They are crazier Jansenists than the old convulsionaries. They shout " Allah " till they are entirely exhausted, and fall to the ground with the hope, only to arise to enter Heaven. Here I abandoned the court for some days to their pleasures, and climbed, at the peril of my life, up and down the Tschetterdan, by following the stony path of this mountain stream, instead of the undiscoverable bridle-paths. I felt the desire to rest my mind, my speaking organs, my ears and my eyes, dazzled with the lights. For they struggle even at nights with the sunlight, which shines the whole day only too violently upon our town. Only you, dearest marquise, understand how to shine always, without fatiguing. I concede this virtue to you alone, not even to the stars.

CATHERINE II OF RUSSIA

(1729–96)

ANIMATED by the spirit of the French philosophers of the eighteenth century, the beautiful German Empress was a masculine, beneficent, and ruthless autocrat at the same time. Having organised the conspiracy against her husband, Peter III, which brought about his downfall and assassination, Catherine was notorious for her many amours of unbridled licence. It is more as a curiosity than as an ideal love letter that we quote the present epistle to an Unknown. Was it to Prince Soltykoff, Poniatowski, Count Orloff (who murdered her husband), Potemkin, or one of the many others ?

When I commenced this letter, I was happy and joyful, and my thoughts passed so rapidly that I did not know what became of them. It is so no longer ; I am plunged in grief and my happiness is no more ; I thought that I myself would have died from the irreparable loss which I have just sustained, eight days ago, of my best friend. With sobs, I have the misfortune to inform you that General Lauxkoi is no more ; and my room that used to be so agreeable to me, has become an empty den in which I drag myself painfully about like a shadow. I cannot see a human face without sobs depriving me of speech. I can neither sleep nor eat ; reading bores me and writing is beyond my strength. I do not know what will become of me, but what I do know, is that in all my life I have never been so unhappy than since my best and lovable friend has thus abandoned me. I opened my drawer, I found this sheet commenced, I traced these lines, but I can go no further. . . .

THE PHILOSOPHERS AND THEIR LADY
ADMIRERS

DENIS DIDEROT TO SOPHIE VOLAND
(1713–84)

INTELLECTUALLY stronger than Voltaire or Rousseau, Diderot had not their high literary gifts, but he too, by his encyclopædic work, which served as a proselytising medium for the free-thinking and sceptical philosophers, was one of the forerunners of the French Revolution. In the frivolous period of the middle-eighteenth century he observes the ills of the working classes, and writes about them to his mistress, Sophie Voland, much more his intellectual equal than his narrow-minded and bigoted wife. His life was continually embittered by impecuniosity, eventually relieved by the munificence of the Empress of Russia, Catherine II, who allowed him a pension.

GRANDVAL, *November 1st, 1759.*

. . . since this morning I hear the workmen beneath my window. The day has hardly begun to break, but they are at it ; spade in hand they dig the earth, they push wheelbarrows. They eat a piece of black bread, they quench their thirst at the running brook ; at midnight they sleep for an hour on the bare earth ; soon they take up their work again. They are merry, they sing, they crack coarse jokes with each other, which liven them up, they laugh. At night they find their naked children round a smoking hearth, a repulsive and dirty peasant woman, a bed from dried straw, and yet their lot is neither worse nor better than mine. Tell me, you who have suffered much, does the present seem harder for you than the past ? . . . I am torturing myself the whole morning, running after a thought which escapes me. I had come down sad, and heard speak of the general troubles. I seated myself without appetite at a sumptuous table, my stomach was still overloaded from yesterday's dinner, and I went on overloading it with food anew ; I took a stick and went for a walk, in order to digest and to feel easier. I came back and deluded myself at the gaming-table that I was whiling the heavy hours away. I had a friend, from whom there was no news. I was far away from my lady-love, for whom I yearned. Worries in the country, worries in the town, worries everywhere. He who knows not care, is not to be found amongst the children of men. Everything is dispelled; the Good by the Evil, the Evil by the Good, and Life is Vanity.

Perhaps we shall drive to-morrow evening or Monday morning to town for a day. I shall see my lady-love, for whom I have been yearning, and shall find the taciturn friend, from whom I had no news. But I shall lose them again on the following day, and the more I was conscious of the happiness of being near to them, the more I shall suffer at the parting.

So it goes always. Turn or twist yourself as you will, everywhere you find a crumpled roseleaf, which bruises you. . . I love my Sophie, my tenderness for her obscures my eyes to every other interest.

I see only misfortune, which could befall me in this world ; but this misfortune is many-headed, and I see it in a hundred shapes. Passes there a day on which she does not write me, " What's the matter with her ? Can she be ill ? " And thus the Chimeras flutter round my head and torture me.

Has she written me ? It haps that I misinterpret a chance word, and go out of my mind. A human being can neither advance nor delay his destiny. His good and bad fortunes are under the inexorable influence of a mighty planet. The wider his sympathies the less there remains for the individual. An only love, and all the feelings are concentrated on it. It is the miser's hoard.

But I feel that I am digesting badly, and all this jaundiced philosophy comes from a stomach out of order. But whether with overloaded or empty stomach, whether sad or merry, I love you, my Sophie, always the same, only the sentiment takes on a different colour.

GRANDVAL, *October* 15/20, 1760.

. . . Just now there is a terrific thunderstorm, with rain, hail, and snow all mixed up, and in the midst of this storm, a whole caravan descends on us from Sussy. There are about ten or twelve of them as stupid as bodies can be. The first moment was very noisy, but after the caresses, with which women and dogs overwhelm each other, when they meet, they quieted down and chattered about a thousand indifferent things. Talking about purchases and furniture, the baron said that he observed the depravity of our manners and the diminished taste of the nation by the number of secret pieces of furniture [secretaires] of all kinds.

I said, on the other hand, I only saw this therein, that people loved each other much the same, and only had increased the habit of writing and saying so. A Mademoiselle d'Ette, formerly as beautiful as an angel, tho' nothing of this has remained but a sparkle of diabolic wit, answered : in order to love sincerely, people of to-day had too many other things in their heads. I answered, that in former times, one drank more than now, one gambled not less, one hunted, rode, went shooting, whiled away time by playing ball, lived in one's own house, had a few friends, frequented the inns, did not admit young people into company, the young girls lived practically cloistered, even the mothers one hardly saw, the men went one way and the women another. Now we all live jumbled up, let young people of eighteen enter company, gamble from boredom, live apart, the children sleep together in one apartment, the bigger ones each with their separate rooms : life is partitioned off into two occupations, philandering [*galanterie*] and business.

A man is to be found in his room or in his dwelling either with a client or a mistress. Imagine for a moment that a nation were to be suddenly seized with a universal craving for music, it is sure that never before would so many bad compositions, such singing out of tune, such bad playing be heard. But on the other hand, everybody with talent for composition or execution would be forced to show it ; never before would so much good music be performed, never before such good singing, never before so many delightful melodies.

Now to point the moral.

As the spirit of philandering [*galanterie* at this period might be translated as immorality, and this is how Diderot as a moralist meant it.—ED.] is universal, there exists perhaps to-day more indecency, more deception, more immorality than ever before ; but we also find more reliability, more candidness, more honest inclination, more love, more delicacy, more durable passion than at earlier times. Those who are born to love and be loved sincerely, do love and are loved sincerely. And the same thing will hold good in other instances. More people practise it, more do it well, more will do it ill.

When the lawgiver promulgates a law, what takes place ? It gives fifty evil-doers the opportunity to infringe it, and ten righteous ones to abide by it, faithfully. The ten good ones become thereby a little better, the fifty bad ones a little worse, and the human race will merit a little more blame and a little more praise.

To make laws for a people means to increase its powers for good and bad, that is, if one may say so, to encourage it to great crimes and to great virtues. . . .

Imagine amongst us a man, who having sought to take the life of his ruler, is caught and sentenced to be tortured with iron screws, to have boiling metal poured over him, to be dipped into seething pitch, to be stretched on the rack, to be torn apart by horses. He has had this terrible sentence read to him, he has listened to it and then answered coolly : " The day will be a hard one " ; at once I should imagine there must breathe beside me a soul of the mould of Regulus, who, when a great universal or personal cause demanded it, would enter a cask studded with nails without changing colour.

How now ! Crime should be able to produce allurements, not to be equalled by virtue ? Does there not rather exist in the world something in this very virtue which can inspire a true and durable devotion ? By the expression virtue, I understand, as you well comprehend, Fame, Love, Patriotism, in a word, all the motives of great and high-minded souls. Besides it is possible that beings who are inclined to bold enterprises, may be cast, through entirely fortuitous circumstances, the one on the side of honour and the other on the side of shame. Who is the arbiter of our fate ? Who can predict the Future ? . . .

JEAN JACQUES ROUSSEAU

(1712–78)

The chief qualities of Jean Jacques Rousseau, the French philosophic writer, was a susceptibility to emotion, almost bordering on hysteria, a self-consciousness unsurpassed by that of the most awkward schoolgirl, a total absence of moral sense, an inordinate vanity, æsthetic perceptions of no mean order, and an exquisite gift of literary expression. After living on terms of intimacy with Madame de Warens, he formed a connection with Thérèse le Vasseur, a girl from Orleans, by whom he had five children, all of whom he sent to the foundling hospital, While writing his *Héloïse* on the estate of Madame d'Epinay, he becomes acquainted with the Countess d'Houdetot, and falls in love with her, although he knows, to his grief, that she is attached, not to him but to the Marquis de Saint-Lambert.

Rousseau to the Countess Sophie d'Houdetot

EREMITAGE, *June* 1757.

Come, Sophie, that I may torture your unjust heart in order that I, on my side, may be merciless towards you. Why should I spare you, whilst you rob me of reason, of honour, and life ? Why should I allow your days to pass in peace, you, who make mine unbearable !—Ah, much less cruel would you have been, if you had driven a dagger into my heart, instead of the fateful weapon, which kills me ! Look what I was and what I am now ; look to what a degree you have abased me. When you deigned to be mine, I was more than a man ; since you have driven me from you, I am the least of mortals. I have lost all reason, all understanding, and all courage ; in a word, you have taken everything from me ! How could you determine to destroy your own handiwork ? How can you dare to consider him as unworthy of esteem, whom you honoured once with your graciousness ? Ah, Sophie, I beseech you, do not be ashamed of a friend, whom you once favoured. For your own honour I demand you to render me an account of myself. Am I not your property ? Have you not taken possession of me ? That you cannot deny, and as I belong to you in spite of myself and of yourself, so let me at least deserve to be yours. Think of those times of happiness, which, to my torture, I shall never forget. That invisible flame from which I received a second, more precious life, rendered to my soul and my senses the whole force of youth. The glow of my feelings raised me to you. How often was not your heart, filled with love for another, touched by the passion of mine. How often did you not say to me in the grove by the waterfall, " You are the most tender lover, that I can imagine ; no, never did a man love like you ! " What a triumph for me, such a confession from your lips ! Yes, it was real ! it was worthy of the passion from which I demanded so ardently, that it should make you receptive, and with which I wished to awake in you a compassion that you now regret so bitterly. . . .

O Sophie ! after all the sweet moments the thought of an eternal renunciation is terrible for him, whom it saddens deeply that he cannot identify himself with you. What ! your touching eyes will never droop again before my glances with that sweet shame, which so intoxicated me with sensuous desire ? I am never more to feel that heavenly shudder, that maddening, devouring fire, which quicker than lightning . . . oh, inexpressible moment ! What heart, what god could have experienced you and resisted ? .

FRANÇOIS MARIE AROUET DE VOLTAIRE.
(1694–1778)

French writer, son of an official, is best known for the stream of satires, epigrams, odes, and epistles that poured from his inexhaustible pen. His dramas are ill-constructed, but they abound in clever character-sketches and wit. To-day his poetry is never read, and his tragedies are never acted. But his real genius first showed itself in the vivid, detailed, and various descriptive writings of his *Lettres Philosophiques*, or letters on England, where he lived for three years. Voltaire may be called the first journalist of genius, and as such, when he was past sixty, he poured forth under a multitude of pseudonyms that stream of witty and mordant criticisms on the evils of the existing régime in his inimitable style. His most serious affair was, as youthful adorer, with Olympe Dunoyer in The Hague ; but as he grew older he never allowed love of woman, or indeed love of anybody excepting himself, to interfere with his self-centred objectives.

Voltaire to Olympe Dunoyer

THE HAGUE, 1713.

I am a prisoner here in the name of the King; they can take my life, but not the love that I feel for you. Yes, my adorable mistress, to-night I shall see you, and if I had to put my head on the block to do it. For Heaven's sake, do not speak to me in such disastrous terms as you write; you must live and be cautious; beware of madame your mother as of your worst enemy. What do I say? Beware of everybody, trust no one; keep yourself in readiness, as soon as the moon is visible; I shall leave the hotel incognito, take a carriage or a chaise, we shall drive like the wind to Scheveningen; I shall take paper and ink with me; we shall write our letters. If you love me, reassure yourself, and call all your strength and presence of mind to your aid; do not let your mother notice anything, try to have your picture, and be assured that the menace of the greatest tortures will not prevent me to serve you. No, nothing has the power to part me from you; our love is based upon virtue, and will last as long as our lives. Adieu, there is nothing that I will not brave for your sake; you deserve much more than that. Adieu, my dear heart!

AROUET.

AGE OF CLASSIC ROMANTICISM IN GERMANY

JOHANN HEINRICH PESTALOZZI
(1746–1827)

We, who hear so much of Madame Montessori these days and her child-training, are apt to forget that the system was discovered and elaborated originally by the Swiss reformer Pestalozzi, who attempted to carry out Rousseau's teaching of a return to nature, educating his child after the fashion of *Emile*. The basis of the Pestalozzian system was the application of psychology to child teaching and the use of manual in conjunction with mental training. The modern application of business management, elaborated by the American engineer Taylor, is based on the same principle, that of developing the inborn potentialities of the individual, rather than by superposing cut-and-dried knowledge like a porous plaster. Although imbued with the purest ideals as a reformer, yet unfortunately Pestalozzi lacked practical and administrative ability to carry out his far-reaching schemes. The correspondence between him and his bride, the seven-years-older Anna Schulthess (daughter of a well-to-do merchant in Zurich, whom he married after her parents' opposition in 1769), sufficiently indicates Pestalozzi's tendency to sentimentality, the so prevalent Teutonic *Schwaermerei* which pervades German young people's literature of the eighteenth century, and which they are not free from even to-day.

Anna Schulthess addresses Pestalozzi as " my best friend, upright, honest youth "—" innocent youth " —" the chosen of my heart "—" I have received thee from the hand of my God," " thou me, so that the one may encourage the other, to achieve the final purpose of his intentions." And so forth !

Pestalozzi replies to Anna Schulthess

FROM HOENGG, *September 24th,* 1769.

My Nanetten ! everybody is at present in church, I am alone. I want to write to you, if I perhaps might have to wait a moment when I am at the plough, so that I might say to you soon, as soon as I am there, that I am joyful, and that even *without you*—do you believe it—I am joyful here. Nanetten, you also would be joyful, if you were here, and I am also, I must tell you, not quite without you here, not a moment, without thinking of you, you there and joyful.

My child, the present day is bright, and so also my soul ! I saw innocent, beautiful children. One I took away from the others on my lap. Oh that you had been there, I had handed it you on your lap. It was the most beautiful child of the village ! We would both have kissed it, and then, full of hope, wishes, and joy, ourselves ! Now I kissed alone, yet always twice, once for you. Nanetten, no children in the town are so beautiful, and they are not so reposeful, they are not so healthy, but our children shall be beautiful, shall be strong and healthy and reposeful like this one.

Nanetten, I am quiet and bright and happy, and even if you send me away, without kissing me, yet I am joyful. My heart laughs in my bosom ; where I am, there I think of you.

My child, I sat to-day on a low, ripening fruit-tree ; the branches bent down, as to an armchair. Gentle, midday zephyrs whispered through the leaves, and above me was shade. Next to me, there was another bending branch, similar to an armchair, a shady seat, cool from the wafting zephyr. There, I thought, there you ought to be sitting, just opposite me ; it was the better seat, I left it unoccupied for you. Upon my branch I read your letter, then I glanced at the empty branch and wished you were there, then hand could have reached hand and lip to lip, there I would not be shy, as beneath over-heated roof-slates.   So joyful am I here.   What meanwhile do you ?   Whatever it may be, you are surely thinking of me and of the countless hours, in which I live banished, without a kiss !   You think of your bad, bad deed, Nanetten ! Therefore you must not be shy any more !   This once I have tolerated it—but there is a knock !   Church is over.   Nannette, how have I spent, how have you spent the time ?

. . . again a moment for you !   Evening is drawing in ; I am beginning too often to count the moments —how long will it be till to-morrow morning ?   I will not tell you, if I do not sleep, from longing for the morning, and whether I perchance get up often and look, if it is not soon 4 o'clock—I will not tell you, when I am angry with the tiresome watchman, that he does not call the morning—all that I will not tell you.   Yet if you have remorse for your sin, and will do penance and also tell me, how you have counted the hours, I will tell you everything.

Nanetten, sleep well and dream of the beloved

PESTALOZZI.

HEINRICH VON KLEIST

(1777–1811)

The name of Heinrich von Kleist is but little known in English-speaking countries.   He may be classed amongst that little band of German romantic poets around Goethe, and particularly as the one great German dramatist after Schiller's death, with his *Penthesilea* and his *Kaetchen von Heilbronn*.   His tendency to depression, only increased by his relations to Frau Henrietta Vogel, who was suffering from an incurable disease, led him to commit suicide in his thirty-fourth year. The following letter is quoted as a literary curiosity in the profusion of its loving epithets. Lovers have a habit of applying endearing diminutives to the beloved object, which range through the entire gamut of natural history, both complimentary and otherwise. Some terms of endearment are purely onomatopoeic, agglomerative endearing sounds of no meaning. Such flattering appellations as the French use, " my little green dog," " my cabbage" or " my little horse " are purely personal; whereas Kleist, at any rate, has given his endearments a pantheistic tinge, in identifying his beloved with any or everything not only of the concrete world around him, but with every idea or abstraction his mind is capable of. For lovers in search of a new range of epithets, this effusion may serve as a useful and stimulating glossary.

Kleist to Adolfine Henriette Vogel

BERLIN, *after Michaelmas* 1810.

My Jettchen [little Henrietta], my little heart, my dear thing, my dovelet, my life, my dear sweet life, my life-light, my all, my goods and chattels, my castles, acres, lawns, and vineyards, O sun of my life, Sun, Moon, and Stars, Heaven and Earth, my Past and Future, my bride, my girl, my dear friend, my inmost being, my heart-blood, my entrails, star of my eyes, O dearest, what shall I call you ?

My golden child, my pearl, my precious stone, my crown, my queen and empress. You dear darling of my heart, my highest and most precious, my all and everything, my wife, my wedding, the baptism of my children, my tragic play, my posthumous reputation. Ach ! you are my second better self, my virtues, my merits, my hope, the forgiveness of my sins, my future and sanctity, O little daughter of Heaven, my child of God, my intercessor, my guardian angel, my Cherubim and Seraph, how I love you !

JOHANN CHRISTOPH FRIEDRICH VON SCHILLER

(1759–1805)

Schiller, one of Germany's greatest poets and dramatists, is one of the most sympathetic figures in literature.   He was a man of singular purity of character, with a mind ambitious of reaching the highest.   In spite of bodily weakness and the frowns of fortune, he strove to attain the ideal in life and art.   Strikingly handsome, after various love-affairs he liberated himself from the influence of Frau von Kalb, to succumb to the charm of the two delightful and witty daughters of Frau von Lengefeld, to one of whom, Lotte, he became engaged, and eventually married in 1790.

He writes from Leipzig to Lotte von Lengefeld

August 3rd, 1789.

Is it true, dearest Lotte ? may I hope that Karoline has read in your soul and has answered me out of your heart, what I did not have the courage to confess ? Oh, how hard this secret has become for me, that I, as long as we have known each other, have had to conceal ! Often, when we still lived together, I collected my whole courage and came to you with the intention to disclose it to you—but this courage always forsook me.   I thought to discover selfishness in my wish, I feared that I had only my happiness in view, and that thought drove me back.   Could I not become *to you* what you were to me, then my suffering would have distressed you, and I would have destroyed the most beautiful harmony of our friendship through my confession.   I would have also lost that, what I had, your true and sisterly friendship. And yet again there come moments, when my hope arose afresh, wherein the happiness, which we could give each other, seemed to me exalted above every, every consideration, when I considered it even as noble to sacrifice everything else to it.   You could be happy without me—but not become unhappy through me. This I felt alive in me—and thereupon I built my hopes.

You could give yourself to another, but none could love you more purely or more completely than I did. To none could your happiness be holier, as it was to me, and always will be. My whole existence, everything that lives within me, everything, my most precious, I devote to you, and if I try to ennoble myself, that is done, in order to become ever worthier of you, to make you ever happier. Nobility of souls is a beautiful and indestructible bond of friendship and of love. Our friendship and love become indestructible and eternal like the feelings upon which we establish them.

Now forget everything, that could put constraint on your heart, and allow your feelings to speak alone. Confirm to me, what Karoline had allowed me to hope. Tell me that you will be *mine* and that my happiness costs you no sacrifice. Oh, assure me of that, it only needs a single word. Our hearts have a long time been close to each other. Allow the only foreign element which has hitherto been between us to vanish, and nothing, nothing to disturb the free communion of our souls. Farewell, dearest Lotte! I yearn for a quiet moment, to portray to you all the feeling of my heart, which, during that long period that this longing alone dwells in my heart, have made me happy and then again unhappy. How much have I not still to say to you. Do not delay to banish my unrest for ever and always, I give all the pleasures of my life into your hand. Oh, it is such a long time that I have pictured you under no other shape than that of your portrait. Farewell, my most precious!

GOETHE
(1749–1832)

Goethe, most universal of German poets, with his *Faust* and numerous works on widely different subjects

(1)   (2)   (3)

(1) HERR VON SCHILLER.   (2) CHARLOTTE VON SCHILLER.   (3) GOETHE.

(from colour theories to elective affinities), was Germany's Admirable Crichton of the eighteenth century. Handsome, well-born, living a well-to-do life in patrician Frankfurt and grandducal Weimar, he rang the changes on many and varied love-affairs, his theory of love being elucidated in his work *Elective Affinities*, wherein he preaches following one's inclination in spite of conventional trammels.

Young Geothe to Kaetchen Schoenkopf

When he was seventeen (1766) his early love-affair was with Kaetchen Schoenkopf, daughter of a Frankfurt wine-merchant, his youthful passion not being reciprocated on account of Goethe's continual bickerings of jealousy.

FRANKFURT, *November 1st,* 1768.

MY DEAREST FRIEND,—Still so bright, still so malicious, so skilful, in presenting good from a false side, so unmerciful, to laugh at a sufferer, to ridicule one who complains, all these amiable cruelties are contained in your letter ; and could the countrywoman of Minna write differently ?

I thank you for a reply so unexpectedly quick, and beg you to continue, in future, to think of me in pleasant, bright hours, and, if it were feasible, to write to me ; to realise your loveliness, your brightness, your wit is one of the greatest pleasures for me, it may be as supercilious, as bitter, as it will.

What kind of a figure I have cut, I know best of all, and the part my letters play, I can imagine. If one calls to mind how others have fared, one can guess, without having the gift of reading the future, how one will be treated ; I am satisfied.

It is the usual fate of those who have passed away, that those who are left and those who come after should dance upon their graves.

How goes it with our principal master of ceremonies, our director, our friend Schoenkopf ?

Does he still occasionally give a thought to his first

actor, who during all this time, in every comedy and
tragedy, did represent the difficult and irksome parts
of lover and mourner, so well and life-like as possible ?
Have you discovered another, who would like to fill
my position, though it be not so efficiently filled?
You will sooner find ten actors for Duke Michael,
than one for Don Sassafras.   Do you take my meaning ?

Our good Mama has had me reminded of Starck's
handbook, I shall not forget it.   You have had me
remembered to Gleim, I shall forget nothing.   During
my absence, as well as during my presence, I am solicitous of satisfying the desires of those whom I love.   I
often have in mind your library, it shall be augmented
at earliest, rely on it.   Even if I do not always keep my
promises immediately, yet I often do more than promise.

You are right, my friend, that I am now being,
punished for what I have sinned against Leipzig ;
my sojourn here is as unpleasant, as my Leipzig one
might have been agreeable, if it had suited certain
people to render it agreeable for me.

If you wish to scold me, you must be just ; you
know what makes me discontented, wayward and
ill-tempered ; " the roof was sound, but the beds
might have been better," says Franziska.

By the way, how goes it with our Franziska, is
she soon to make her peace with Justus ?   I think so.
As long as the sergeant was still there, well, she remembered her promise ; now that he has gone to Persia,
well then, out of sight, out of mind, she would rather
take a serving-man, whom she would not dream of
otherwise, than none at all.   My greetings to the
dear girl.   You are up in arms against the compliment
addressed quite exclusively to your neighbouring
miss.   What remains over for you then ?   What a
question to ask !   You have my whole love, my whole
friendship and the most comprehensive of compliments
does not contain one-thousandth part of that, as
you very well know, although you behaved so to
plague or entertain me in your letter P.E. in that
part about leave taking pp. which I overlook.

Show this letter, and may I beg of you, all my letters, to your parents, and if you wish, to your friends, but to no one else ; I write, as I have spoken, sincerely, and in doing so, I might wish that no one should see it, who might distort its meaning. I am, as always, incessantly and completely yours,

G.

Goethe to Charlotte Kestner (née Buff)

Goethe's heart (after weathering an idyllic attachment to Frederike Brion, the daughter of the pastor at Strassburg, where he was working for his examination as licentiate) was in serious danger owing to his passion for Charlotte Buff, of Wetzlar, who was engaged to and eventually married his friend Kestner. Even after her marriage, he still carried on a passionate correspondence with her, his soul-turmoil being embodied in his *Sorrows of Werther*, a book which had an immediate and universal success all over Europe.

FRANKFURT, *August* 26/31*st*, 1774.

Who goes this very moment out of my room ? Lotte, dear Lotte, you will not guess it. You will guess a whole row of distinguished and undistinguished people rather than Frau Katrin Lisbet, my own stocking-laundress from Wetzlar, the gossip, whom you know, who loves you as we all do, who all your life have been about you ; she can no longer get a living in Wetzlar, and my mother hopes to get her a job. I took her up into my room, she saw your silhouette, and exclaimed " Ach ! my darling Lottchen." In spite of all her toothlessness, full of sincere emotion. Out of sheer joy she kissed my coat and hand, and related about you, how horrid you were, and afterwards a good child and had kept silence, when she was beaten on your account, for taking you to Lieutenant Meyer, who was in love with your mother, and wanted to see you and give you presents, which she will not permit pp. everything, everything. You can imagine how precious the woman was to me, and that I shall look after her.

Goethe to Charlotte Buff

If bones of saints, and lifeless rags, which have touched the bodies of those saints, merit adoration and preservation and care, why not the human creature, which touched you, bore you on her arm as a child, took you by the hand, that creature from whom you, no doubt, have begged for many things ? Thou, Lotte, hast begged! and this creature should not ask me for anything. Angel of Heaven! Dear Lotte, one thing more. That made me laugh. How often you annoyed her with your hands dangling, like you do let them, I imagine, even now; she imitated you at it, and it seemed to me, that your spirit was about me, and about Karlinchen and Lenchen, everyone, and everything I had not seen, and had seen, and finally there was Lotte, and Lotte and Lotte, and Lotte, and Lotte, and without Lotte nothing but Want and Mourning and Death. Adieu, Lotte, not a word more to-day, 26th August.

.   .   .   .   .   .

Yesterday the 26th, I had begun a letter to you ; here I sit now in Langen, between Frankfurt and Darmstadt, awaiting Merken, whom I have asked to come here, and I am so minded, to write to you. To-day, two years ago, almost the whole day I sat by your side ; beans were being cut up until about midnight, and the 28th was commenced ceremoniously with tea and friendly faces !

O Lotte, and you assure me with all the frankness and simplicity of your soul, which I valued so much in you, that you both still love me, for look, it would be truly saddening, if the course of time were to overwhelm us too. I shall shortly send you a prayer book, treasure casket, and whatever you like to call it, in order to confirm you morning and evening in the pleasant reminiscence of friendship and love. . . .

Frau von Stein, Goethe's senior by seven years, the wife of a Weimar Court official, a woman of great charm and will-power, was for many years Goethe's affinity and Egeria at the little grandducal court, a relationship which was only broken years afterwards, when, on returning from Italy, Goethe entered into relations with the young and pretty daughter of another Weimar official, Christine Vulpius.

Frau von Stein to Goethe

February 1776.

The world is beginning to become lovable again, I had renounced it so entirely, lovable through you. My heart reproaches me, I feel that I am preparing tortures for you and me. Half a year ago, I was ready to die, I am so no longer.

Goethe to Frau von Stein

WEIMAR, *July 16th*, 1776.

On the evening of the 16th. One word more. Yesterday as we rode at night back from Apolde, I was alone in front with the hussars. They were bandying quips with each other ; I heard them, heard them not, riding on lost in thought. Then it struck me, how fond I am of the neighbourhood. That country ! The Ettersburg ! the soft hillocks ! and it shot through my mind ; supposing you had to leave this too sometime ! the country, where you have found so much, found every happiness, that a mortal can dream of, where you float, between pleasure and displeasure, in an eternally harmonious existence, if you were forced to leave that too with a staff in your hand, as you have left your fatherland. Tears came into my eyes, and I felt myself strong enough, to endure that too. Strong ! that means ! In the Dumps !

Many of Goethe's letters are descriptive of his travels and of the historic events he witnesses, in his capacity of trusted representative of the Grand

Duke of Hesse-Darmstadt. His long sojourn in Italy estranged him from Frau von Stein and he writes imploringly to her after she has broken her long silence in writing him.

December 23rd, 1786.

Only let me thank you for your letter! Let me forget for a moment the painful part of its contents. My love! my love! Let me beg from you on my knees, imploringly, make my return to you easier, that I may not remain banished in the wide world.

Pardon me generously for my sins towards you, and raise me up. Tell me oft and at length, how you live, that you are well, that you love me. In my next letter I will let you know my travel-itinerary, what I had proposed doing, and may Heaven let it prosper. Only I beg of you; do not regard me as separated from you, nothing in the world can replace to me, what I should lose both in you and in my circumstances there. May I bring back the strength to suffer more manfully every contrariety. Do not open the boxes, I beg, and be without anxiety. My greetings to Stein and Ernest, I thank Fritz for his letter, let him write often to me, I have already begun to collect for him, he shall have what he asks for.

That you are ill, ill through my fault, oppresses my heart to such an extent, that I cannot describe it to you. Forgive me, I myself have been struggling between death and life, and no words can render the state I was in. This fall has brought me to my senses. My love! My love!

Goethe to Christiane Vulpius

In spite of his protestations to Frau von Stein, the old sinner, upon his return from Italy, had succumbed to the youthful charm and attractions of Christiane Vulpius, and envelops her with his usual word-spinning incantations—

VERDUN, *September 10th, 1792.*

I have written you many little letters, and do not know, when they will reach you one by one. You are informed once more that I am in good health, you know that I love you heartily. Would that thou werest only now by my side. There are everywhere large wide beds and thou shouldst have no cause to complain, as sometimes happens at home. Ach, mein Liebchen! There is nothing better than to be together. We will never cease to repeat this, when we are with each other again. Only think! We are so near to Champagne and find no good glass of wine. On the Frauenplan [A street in Weimar.—ED.] it will be better as soon as my Liebchen is in charge of kitchen and cellar. Be a good home-treasure, won't you, and prepare for me a pleasant dwelling. Look after the boy [*das Buebchen*] and cherish my love. Cherish my love, I beg, for I am sometimes jealous in my thoughts and imagine that another could please you more, because I find many men handsomer and more agreeable than myself. But that is not for you to notice, rather you must think me the best of all, because I love you awfully and nothing pleases me outside of you. Often I dream all sorts of confused stuff about you, but always, that we love each other. And let it remain at that.

From my mother I have ordered two mattresses and feather pillows and all kind of fine things besides. Only see to it, that our little house be very orderly, care will be taken for the rest. In Paris many things are to be had, in Frankfurt there is besides another little Jew store. To-day a small basket of liqueurs was sent off, and a packet of confectionery; things will continually arrive for the housekeeping. Cherish my love, and be a faithful child, everything else will follow. As long as I had not your heart, what use had I for the rest ? Now that I have it, I should like to keep it. It is for that, I am yours. Kiss the child, greeting to Meyer and love me.

(*Note.*—By Christine Vulpius, Goethe had several children, and, in spite of his rooted objection to marriage, married her in 1806, nearly twenty years afterwards, just before he completed his masterpiece,

Faust, in 1808. But he lived to regret his marriage, for shortly afterwards he fell in love with Minna Herzlieb, of Jena. Fortunately for him, his heart-affairs generally found an outlet in literature, this last one leading to his writing his *Wahl-verwan-schaften* (*Elective Affinities*), in which he preaches the doctrine of following one's own inclinations in love-affairs. But even after his wife's death in 1816, the old warhorse was still susceptible to the trumpet of love, for even as late as 1823, when seventy-four years old, he indulged in an almost youthful passion for a young lady whom he met at Marienbad. But this was the last of his amatory excursions, Goethe dying in 1832, when eighty-three years of age.)

COUNT GABRIEL HONORÉ DE MIRABEAU
(1748-91)

THE young and handsome nobleman, after wasting his own and his wife's fortunes, had been imprisoned by his father's request in the Château d'If (the memorable scene of Dumas's *Monte Cristo*). There the young Mirabeau fascinated Madame Sophie de Mounier the young wife of an old magistrate, and eloped with her until arrested and imprisoned again. At the outbreak of the French Revolution, elected to the States-General, he again exerted his magnetic influence upon men ; and had Louis XVI trusted him, the Revolution might have had a less sinister issue. But the great orator's triumphs in the Assembly were mainly rhetorical and superficial, and he failed to stem the tide of revolution. His letters to Sophie de Mounier are considered in France as classics in love-letters.

Mirabeau to Sophie

To be with the people one loves, says La Bruyère is enough—to dream you are speaking to them, not speaking to them, thinking of them, thinking of the most indifferent things, but by their side, nothing else matters. O mon amie, how true that is ! and it is also true that when one acquires such a habit, it becomes a necessary part of one's existence. Alas ! I well know, I should know too well, since the three months that I sigh, far away from thee, that I possess thee no more, that my happiness has departed. However, when every morning I wake up, I look for you, it seems to me that half of myself is missing, and that is too true. Twenty times during the day, I ask myself where you are ; judge how strong the illusion is, and how cruel it is to see it vanish. When I go to bed, I do not fail to make room for you ; I push myself quite close to the wall and leave a great empty space in my small bed. This movement is mechanical, these thoughts are involuntary. Ah ! how one accustoms oneself to happiness. Alas ! one only knows it well when one has lost it, and I am sure we have only learnt to appreciate how necessary we are to each other, since the thunderbolt has parted us. The source of our tears has not dried up, dear Sophie ; we cannot become healed ; we have enough in our hearts to love always, and, because of that, enough to weep always. Let those prate who affirm that they have shaken off a great affliction by virtue or by strength of mind ; they only became consoled because they are weak and on the surface. There are losses one must never be reconciled to ; and when one can no longer bring happiness to what one loves, then one must bring misfortune. Let us speak the Truth itself, it must be ; and this delicate sentiment, whatever one may say, is in the nature of a tender love. Would Sophie not be in despair, if she knew her Gabriel consoled ?

MADAME ROLAND

(1754–93)

The wife of Jean Marie Roland de la Platière, Marion Jeanne Philipon, daughter of a Paris engraver, had studied Voltaire, Rousseau, Diderot, revelled in scientific studies, and at eighteen demanded " a philosopher " as a husband, and found him in Roland. Talented, courageous, enthusiastic for ideals, beautiful but of doubtful morality, she inspired the Girondists, who used to meet at her Paris house, and suffered death, in which she displayed a noble fortitude, by the guillotine. Amongst her several lovers, we select

(1) FRANÇOIS RENÉ DE CHATEAUBRIAND.   (2) MADAME DE STAËL.
(3) MADAME ROLAND.

a letter of hers to the deputy Leonard Buzot, written from prison shortly before her execution.

Madame Roland to Leonard Buzot

(From prison) *June 22nd*, 1793.

How often do I not re-read your letters! I press them to my heart, I cover them with my kisses. I did not expect any more. Without success I asked for news of you from Madame Cholet. I wrote once to M. le Tellier in Evreux, so that you should receive a sign of life from me, but the postal connection is interrupted. I did not want to send you anything direct, because your name would suffice for the letter to be intercepted, and I might besides attract suspicion to you. Proud and calm I came here, with wishes for the defenders of liberty and some hopes for them. When I heard of the decree of arrest that had been promulgated against the twenty-two, I exclaimed " My country is lost." I remained in painful anxiety, before I had certain news of your flight, and the decree issued for your arrest frightens me anew. This horrible thing is no doubt due to your courage; since I know that you are in the Calvados, I regain my equanimity. Continue in your noble endeavours, my friend. Brutus despaired too soon of the Roman safety at the battle of Philippi. As long as a republican still breathes, is free, has his courage, he must, he can be useful. The south of France offers you in any case a refuge, and will be the asylum of honourable men. Thither you must turn your looks and wend your steps. There you will have to live, in order to serve your fellows and to exercise your virtues.

I personally shall know how to wait quietly, until the reign of justice returns, or shall undergo the last acts of violence, of tyranny in such a manner, that my example too will not be without utility. If I have feared anything, it was only, that you might have intervened impetuously on my behalf. My friend! If you save our country, you also bring about

8

my salvation. I shall be prepared to breathe my last with resignation, if I know that you are serving your country successfully. Death, tortures, sufferings, mean nothing to me, I can face them all. Be without fear, I shall live to the last hour of my life, without wasting a moment in the restlessness of unworthy excitement. . . .

Without fear ! We cannot cease to be worthy of those feelings, with which we mutually inspire each other. Thus one cannot become unhappy. Farewell, my friend, farewell, my dearly beloved !

CAMILLE DESMOULINS
(1760–94)

A young advocate in Paris, he threw himself into the arms of the Revolution, enthusiastic for Freedom and Equality. Haranguing the multitude in 1789 in the Palais-Royal, he created the distinctive sign for the revolutionaries, by fixing a leaf into his hat, from which originated the cockade. About this time he married Lucile Duplessis, a beautiful, witty woman, whom he loved passionately. With Danton he founded the Club of the Cordeliers. Owing to his demands for clemency, and his attacks on the tyranny of the terror-ists, Robespierre had him guillotined. His wife, who had moved heaven and earth to save him, went to the guillotine a fortnight afterwards, though only twenty-three years of age. Even in death, he still makes the gesture of the noble Roman wrapping his toga around him.

Camille Desmoulins to his Wife Lucile
On the 2nd Germinal, the II Decade, at 5 o'clock in the morning April 1s
1794.

(Copy of my letter, which you have perhaps not received.)

Beneficent slumber has helped to obliterate my sufferings. When one sleeps, one has not the feeling

of being in prison, one is free. Heaven had mercy
for me. Only a moment ago, I saw you in my dream,
I embraced you one after another—you Horace, and
you, Daronne, who were at home. Our little one
had lost an eye, and I saw upon it a bandage. And in
my distress at this, I woke up. I found myself in
my dungeon. Day was dawning. I saw you no more,
my Lolotte, and could not hear you, for you and your
mother, you had spoken to me, and Horace, without
feeling his pain, had said " Papa, papa." Oh, the
cruel ones, who deprive me of the joy to hear these
words, to see you and to make you happy. For
that was my only ambition and my only conspiracy. . .

I have discovered a crack in my cell. I put my
ear to it, and heard a sigh. I hazarded a few words,
and heard the voice of a sick man suffering. He
asked me for my name, which I told him. " My
God ! " he exclaimed, and sunk back on his couch.
" I am Fabre d'Eglantine. But you are here ?
Has then the counter-revolution been successful ? "
We did not dare to talk with one another, in order
that hatred might not deprive us of the poor consolation, and so that one might not hear us and separate
us from each other, to place us in still closer confinement. Beloved, you cannot imagine what it means to
be in the dark, without knowing the reason, without
being interrogated, without a single newspaper. It
means to be at the same time living and dead. Or
alive and to feel oneself in a coffin. They say, that
innocence is at rest and full of courage. Oh, my
precious Lucile, that would be true, if one were
God.

At this moment the commissaries of the Republic
came to interrogate me, whether I had conspired
against the Republic. How ridiculous ! how can they
so insult the purest Republicanism ! I see the fate
which awaits me. Farewell, my precious Lucile, my
Lolotte, my good Lou, say farewell to my father for
me. You see in me an example of the barbarity
and ingratitude of man. As you see, my fear was

well founded, my premonition right every time. But
my last moments shall not dishonour you. I was the
husband of a woman of divine virtue, I was a good
husband, a good son, I would also have been a good
father. I follow my brothers who have died for the
Republic. I am certain to take with me the esteem
and the pity of all friends of virtue, of freedom, and
of truth. I die at thirty-four years of age, and yet
it is a miracle that I have passed through so many pitfalls
of the Revolution during five years, and that I am still
alive. I rest my head with confidence on the pillow
of my all too numerous writings, but they all breathe
the same love of humanity, the same wish, to make my
fellow-citizens free and happy, those whom the axe
of St. Just will not fall upon. I see that power intoxi-
cates almost all men and that they all say with Diony-
sius of Syracuse, "Tyranny is a beautiful gift."
However, console yourself, disconsolate widow, Hector's
widow, for the inscription on the grave of your unhappy
Camille is more glorious: it is that of Cato and Brutus,
the murderers of tyrants. My beloved Lucile, I
was born to make verses and to defend the unfortunate.
In this hall, where I fight now for my life, I defended
four years ago for whole nights a mother of ten children,
who could find no advocate. In front of the same
bench of jurors, who now murder me, I once appeared,
when my father had already lost a great law suit,
suddenly like a miracle in the midst of the judges.
Then at least weeping was no crime. My emotional
speech knew how to move them, and I won the case,
which my father had already lost. Such a conspirator
am I! I never was any other. I was born, in order
to make you happy, in order to create for us both,
with your mother and my father and some intimate
friends, a Tahiti. I dreamt the dreams of the Abbé
St. Pierre. I dreamt of a republic, the idol of all
men, I could not believe that men are so unjust and
so cruel. How could I imagine that a jovial allusion
towards colleagues in my writings could obliterate
so many services. I do not conceal from myself that

I fall as a victim of those pleasantries and of my friendship for the unfortunate Danton. I thank my murderers for this death with him and Phélipeaux. My colleagues, my friends, the whole " mountain," which, with the exception of a few, has encouraged me, congratulated me, kissed me, pressed my hand in thanks, has been so cowardly as to desert me. Those who have said so much to me, and even those who condemned my newspaper, none of them can seriously consider me a conspirator. The freedom of the press and opinion has no longer any defenders, we will die as the last republicans, even though we had to pierce ourselves with our own swords like Cato, if there had been no guillotine.

MADAME RÉCAMIER AND HER ADMIRERS

Madame Récamier

(1777–1849)

THE story of Madame Récamier, whose classical beautiful features and figure harmonised so well with the Empire style, as we see in her celebrated portrait by the painter David, in the Louvre, really constitutes a panorama of the period, during which every celebrated Frenchman of the times frequented her salons. Love-letters are extant (and quoted in this collection) to her from such diverse adorers as Lucien Bonaparte, Benjamin Constant, and Chateaubriand, to all of whom she appears to have been equally gracious and attractive without having ever given cause for scandal. Married to the rich banker, Récamier, in 1793 (he was forty-two and she fifteen), her life seems to have been perfectly pure, and apart from her classical beauty, she attracted through her charm of conversation and her sympathetic manners. Banished by Napoleon in 1811, because of her friendship with Madame de Staël and the *ancien régime*, she joined Madame de Staël in banishment, only returning to Paris at the Restoration, dying there from cholera in 1849.

LUCIEN BONAPARTE (1775–1840), Napoleon's next brother, was twenty-four years old when he met Madame Récamier, and declared his passion, pretending to give a literary flavour to his letters by addressing them to Juliet from Romeo. But after a year's incessant courtship, Lucien retired discomfited. Madame Récamier's Christian name was Juliette.

MADAME RÉCAMIER.

Lucien Bonaparte to Madame Récamier

VENICE, *July 27th.*

Romeo writes to you, Juliette; if you were to refuse to read it, you would be more cruel than our parents, whose long quarrels have just finished; without doubt these terrible quarrels will not be renewed.

Only a few days ago, I only knew you by reputation. I had seen you several times in the temples and in the festivities; I knew that you were the most beautiful; a thousand mouths repeated to me your praises, but these praises, and your attractions had struck without dazzling me. . . . Why did the peace deliver me to your sway? The peace!—it is to-day in our families, but the trouble is in my heart. . . .

I have seen you since. Love has seemed to smile on me—seated on a circular bench, alone with you I have spoken, I seemed to hear a sigh issue from your bosom! Vain illusion! Recovered from my error, I have seen indifference with a tranquil forehead seated between us two;—the passion which masters me, expressed itself in my discourses, and yours bore the amiable and cruel imprint of pleasantry.

O Juliette! life without love is only a long sleep; the most beautiful of women must have feeling; happy the mortal who will become the friend of your heart.

BENJAMIN CONSTANT (1767–1830).—Henri Benjamin Constant Rebecque (to distinguish him from his namesake, Jean Joseph Benjamin Constant, the French painter, who lived in the nineteenth century), a French statesman " constant in inconstancy " towards the Republic, Napoleon, and the Restoration in turn, was very changeable in his many love-affairs, seeking diversions in his many intrigues.

Benjamin Constant to Madame Récamier

September 3rd, 1814.

To-morrow evening, to-morrow evening? What is that evening to me? It will commence for me at five o'clock in the morning. To-morrow is to-day. Thanks to God, yesterday is passed. I shall therefore be at your door at nine o'clock. They will tell me that you are not there. I shall be there between ten and eleven, will they still tell me that you are not there ?

I suffer in advance from that which I shall suffer. I wager that you do not believe me. That is because you do not know me. There is in me a mysterious point. So long as that is not reached, my soul is unmoved. If it is touched, everything is decided. There is perhaps still time.

I think only of you, but I may perhaps still combat myself. I have seen nothing but you these last two days. All the past, all your charm that I have always feared, is entered into my heart. It is a fact that I have difficulty in breathing while writing to you. Take care of that, you can render me too unhappy not to be unhappy yourself because of that ; I have never more than one thought. You have wished it so ; that thought is you. Politics, society, everything has disappeared. I seem mad to you perhaps ; but I see your look, I repeat to myself your words, I see that schoolgirl air, which united so much grace to so much " finesse." I am right to be mad. I would be mad not to be so. Till this evening then. Mon dieu ! If you are not the most indifferent of women, how much you will make me suffer in my life ? To love is to suffer. But it also means living, and since so long a time I have not been living. Perhaps I have never lived such a life. Once again, till to-night.

Benjamin Constant to Madame Récamier

January 1815.

It is four o'clock in the morning. I ought to go to bed instead of writing, but I cannot go. I left you three hours ago. I only thought of you, I cannot refrain from telling you so. You promise me friendship, a friendship a little different from that which you grant to the crowd of your friends.

I thank you for that. I consecrate to you my entire life, the wit I may possess, the faculties, the physical and moral forces, in exchange for this friendship so insufficient but so precious. I only live for that, I swear to you ; and, if I exaggerate, I beg God to deprive me of this only good which sustains me in this world. I swear to you that never, neither by night nor by day, at no time whatever, in the midst of no business of any sort, does your image leave me.

My love is a constant sensation which nothing suspends, which nothing interrupts, which is alternatively absolute devotion which has its sweetness, and an agony so fearful, that if you were to prolong it twice twenty-four hours, you would kill me. Have you not seen yesterday again your power ? Do you not feel that every time I speak to you of anything else than my feeling for you, it is a sacrifice that I make. But what sacrifice would I not make to enable me to see you and to hear you ! If you knew what enchantment I feel when you speak rather more freely than usual, with a little openness and confidence ! how every one of your words goes down into my heart, how my soul fills itself with you ! how a repose, a momentary happiness, replace the agitation which devours me elsewhere ! Oh, if you loved me as I love you, what happiness would we not enjoy ! What certainty would we not have the one from the other in life ! If, in awaking, you were to think with pleasure of this feeling which surrounds you, which embraces from the smallest details up to the greatest interests of your existence, which associates itself to every one of your thoughts ; which, if you would permit it, would not leave a single one of your emotions, not one of the needs of your heart without reply ; of this feeling so exempt of all egoism, which finds in devoting itself the happiness which others seek in self-love and in success ; which is a stranger to all other calculations ; for which neither glory nor power, nor fortune, nor amusement exist in so far as they are not means to come to you and to serve you or please you, how much fuller would not your life be and how much stronger! how this indecision which torments you would become happiness. For, every detail of life, every movement of the soul, every interest, even a vulgar one, would be a cause of union, an occasion of sympathy, and the objects which tire you or are indifferent to you would take on importance, as if to prove to you that you are uniquely understood, cherished, adored. Say well to yourself at least that, if your character, your will, your memories, make you disdain this happiness, the certainty, which must be at the bottom of it, exists nevertheless, that you dispose of me as an instrument which replies to every thought, to every emotion of yours, and which would only cease to reply thereto if you wanted to break it. Do not break it. You have been very near to doing this more than once; but to-day, you can have neither fear nor distrust.

It was during Madame de Staël's last illness that M. de Chateaubriand met Madame Récamier, but not till 1818 did the noble author of *The Genius of Christianity* become an assiduous visitor. One of the most precise of men, in that every morning early he indited a note to Madame Récamier, and visited her so invariably punctually at three o'clock in the afternoon, that the neighbours set their clocks by him when seeing him pass.

But his appointment as ambassador obliged him to travel. When French Ambassador in London (where he had lived in exile as *émigré* twenty years before) he writes:

Vicomte de Chateaubriand to Madame Récamier

LONDON, *Tuesday, April 9th,* 1822.

I have great need to receive a line from you. I wrote to you from Calais and Dover. I am now here in London, where I have only sad reminiscences, and where I am very lonely, whatever you may think and say about it. I do not take a step here without recognising something which reminds me of my sufferings and my youth, the friends I have lost, the world that has gone, the hopes I used to buoy myself with, my first works, my dreams of glory, and, *enfin*, all that which makes up the future of a young man who feels himself born to something. I have grasped some of my chimeras, others have escaped me, and all that was not worth the trouble I took over it. One thing remains to me, and as long as I shall preserve that, I shall console myself about my grey hairs, and with what I have missed on the long road that I have travelled since thirty years.

Chateaubriand to Madame Récamier, from London

May 31st, 1822.

With what joy have I now seen again the little handwriting. All the posts which arrived without a solitary word from you, broke my heart. How mad I am to love you thus, and why do you abuse so much of your power ! How could you believe for a moment what one can have told you ? I hate mortally those who have done me so much harm, whoever they may be. We shall explain things ; but, meanwhile, let us love each other, that is the means of getting rid of our enemies. If you had gone to Italy, I would have followed you.

VICOMTE RENÉ DE CHATEAUBRIAND

(1768–1848)

We have seen in the correspondence with Madame Récamier, Chateaubriand after the Restoration as French Ambassador. But before this, when living in poverty as an *émigré* in England, he had written his best-known work, *The Genius of Christianity*, on which his fame rests. Chateaubriand is celebrated as the first great writer of poetical prose in France, as well as for his romantic praise of Christianity ; he was always a great favourite of the high-born ladies of the *ancien régime*, from whose letters we quote. His inordinate vanity was the cause of many of his misfortunes.

Chateaubriand to Madame de Custine

You cannot conceive what I suffer since yesterday; they wanted me to go away to-day. I have obtained, by special favour, that they should give me at least till Wednesday. I am, I assure you, half mad, and I believe that I shall end, by handing in my resignation. The idea of leaving you, kills me. As a climax of misfortune I shall not be able to see you before two o'clock this afternoon.

In the name of Heaven, do not go away. Let me see you once more at least! Are you ill?

Saturday morning.

And a further letter:

If you knew how happy I am and unhappy since yesterday, you would take pity on me. It is five o'clock in the morning. I am alone in my cell. My window is opened on the gardens which are so fresh, and I see the gold of a beautiful sun rising which is showing itself above the quarter where you live. I think that I shall not see you to-day and I am very sad. All this resembles a romance; but have not romances their charms? And is not all life a sorry romance? Write to me; that I may at least see something that comes from you! Adieu, adieu! until to-morrow. Nothing new about the accursed voyage.

Sunday morning.

Chateaubriand to the Countess de Duras

June 18th, 1813.

Saturday, I shall be in Paris, and I shall see you Sunday after the Mass. I have many things in my soul that I would like to say to you, but I suffer so that I have difficulty in seeing the words which I

write. Good night, dear sister ! I am going to bed
thinking of you and the song of a nightingale which
comes back every spring into my little tower. He
arrived the day before yesterday. I am counting
on teaching him the name of *mon amie.*

End December 1813.

Dear sister, see whether I love you ! I am giving
up this morning a great hunting meeting in order to
write to you. . . . I cannot say how happy I was
to see you again. My attachment for you increases
every day. I am, as I have told you, the most sterile
of men in the expression of my feelings. I only have
one formula, and when I have said " I love you," I
have said everything. That makes letters so short
that I am ashamed of it. To lengthen them, I
ought to speak of myself, and do you not know this
poor me ? . . . Good day, dear sister.

MADAME DE STAËL
(1766–1817)

Daughter of Necker, the great French financier
under Louis XVI, she had to flee at the outbreak of
the French Revolution, while her quarrel with Napoleon in 1804 and her banishment lasted till his downfall.
A woman of brilliant parts, leader of the Paris salons,
her marriage being unhappy, she cultivated a passion
for Benjamin Constant, the man of inconstancy, in
1794, whom we have also referred to in connection
with Madame Récamier. After her husband's death,
she married a young officer of the Hussars in 1811.

Madame de Staël to Benjamin Constant

October 1st, 1804.

DEAR FRIEND,—Rejoice with me if Providence allows
me to descend before you into the tomb. After
the death of my father, I could not possibly endure
yours. I shall follow the admirable man, beloved of

you, and shall await you there with a heart, which God will pardon, because it has loved much. Look after my children ! In the letter which you are to show them, I exhort them to love in you, a man whom their mother has loved so much. Ah ! this word " loved " that was our fate, what does it mean in the hereafter ? My father's Creator is a kind Being. Pray to Him, my friend, through Him the dead stands in communication with the living. You know that by an arrangement between us a house bought by M. Fourcault for Madame de Nassau in the Rue des Mathuzins belongs to us, both under the stipulations that the interest belongs to you, and the capital, after you, to my daughter. If you would rather sell it, you must invest the money in a way approved of by the guardians, but the interest remains yours to your death. Farewell, my dear Benjamin, I hope that you at least will be near me when I die. Oh, I did not close my father's eyes : will you close mine ?

NECKER STAËL DE HOLSTEIN.

NAPOLEON (1769–1821) AND JOSÉPHINE
(1763–1814)

TWENTY-SIX years old, of provincial manners, and of negligent attire, the young, pale-faced, dark, and long-haired General, known to Barras as Buona-Parte, new to Paris and its luxuries, is approached by a soi-disant lady of fashion, Joséphine de Beauharnais. He is too naïve to notice that the charming Creole is already past her first youth, at thirty-two, and at her wits' ends to scrape acquaintance with him as one of the coming men in the new régime.

With the passion of youth, to him she is a delightful woman, and a lady of the " ancient French society." Fifteen days after his first visit in 1795 there is a *liaison*, and six months later he marries her. Two days later the young General is on his way to the army of Italy. He inundates her with letters, almost from every posting-station. In his letters, nothing but love and passion. The future does not worry him ; he is master of his destiny ; but his whole soul is in his letters to the only woman he really loved.

Letter on letter to Joséphine :

" If I am ready to execrate this life, I put my hand upon my heart, thy portrait beats there ; I look at it, and love is for me absolute happiness, and everything is smiling excepting the time when I see myself absent from my friend."

For her, in fifteen months from this month of April 1796, six victories, twenty-one standards taken, Piedmont forced to capitulate. He sends Junot to Paris with the trophies and to bring her back with him.

" Quick, I warn you, if you delay, you will find me
ill ; the fatigues and your absence are too much at
once."

All during the strain of ill-health, he has one thought,
" Thou wilt return, n'est ce pas ? Thou wilt be here
by my side, on my heart, in my arms ! Take wings,
come, come ! "

Joséphine is in no hurry. For the first time in
her life she is, as wife of the Commander-in-Chief
of the Army of Italy " quelqu'un "—a person of
importance. He, hoping, raging, tortured with jealousy, anxiety, desire, sends courier upon courier.
What is she doing ? What is she thinking about ?
Has she then taken a new lover " of nineteen years,
no doubt ? "

" If it were true, fear the poignard of Othello,"
and she, smiling, says with that slight Creole lisp,
" He is funny, Bonaparte." Her pretext is that she
is ailing, that it is the beginning of an accouchement.
Bonaparte is full of self-reproach.

" I am guilty of so many wrongs towards you, that
I do not know how to expiate them. I accuse you of
staying in Paris, and you were there ill ! Forgive me,
my good *amie* ; the love you have inspired me with
has bereft me of reason ; I shall never recover it. One
does not become cured of that sickness. My presenti-
ments are so mournful that it would suffice me to
see you, to press you to my heart and to die together.
. . . A child as adorable as its mother will see the
light in your arms. Unfortunate me, I would content
myself with a day ! "

But Joséphine has to realise that these pretexts
will not stall off her passionate Corsican any longer.
He will not stand it. He threatens, if his wife does
not come, to resign his command, to abandon everything, to come back himself. So Joséphine, in tears
and with an unwilling heart, tears herself away, and
accompanied by her pet dog Fortuné, Joseph (Napoleon's brother), Junot, and several domestics, jogs
off in her chaise to the seat of war. Bonaparte, hearing

NAPOLEON I.

of the chaise-party close to Milan, begs Joséphine to
join him at Verona. " I need you, for I am going to
be very ill."

But she awaits him at Milan, and he hurries there.
Two days of outpourings of love, of passionate caresses.
But the complications of war become threatening, he
has to hurry away, though writing her every day a
long love-letter.

" Ah, I beg of you, let me see some of your defects ;
be less beautiful, less gracious, less tender, less kind,
above all ; above all, never be jealous ; never shed
tears ; thy tears bereave me of reason, burn my blood.
. . . Come and rejoin me, at least, so that before
dying we are able to say to each other, ' We were
happy so many days ! ' "

But though these passionate effusions of a young
man become gradually appeased, yet his wife is still
the only woman that he loves. " I love my wife,"
he says to Madame de Staël. She is no longer pretty.
" She is nearly forty, and she looks it." Never mind !

For Bonaparte, she does not grow older, and all
through his life, however much she may deceive him,
she will always remain the adored one dominating
his senses and his heart. The following short selection
of his rapid epistles give us a picture of his love.

To Joséphine at Milan

VERONA, *November* 13*th*, 1796.

I do not love thee any more ; on the contrary, I
detest thee. Thou art horrid, very awkward, very
stupid, a very Cinderella. Thou dost not write me
at all, thou dost not love thy husband ; thou knowest
the pleasure that thy letters afford him, and thou
dost not write him six lines of even haphazard scribble.

What do you do then all the day, Madame ? What
matter of such importance is it that takes up your
time from writing to your very good lover ? What
affection stifles and pushes on one side the love, the
tender and constant love, which you have promised

him ? Who can be this marvellous, this new lover who absorbs all your instants, tyrannises your entire days, and prevents you from being solicitous about your husband ? Joséphine, beware, one fine night the doors will break open and I will be there.

In truth, I am anxious, my good amie, at not receiving your news ; write me quickly four pages, and say those amiable things which fill my heart with sentiment and pleasure.

I hope before long to press you in my arms and shall shower on you a million burning kisses as under the Equator.

BONAPARTE.

To Joséphine at Genoa
MILAN, *November 27th*, 1796, *three o'clock afternoon.*

I arrive at Milan, I rush into your appartement, I have left everything to see you, to press you in my arms . . . you were not there ; you run to towns where there are festivities ; you leave me when I arrive, you do not care any more for your dear Napoleon. It was a caprice, your loving him ; fickleness makes you indifferent to him. Accustomed to dangers, I know the remedy for the worries and ills of life. The misfortune that overtakes me is incalculable ; I had the right to be spared this.

I shall be here till the 9th in the evening. Do not put yourself out ; run after pleasures ; happiness is made for you. The entire world is too glad to be able to please you, and only your husband is very, very unhappy.

BONAPARTE.

A Letter from the First Consul Bonaparte to his Wife (during the Marengo Campaign, 1800)
LAUSANNE, *May 13th*, 1800.

I am since yesterday at Lausanne, I leave to-morrow. My health is sufficiently good. This country is very beautiful. I see nothing inconvenient, ten or

(1) MADAME DU BARRY.   (2) JOSÉPHINE.

twelve days from now, in your coming to meet me ;
but you would have to travel incognito, and not say
where you are going, because I do not wish anyone
to know what I am about to do. You can say that
you are going to Plombières. I will send Moustache
[the First Consul's courier], who has just arrived. A
thousand tendernesses to Hortense. Eugène will
only get here in eight days ; he is on the way.

BONAPARTE.

*Letters from the Emperor Napoleon to the Empress
Joséphine*

To the Empress at Munich, *December 19th,* 1805.

Great Empress, not a letter from you since your
departure from Strassburg. You have passed at Baden,
at Stuttgart, at Munich, without writing us a word.
That is not very admirable nor very tender ! I am
still at Brunn. The Russians are gone ; I have a
truce. In a few days I shall decide what I shall do.
Deign from the height of your greatness, to occupy
yourself a little of your slaves.

NAPOLEON.

To the Empress at Mayence (1806)
November 6th, 9 *o'clock in the evening.*

I have received your letter wherein you seem to
be annoyed at my adverse criticisms about women ;
it is true that I hate intriguing women above everything. I am accustomed to kind women, sweet and
conciliating ; it is those that I like. If they have
spoilt me, it is not my fault ; it is yours. Besides,
you will see that I have been very kind for one who
showed herself as a woman of feeling and kindness,
Madame d'Hatzfeld. When I showed her her husband's letter, she said to me with sobs, deep feeling
and naïvely : " Ah, *truly that is his signature !* "
Whilst she was reading, her accent went to the soul ;
I was sorry for her. I said to her : *Well, Madame,
throw that letter into the fire ; I shall no longer be*

powerful enough to have your husband punished! "
She burnt the letter and seemed very happy to me.
Her husband since then is much composed ; two hours
later he would have been lost. You see thus that I
love kind, naïve, and sweet women ; but that is
because those alone resemble you.

Adieu, mon amie, je me porte bien.

NAPOLEON.

To the Empress at Paris

Mon amie, your letter of 20th January has pained
me ; it is too sad. You see, there is the drawback
in not being somewhat religious ! you should say,
the happiness of others constitutes my glory : that
is not conjugal ; you should say, the happiness of
my husband constitutes my glory : that is not maternal;
you should say, the happiness of my children constitutes my glory ; well then, as nations, your husband,
your children, cannot be happy without a little glory,
you should not make such a boast about it. Joséphine,
your heart is excellent, and your reason feeble ; you
feel marvellously true, but you reason less well.

Now that is enough quarrelling ; I want you to be
gay, contented with your lot, and for you to obey, not
in grumbling, and shedding tears, but from gaiety of
heart, and with a little happiness. Adieu, mon amie ;
I leave to-night to make the round of my advance-
posts.

NAPOLEON.

Letter from the Empress Joséphine after her Divorce from Napoleon

NAVARRA, *April* 1810.

A thousand, thousand tender thanks for not having
forgotten me. My son has just brought me your
letter. With what ardour I read it and yet I spent
much time on it ; for there was not a word in it
that did not make me weep. But those tears were so
sweet. I found again my whole heart, and such as

PRINCESS BORGHESE (PAULINE BONAPARTE).

it will always be; there are sentiments which are
life itself, and which can only finish with it.

I would be in despair if my letter of the 19th
had displeased you; I do not entirely remember
its expressions; but I know what very painful sentiment had dictated it, it was the chagrin not to have
had news from you.

I had written you at my departure from Malmaison;
and since then, how many times did I not wish to write
to you! But I felt the reason of your silence, and
I feared to be importunate by a letter. Yours has
been a balm for me. Be happy; be it as much as
you deserve it; it is my entire heart that speaks to
you. You also have just given me my share of happiness, and a share very vividly felt; nothing can equal
the value for me of a mark of your remembrance.

Adieu, my friend; I thank you as tenderly as I
shall always love you.

JOSÉPHINE.

Napoleon to Madame Walewska

On January 1st, 1807, the Emperor, on his way to
Warsaw, meets with beautiful Madame Walewska,
the young eighteen-year-old wife of an old Polish
nobleman, enthusiastic at the arrival of the saviour
of Poland. After the State ball, he writes her the
following billet-doux.

I have seen only you, I have admired only you, I
desire only you. A very prompt reply to calm the
impatient ardour of

N.

And the second note he sends back, reads:

Have I displeased you, Madame? I had, however, the right to think the contrary. Have I been
mistaken? Your eagerness has diminished, whereas
mine increases. You take away my rest! Oh! give
a little joy, and happiness to a poor heart all ready to

adore you. Is a reply so difficult to obtain? You owe me two.

N.

A third billet reads:

There are moments when too much elevation weighs heavily, and that is what I feel. How shall I satisfy the longing of a smitten heart, which would throw itself at your feet, and which finds itself checked by the weight of high considerations paralysing the strongest of desires? Oh! if you would. . . . There is nobody but you who can remove the obstacles which separate us. My friend Duroc will make the means easy for you.

Oh, come, come! all your desires shall be granted. Your country will be dearer to me when you have pity on my heart.

N.

And finally:

Marie, my sweet Marie, my first thought is for you, my first desire is to see you again. You will come again, will you not?

You have promised it. If not, the eagle will fly to you! I shall see you at dinner, the friend has said so. Deign then to accept this bouquet; let it become a mysterious bond to establish between us a secret relation in the midst of the crowd which surrounds us. Exposed to the looks of the multitude, we can understand each other. When my hand presses my heart, you will know that it is entirely occupied with you; and to reply, you will press your bouquet! Love me, my charming Marie, and let not your hand ever leave your bouquet!

N.

Napoleon and Luise, Queen of Prussia

Queen Luise of Prussia (1776–1810), the beautiful and high-minded queen of the weak-willed monarch, Frederick William III of Prussia, humbled herself

QUEEN LUISE OF PRUSSIA.

in vain to induce Napoleon to reduce the harsh terms of the Peace of Tilsit, in 1807, by which Prussia lost half her kingdom.

The Prince of Hardenberg, the Prussian Foreign Minister at the time, had incurred Napoleon's particular hatred through overtures to England, in opposition to his policy, and though the beautiful Queen implored her husband not to give way, Hardenberg was dismissed at Napoleon's demand.

Queen Luise of Prussia to her Husband, King Frederick William III of Prussia

June 27th, 1807.

I clearly recognise the whole magnitude of your friendship in your writing so exhaustive a letter at a moment, when your mind must be distracted beyond all measure. I am in an indescribable condition on your behalf, on behalf of the good cause, and the outcome of this moment. In your letter there are observations capable of sending one out of one's mind. While I can appreciate your eagerness to visit one another, yet what I cannot conceive and never shall conceive is the stay of the three crowned heads in Tilsit, and I really believe that you are making merry at my expense in writing me this. The thing is impossible. However, one thing I implore you to "lay well to heart," namely, to summon in this matter all the energy you are capable of, and to agree to nothing which would destroy your independence. Misfortune must, at all events, have taught us the great lesson that we are "so inured to privations that such a measure of sacrifice," the sacrifice of territory, must be as nothing compared to the sacrifice of freedom.

Let Napoleon take, if he will, half the territory that was yours, if you only retain full possession of what is left to you, with the power of doing good, of making the subjects which God will grant you, happy, and in politics, of entering into such alliances to which honour calls and your sentiments incline.

Hardenberg must not be sacrificed under any circumstances, if you do not want to take the first step towards slavery and to incur the contempt of the whole world. You have two means of saving him : the first is the Emperor Alexander, who from his settled belief and his friendship for you will require his whole eloquence to convince the enemy of the right; secondly, you yourself, my friend, speak very well, once you are thoroughly prepared. In your place, I would say to Napoleon that he must realise the slender chances of your acceding to his request, as it would mean depriving you of your best servitor ; that would be analogous to your demanding the removal of Talleyrand, who serves him excellently, but gives you cause for complaint, and whom you do not trust, so that he could see for himself, you were solidly together, the pair of you. I venture once more earnestly to beg you to summon up all the will-power you possess in this affair. I repeat it : what is the sacrifice of territory in comparison to the sacrifice of liberty of mind, of honourable behaviour, in a word, of independent power ? You would become a poor thing, contemptible to Napoleon, held up to the ridicule of the world.

Is there no prospect of a Universal Peace ? Is it not felt that this alone can save us, such as we are ? Only by a complete agreement between Northern Europe can there still be hope to escape slavery, the fate of being swallowed up and consumed by the hydra, one by one. The principle you have so often announced for Northern Europe, must now be obeyed by Northern Europe. " All for one, one for all."

I distrust this stay in Tilsit very much ; you and the Emperor, who are honour itself, against cunning, the devil.

" Doctor Faust and his Famulus," that will never succeed ; and no one is able to cope with such shiftiness. So much the worse, " and the Lord be praised."

Adieu, my dear friend, I leave you to drag myself anywhere it may hap. How shall we meet again ?

FREDERICK WILLIAM KARL.

I fear, unhappier than on leaving you, for I know nothing more horrible, nothing more terrible, than to be his friend, whose bosom conceals nothing but Misfortune, Despair, and Death. Adieu! May the God of Mercy bless you, may He grant you those favours, which I wish you!

May prayer give you strength; it does not desert those who do not desert it. Only stand firm; make no concessions that might be hurtful to your independence. The Emperor must and will support Hardenberg, just as you do. Adieu, thousand times, adieu. God be with you, as are also the wishes of your friend, which you are sure of.

LUISE.

Napoleon writes from Tilsit, 1807, to the Empress Joséphine at St. Cloud.

Napoleon to Joséphine

TILSIT, *July 7th*, 1807.

My friend, the Queen of Prussia, dined with me yesterday. I had to be on my guard, as she tried to induce me to make some further concessions to her husband; but I was courteous and upheld my policy. She is very amiable. I shall later give you the details that would be impossible to give you now without being very lengthy. When you read this letter, the peace with Prussia and Russia will have been concluded, and Jérôme recognised King of Westphalia with three millions of population. This news is for you alone.

Adieu, mon amie. I love you and desire to know that you are contented and bright.

NAPOLEON.

HORATIO VISCOUNT NELSON
(1758–1805)

The letters that Nelson wrote to his dear Emma are true sailor's letters, such as Tom Bowling might have

written to his Black-eyed Susan. He met her first
when she was at the zenith of her power and beauty,
as wife of the English Ambassador at Naples, Sir
William Hamilton. " I will neither have P's and
Q's come near you. No, not the slice of a single
Gloster." His own wife—good, humdrum soul—
never inspired him to such enthusiasm, and yet he was
a good husband to her. But simple-minded Nelson
was devoted to the somewhat stagey, full-bosomed
beauty of the erratic former nursemaid, whom a
grateful King and country allowed to die in penury,
in spite of Nelson's dying prayer, " Look after
Emma."

Nelson to Lady Hamilton

August 26th, 1803.

MY DEAREST EMMA,—[says he has received all
her letters.] All your letters, *my dear letters*, are
so entertaining, and which point so clearly what you
are after that they give me either the greatest pleasure
or pain. It is the next best thing to being with
you.

I only desire, my dearest Emma, that you will
always believe that Nelson's your own; Nelson's
Alpha and Omega is Emma! I cannot alter—my
affection and love is beyond even this world! Nothing
will shake it but yourself; and that I will not allow
myself to think for a moment is possible.

I feel that you are the real friend of my bosom, and
dearer to me than life; and that I am the same to
you. But I will neither have P's nor Q's come near
you. No, not the slice of a single Gloster. But if I
was to go on, it would argue that want of confidence
which would be injurious to your honour.

I rejoice that you have had so pleasant a trip into
Norfolk, and I hope one day to carry you there by
a nearer *tie* in law, but not in love and affection than
at present. . . .

LADY HAMILTON.

(He concludes this letter by saying he will send her some sherry and a cask of paxoretti [sic] by the convoy.)

Nelson to Lady Hamilton

" Victory," *September 29th,* 1804.

This day, my dearest Emma, which gave me birth, I consider as more fortunate than common days ; as by my coming into this world, it had brought me so intimately acquainted with you, whom my soul holds most dear. I well know that you will keep it and have my dear Horatia to drink my health. Forty-six years of toil and trouble ! How few more the common lot of mankind leads us to expect, and therefore it is also time to think of spending the few last years in peace and quietness.

Nelson's Last Letter

This letter was found open in Lord Nelson's desk after the battle of Trafalgar—when brought to Lady Hamilton, she wrote on the last page :

" O miserable, wretched Emma !
O glorious and happy Nelson ! "

" Victory, *October* 19th, 1805, noon ;
Cadiz, S.S.E. 16 leagues.

My dearest beloved Emma and the dear friends of my bosom,—The signal has been made that the enemy's combined fleet is coming out of port.

We have very little wind, so that I have no hopes of seeing them before to-morrow. May the God of Battles crown my endeavours with success ! at all events I shall take care that my name shall ever be most dear to you and Horatia, both of whom I love as much as my own life ; and as my last writing before the battle will be to you, so I hope in God that I shall live to finish my letter after the battle. May Heaven keep you, prays your Nelson and Bronte.

October 20th.—In the morning we were close to the mouth of the straights, but the wind had not come

far enough to the westward to allow the combined
fleets to weather the shoals of Trafalgar, but they were
counted as far as forty sail of ships-of-war which I
suppose to be thirty-four of the line and six frigates.
A group of them was seen off the lighthouse of Cadiz
this morning, but it blows so very fresh, I think (. . .)
weather, that I rather believe they will go into harbour
before night.

May God Almighty give us success over these fellows
and enable us to get a Peace.

FIELD-MARSHAL GERHARD LEBERECHT VON BLUECHER
(1742–1819)

Old Field-Marshal " Forwards," as was his nick-
name, was always notorious for the bluntness of his
speech and manners, which had caused Frederick the
Great to dismiss him when a young officer, telling him
to " betake himself to the devil." When war was
declared against Napoleon in 1813, Bluecher, now
cavalry general, was placed in command of the German
troops in Silesia, which he delivered. He defeated
Marmont at Moeckern near Leipzig, and for this
victory he was appointed Field-Marshal, as he describes
to his wife. In 1814 Bluecher crossed the Rhine with
his army, joined up with the main army, and, in
spite of the doubtful issue of the battle of Brienne,
marched on to Paris.

He writes to his wife, Amalie, a typical old soldier's
letter, full of alarums and excursions. His simple-
minded letters, which really take the form of dispatches,
are imbued with a good deal of personal vanity. The
one after the battle of Brienne will suffice.

BRIENNE, *February 2nd,* 1814.

DEAR WIFE,—The great blow has been struck. Yesterday I collided with the Emperor Napoleon. The
Emperor of Russia and our King arrived as the battle

commenced. Both monarchs transferred everything
to me and were onlookers of the struggle. At one
o'clock midday I attacked the enemy. The battle
lasted until in the night, and only at ten o'clock had I
driven the Emperor Napoleon from all his positions.
Sixty cannons and over three thousand prisoners fell
into my hands. The number of the dead is very
great, for the exasperation had reached the highest
degree. You can imagine how much thanks I garnered
from the monarchs. Alexander pressed my hand and
said, " Bluecher, to-day you have set the crown on
all your victories ; men will bless you."

I could have dropped from fatigue and I slept five
hours without waking. To-day early I had to attack
my enemy once more and disperse him entirely. Now
he is in retreat on Paris. We follow him in his footsteps. Whether he will now still remain Emperor of
France, remains to be seen. If he retains the crown,
he must look upon it as a present from the hand of
our monarchs. My staff wishes to be remembered.
to you. To our surprise, all have remained unwounded
You can now with surety hope for an early peace, and
I look forward to your return. Inform all my acquaintances and the good Breslauers of this great
event. I shake so, that I cannot write any more. But
I am well and lifelong your truest [Bluecher], who
loves you heartily.

BLUECHER.

One realises, in reading the old warrior's simple
epistles, how Bluecher, after the battle of Waterloo,
could instruct his Chief of Staff, Gneisenau, to sit
down and write the description of " how we did it."

DUKE OF REICHSTADT (NAPOLEON II)
(1811–32)

The son of Napoleon and Marie Louise having the
title of King of Rome, he was practically a prisoner
all his short life in Schoenbrunn, near Vienna. Metter-

nich saw to it that he remained a weakling. In Rostand's play *L'Aiglon*, is finely portrayed the spirit of the caged "Eaglet" beating out his life against the bars of his cage. The following letter is an historic document to bear out the poet's interpretation of the noble aspirations of Napoleon's unfortunate son.

The King of Rome to the Archduchess Sophie

You said to me, "With you, love is only a ruse of ambition." I have long reflected upon this statement. I sounded all the folds of my soul; I made a severe survey of everything I have to fear, without rejecting that which I may have to hope; I judged myself without prejudice . . . yes, without prejudice, and I maintain that is possible. Well, then, the result of this examination is that I love you without an afterthought, without being the dupe of any dominant motive; in a word, I am sure that I love you in order to love you.

I love you because you have been generous and kind from frank impulse. You said to yourself, "This poor victim is condemned not to taste of any of the joys which form, alas! a part of the programme. They prohibit him from innocent things, because his nature, in finding itself, might derive forces from them, and could find in them a source of energy. I will permit him to love me," you said, "and the illusions of the heart would throw their prestige on all the arid and desolating realities. . . ."

You see, that to begin with, I loved you out of gratitude. Whatever they may do, I feel in me that it is precisely by what they reproach me for, that I raise myself above the others. I have to render account to the world for my birth; I have to raise myself or fall; the air of the middle regions stifles me . . . I see you smile. Well, you shall see. . . .

When the rays of sunlight spread themselves simultaneously on living nature, they vivify it, and make it fruitful; but when, shining through the convexity of a glass, they unite to a focus, they burn and consume. If all my affections had enjoyed their natural course, love would have acted on me with less energy ; but, in taking possession of all the forces of my nature it has come to represent its entirety . . . oh, be without fear ; the disquieting activity of passion is temperated in me by an indescribable respect which amounts to a religion. The filial sentiment and friendship, from which they have severed my youth, and up to the very Love of Country which alone you will allow me to have, have purified the love of the young man. How can you call weakness a feeling which is the source of all perfection ?

There is a point on which I would claim your indulgence—your pity ! Never jest about my jealousy. . . . I am convinced that nobody loves you as I do, because nobody understands you as I do, and because you are the only one to understand me. I know that you have duties to fulfil, I respect them ; that you are kind to everyone, that is your right ; but there is a degree of intimity from your soul to another soul which it is impossible for me to support. That is not egotism; it is a feeling of exquisite propriety ; we belong both of us to a world apart ; our engagements, though unwritten, are all the more sacred. To what does it serve you to be sublime with minds earth to earth. To expend treasures to nobody's gain. Would you divert the course of the Danube to water a cornfield ? The most beautiful things lose their value in contact with certain others ; a flower is beautiful on the bosom of a young girl, on an altar, even on a tomb ! That is because the thought is completed by analogies or by contrasts. But what effect would a rose produce on a Savoy cake ?

VITTORIO, COUNT ALFIERI
(1749–1803)

ALFIERI, one of the greatest of Italian classical dramatists, was an extensive traveller, and is known to us
for his admiration of English freedom and institutions.
While in Florence, he met the Countess of Albany,
wife of Prince Charles Edward Stuart, and passed
many years in her society in Paris and Alsace. At
the outbreak of the French Revolution, which caused
his fortune to be confiscated, he returned to Italy
and died, at enmity with the world, in Florence. The
following letter is written to an unknown lady in
Siena :

FLORENCE, 1800.

NINA, SWEETEST MISTRESS,—My epistle to you to-day
shall be short. Not that I had not a great deal to
write to you ; but you will probably have neither time
to read an elaborate letter, nor, above all, to answer
it. You know that I love you as much as my life,
and only less than my name. I only left you, because
I loved you too much ; but I shall never forget you.
I recommend this boy to your heart, who is not indeed
my child, but is born under my auspices. I desire
for him only this one thing : that he may equal his
parents in goodness of heart, but may not emulate
them in it, that he, like they, may find it sweet, to
remain idle. I and all my animals are well ; I hope
the same from you and yours. Keep me in good memory and write me a few lines with contents such as
one always particularly likes to hear repeated from afar,

although it just then more subject to doubt and loses in influence. Farewell, dearest.

The tragic writer
ALFIERI.

UGO FOSCOLO

(1778–1827)

The fiery Italian poet and would-be liberator of his country, vents his disappointment at Napoleon's handing over Venetian territory to Austria in his book *Letters of Jacopo Ortis*, originally a love-story after the style of Goethe's *Werther*. One of the greatest of Italian writers and thinkers, his irregular and improvident habits brought him to an early and destitute grave in banishment in London. Of his many love-affairs, we quote a love-letter of his to Isabella Roncioni.

1799.

My duty, my honour, and in particular my fate, force me to go away. Perhaps I shall return. If my misfortunes or death do not keep me away for ever from this holy ground, then will I return, and breathe the same air with you, and my bones will rest in your birthplace. I was determined not to write any more and not to see you again. Yet—no, I will not see you any more! Let me only write these few lines, which are bedewed with my scalding tears. Send me your picture, when and where you are able. If a feeling of pity for an unhappy man still moves you, then do not refuse me this mercy, which weighs heavier than all my misfortune. Even that happy youth, who loves you, can have nothing to say against it. He is beloved in his turn and weeps. May he infer from that, how much more unhappy I am ; he can see you and hear you speak and can mingle his tears with yours. But I, in the hours of my passionate sorrow peopled with terrible phantasmagoria, disgust seizes me of the entire world, a general distrust tortures me, and in a gloomy, lonely state of mind

I shall totter towards the grave, and only be able to
uplift myself, when I cover your holy picture day
and night with kisses; so shall I, even when far in
the distance, take strength and courage to carry on
the burden of my life.   In death my breaking eyes
will be turned towards it.   Thou shalt receive my
last sigh, and I shall take thee upon my bosom with
me down into the grave.

Woe is me, I thought myself more steadfast than
I am!   Do not, for the mercy of God, deny me this
comfort!   Send it to Niccolini; my friend is never
wanting in means and ways. . . . Farewell.   Adieu.
I can say no more.   Kiss little Cecco from me.   While
I write this, I weep like a child.   Adieu, and think
of me sometimes!   I love you and shall always love
you and shall always be happy.   Adieu!   Your loving
Ugo.

PRINCE DE METTERNICH (1773–1859) TO THE COUNTESS DE LIEVEN

As a statesman, we know Metternich principally
through his arrangement of the marriage between
the Austrian Archduchess Marie Louise and Napoleon
I, in order to consolidate Austrian interests; the
care for these eventually also caused him to conclude
the quadruple alliance against Napoleon in 1813, which
led to Waterloo.   The death in captivity of Napoleon's
son, the Duc de Reichstadt, was also the result of
his policy.   Perhaps history might give him the rank
of a lesser Talleyrand, whose venality he possessed,
but not his wit.   Metternich meets the Countess
de Lieven, the wife of the Russian Ambassador at
the Court of St. James, at the Congress of Aix-la-
Chapelle in 1818, and becomes enamoured of her, but
not for long.   He was too self-centred for that.

BRUSSELS, *November 28th*, 1818.

Here is the first letter that I am sending to you to
London.   It will not be the first which you will

receive, for I shall write to you again during your
stay in Paris, but it is destined to make you think of
your friend as soon as you arrive at the place which
must one day bring us closer together.

Mon amie, when one feels like I do, one is accessible
to every shade of feeling; can you conceive that I
prefer to write you to London rather than to Paris ?
I send you back the deposit you confided to me, I
have re-read all my letters and have wept in reading
them.   What is that power which you wield over me?
—that power which you captured so quickly ? Do
you think that I am easy to conquer, that one could
make me feel what is not born and formed in
me beforehand ? You would be mistaken if you
thought so.

[Metternich now describes the incidents which led
to their acquaintance.]

The 28th, I made my first visit to you, full of
ceremony. The hour I passed, seated at your feet,
proved to me that the place was a good one. It
seemed to me, in coming home, that I had known you
for years. . . .

I acquired, in a short time, a great knowledge of
you, of that you which I love more than my life.   In
order to do that, one must have seen everything that
I was enabled to see. You have as much wit as it is
possible to have; you have this in common with all
good women, strong and placed on a scale which raises
them above the immense majority of their sex, *the
need to feel a sentiment which becomes life.*

You notice an emptiness in your home which you
feel the need to fill; your husband is good, loyal,
but he is not what a husband ought to be : the arbiter
of his wife's destinies. You are entirely mine ; never
have I felt a sentiment of tranquillity on this point,
the first of those which constitute happiness such
as you have made me feel.

Mon amie, I who have an almost insurmountable
difficulty in believing that I am loved, I am sure of
you as of myself. Not a thought disturbs this senti-

ment, that of the contrary has not even entered my
head. My good Dorothée, you must have a charm of
truth which I have never encountered ; can you conceive that I must love you more than ever I have
loved ? . . . And then the world thinks that I
cannot love ; let it think what it likes, what does it
matter ?

PIERRE JEAN DE BÉRANGER
(1780–1857)

By the year 1812 this, the greatest of French national
song-writers, after starving in a garret for years, had
found his vocation.   In character simple, disinterested,
and just, his songs were instinct with humanity, and
overflowed with wit, pathos, humour, true and noble
sentiment.   He it was who perpetuated much of the
Napoleonic legend in his verse.   The following letter
gives Béranger's ideas on love.

(*Béranger to X——*)

If you had asked me to guess which verses had shocked
you in the *Grenier* [the *Garner*], I should have told
you. Ah ! chère amie, how differently we understand
Love ! At twenty years of age, I was in this respect
as I am to-day. Thus you have a very poor opinion
of that poor Lisette ? and yet she was such a good-
hearted girl ! so full of life ! so pretty ! I should
even say, so tender ! Well what of it ? Because she
had a husband of sorts who saw to it that she was
well-dressed, you have no patience with her ; you
wouldn't have had the presumption to be like that,
if you had seen her then. She dressed in such good
taste, and everything suited her so well. Besides,
she would have asked for nothing better than to
receive as a gift from me what she was obliged to
buy from another. But how could that be ? I was
so poor ; the most modest day's amusement obliged
me to live from bread-soup for eight days, which I

used to make myself, whilst piling up rhyme upon rhyme, and full of hope of future glory. I only need speak to you of this smiling period of my life, when, without assistance, without assured meals, without education, I dreamt of my future, without neglecting the pleasure of the present, my eyes grow wet with involuntary tears! Oh, what a beautiful thing is youth, since it can extend its charm as far as old age, that age so disinherited and so poor! Employ well as much of it as remains to you, ma chère amie, Love and allow yourself to be loved. I have known this happiness well; it is the greatest of my life.

ROBERT BURNS

(1759–96)

BURNS, greatest of Scotch vernacular poets, was
notorious for his love-affairs. There was always some
new divinity for this worshipper of the fair sex. Besides numerous flirtations, more or less poetical, he
had many serious amours. At the age of fifteen
" Handsome Nell," aged fourteen, Nelly Fitzpatrick,
a fellow field-labourer, attracted his attention. This
" bonnie, sweet, sonsie lass " was " coupled" with
Caledonia's national poet. She initiated him (says
Merydew) in that delicious passion, which he says, in
spite of " acid disappointments, gin-house prudence,
and bookworm philosophy I hold to be the first of
human joys, and our dearest blessing here below."
In 1767, the celebrated Jean Armour (who made him
a father several times and whom he finally married
in 1788) rose in the ascendant, one of the half-dozen
" proper young belles " of Mauchline. In 1780 Miss
Ellison Begbie, who has been identified with the Mary
Morison, held him a close prisoner. In 1786 he
exchanged Bibles as a testimony of lasting love with
Miss Mary Campbell. In 1787 he was introduced to
Mrs. Maclehose, the celebrated Clarinda. Mrs. Maclehose had been deserted by her husband, a West
Indian planter. A friendship more or less platonic
subsisted for a while, after which the poet returned to
Ayrshire, and married his " Mary," or Jean Armour,
who had been turned out of doors by her father, whilst
her lover was prosecuting his written addresses to

Mrs. Maclehose. Ellison Begbie, to whom the following is addressed, was a rustic servant-girl.

Robert Burns to Ellison Begbie (written about 1780)

I verily believe, my dear E, that the pure, genuine feelings of love are as rare in the world as the pure, genuine principles of virtue and piety. . . . I don't know how it is, my dear, for though except your company there is nothing on earth gives me so much pleasure as writing to you, yet it never gives me those giddy raptures so much talked of among lovers. I have often thought that if so well-grounded affection be not really a part of virtue, 'tis something extremely akin to it. Whenever the thought of my E. warms my heart, every feeling of humanity, every principle of generosity kindles in my breast, it extinguishes every dirty spark of malice and envy which are but too apt to infest me. I grasp every creature in the arms of universal benevolence and equally participate in the pleasures of the happy and sympathise with the miseries of the unfortunate.

I assure you, my dear, I often look up to the Divine Disposer of events with an eye of gratitude for the blessing which I hope He intends to bestow on me in bestowing you. I mainly wish that He may bless my endeavours to make your life as comfortable and happy as possible, both in sweetening the rougher parts of my natural temper and bettering the unkindly circumstances of my fortune. This, my dear, is a passion, at least in my view, worthy of a man, and I will add, worthy of a Christian. The sordid earthworm may profess love to a woman's person, whilst in reality his affection is centred on her pocket, and the slavish drudge may go a-wooing as he goes to the horse-market to choose one who is stout and firm, and as we may say of an old horse, one who will be a good drudge and draw kindly. I disdain their dirty, puny ideas. I would be heartily out of humour with myself if I thought I were capable of having so poor a notion of the sex which were designed to crown the pleasures

of society. Poor devils! I don't envy them their
happiness, who have such notions. For my part, I
propose quite other pleasures with my dear partner.

R. B.

(To Ellison Begbie)

. . . Though I be, as you know very well, but an
awkward lover myself, yet, as I have some opportunities
of observing the conduct of others who are much better
skilled in the affair of courtship than I am, I often
think it is owing to lucky chance more than to good
management that there are not more unhappy marriages than there usually are.

It is natural for a young fellow to like the acquaintance of the females, and customary for him to keep
them company when occasion serves ; some one of
them is more agreeable to him than the rest . . .
there is something he knows not what pleases him,
he knows not how in her company. This, I take to
be what is called love with the greater part of us ;
and I must own, my dear E., it is a hard game such a
one as you have to play when you meet with such a
lover. You cannot refuse but he is sincere ; and yet,
though you use him ever so favourably, perhaps in a
few months or, at the farthest, in a year or two, the
same unaccountable fancy may make him as distractedly
fond of another, whilst you are quite forgot.

I am aware that perhaps the next time I have the
pleasure of seeing you, you may bid me take my lesson
home, and tell me that the passion I have professed
for you is perhaps one of those transient flashes I have
been describing ; but I hope, my dear E., you will do
me the justice to believe me when I assure you that
the love I have for you is founded on the sacred
principles of virtue and honour, and by consequence
so long as you continue possessed of those amiable
qualities which first inspired my passion for you, so
long must I continue to love you. Believe me, my
dear, it is love like this alone which can render the
marriage state happy. People may talk of flames

and raptures as long as they please—and a warm fancy
with a flow of youthful spirits may make them feel
something like what they describe ; but sure I am
the nobler faculties of the mind, with kindred feelings
of the heart, can only be the foundation of friendship,
and it has always been my opinion that the married
life was only friendship in a more exalted degree. . . .

It is hard to believe that the author of these letters
is the same who glorifies so many "bonnie lasses,"
that he would shelter with his "plaidie" or, if needs
be, "lay me down and dee" for. If one did not know
that it was Robert Burns, the exciseman, who sings,
in Scots common tongue, the delights of wine, woman,
and song, one could imagine this disquisition on love
to be from the pen of a learned university professor.

Sylvander to Clarinda

December 21st.

I beg your pardon, my dear Clarinda, for the frag-
ment scrawl I sent you yesterday. I really don't know
what I wrote. A gentleman for whose character,
abilities, and critical knowledge I have the greatest
veneration, called in just as I had begun the second
sentence, and I would not make the porter wait. . . .
I do love you, if possibly still better for having so fine
a taste and turn for poesy. I have again gone wrong
in my usual unguarded way ; but you may erase the
word and put esteem, respect, or any other tame Dutch
expression you please in its place.

I believe there is no holding converse or carrying
on correspondence with an amiable woman, much less
a *gloriously amiable, fine woman*, without some mixture
of that delicious passion, whose most devoted slave
I have more than once had the honour of being. But
why be hurt or offended on that account ? Can no
honest man have a prepossession for a fine woman, but
he must run his head against an intrigue ? Take a
little of the tender witchcraft of love and add to it
the generous, the honourable sentiments of manly

friendship, and I know but one more delightful morsel, which few, few in any rank ever taste. Such composition is like adding cream to strawberries; it not only gives the fruit a more elegant richness, but has a peculiar deliciousness of its own. . . .

. . . Why are you unhappy? and why are so many of our fellow-creatures unworthy to belong to the same species with you, blest with all they can wish? You have a hand, all benevolent to give—why were you denied the pleasure? You have a heart formed, gloriously formed, for all the most refined luxuries of love—why was that heart ever wrung! O, Clarinda! Shall we not meet in some state, some yet unknown state of being where the lavish hand of Plenty shall minister to the highest wish of Benevolence, and where the chill north wind of Prudence shall never blow over the flowery fields of enjoyment? If we do not, man was made in vain! . . .

These letters between Sylvander and Clarinda present an interesting and strange mixture of formality and affectation, of sentiment and religion, of lax ethics and intense expression. She has certain nameless feelings which she perfectly comprehends, though the pen of Locke could not define them. These are "delightful" when under the check of *reason* and *religion*. Sylvander answers this letter with considerable warmth, and Clarinda thereupon asks, "Do you remember that she whom you address is a married woman? or Jacoblike would you wait seven years, and even then perhaps be disappointed as he was?" Clarinda checks Sylvander with a happy mixture of dignity and mildness (says her biographer), bespeaking inward purity. "Is it not too near an infringement of the sacred obligations of marriage, to bestow one's heart, wishes, and thoughts upon another? Something in my soul whispers that it *approaches* criminality. I obey the voice; let me cast every kind feeling into the allowed bond of friendship. If 'tis accompanied with a shadow of a softer feeling, it shall be poured into the bosom of a merciful God! If a confession of my warmest, tenderest, friendship does not satisfy you, *duty* forbid Clarinda should do more!"

Eventually they console themselves with the certainty of meeting in " an unknown state of being " in which we must suppose Mrs. Burns was to have no part or share. Clarinda will not admit a love which brings no certificate from the temple of Hymen ; such a love, she says, is not to be heard at the bar of reason. Sylvander promises to remember her in his prayers.

JAMES HOGG (1770–1835), THE ETTRICK SHEPHERD

James Hogg, Scottish poet, song-writer and essayist, is now regarded as the legitimate heir to Burns. " The Witch of Fife," " The Skylark," " When the Kye come hame," and above all, " Kilmeny " are aflame with the truest fire of genius. Margaret Phillips, an acknowledged belle in Edinburgh, preferred the middle-aged, struggling poet to all others, and after waiting ten years, in 1820, Hogg was married to his lady-love.

As often is the case with lovers, he seems, at times, to have doubted whether the marriage would ever take place.

" Tell Walter [her brother] that I'll give him twenty guineas [a matter of some concern to a farmer when grain is so cheap] if he will just bring you over and set you down at my side, and make me free of all the rest of it, save taking you by the hand and making a short awkward bow to the minister, for as to pulling off gloves, you know I never wear any."

" I am far from thinking [he writes] you did wrong in what you communicated to your father. A parent is always a sure confidant. Indeed I have always thought that a young lady, who receives the addresses of a lover out of her father's knowledge or without his approbation had better not receive them at all. . . . I could not cherish a hope of losing you, but some things that you said to me set me a-thinking, and that very seriously, and I am not yet convinced of the prudence of our marriage, considering my years and the uncertain state in which I hang as it were between poverty and riches."

Towards the close of 1819 he writes from Ettrick :

" I see your letter is of an old date, and yet it is several days since I got it ; but at this season I am quite secluded almost from the possibility of communication with this world ; it being only by choice that I got my letters at all. . . . That night before I got your letter, which was on Saturday last, I had such a dream of distress as I never experienced. It was all about your family, and terminated at an old church among graves and gravestones, and strangers.

" But why frighten I my dearest Margaret by the vagaries of such a visionary as I am ;—only the circumstances had made me uneasy and I cannot keep it.

" It was never in view of receiving a fortune with you that induced me to pay my addresses to you, Margaret. On the contrary, you know that I declined an independent fortune that was mine for the taking for your sake, and that it was pure affection made me offer you my hand. 1 had no doubt that your father had the same affection for you that he has for the rest of his family, and judging from my own feelings, perhaps I thought he might have more.

" Whatever portion, therefore, he thinks proper to give or bequeath to you, with that I have made up my mind to be satisfied, and grateful both to him and his memory. But having no fortune of my own to bestow on you, I would scorn to enter into conditions for the woman I loved."

(1)

(2)

(3)

(4)

(1) SIR WALTER SCOTT.
(3) KEATS.
(2) MARY WOLLSTONECRAFT GODWIN.
(4) THE RT. HON. LORD BYRON.

SIR WALTER SCOTT
(1771–1832)

" It was a proud night with me," Sir Walter Scott one day exclaimed, " when I first found that a pretty young woman could think it worth her while to sit and talk with me, hour after hour, in a corner of the ballroom, while all the world were capering in our view."

But, as with most of us, the fancy for pretty young women with whom we first sit out in ballrooms (and later, on the stairs) seldom becomes anything more serious, so it was with Scott, for in the autumn of 1797, he became engaged to Miss Charlotte Carpenter, whom he eventually married. It appears from the lady's correspondence that Sir Walter's family were not altogether pleased that his lady-love was of French parentage, but her letters would certainly be accepted as models of propriety and maidenly deportment by any head-mistress of a High School for Young Gentle-women.

CARLISLE, *October 25th*, 1797.

Indeed, Mr. Scott, I am by no means pleased with all this writing. I have told you how much I dislike it, and yet you persist in asking me to write, and that by return of post. O ! you are really out of your senses. I should not have indulged you in that whim of yours, had you not given me that hint that my silence gives an air of mystery. I have no reason that can detain me in acquainting you that my father and mother were French, of the name of Charpentier; he had a place under Government ; their residence was at Lyons, where you would find on inquiries that they lived in good repute *and in very good style*. I had the misfortune of losing my father before I could know the value of such a parent. At his death we were left to the care of Lord D[ownshire], who was his very great friend ; and very soon after, I had the affliction of losing my mother.

Our taking the name of Carpenter was on my brother's going to India to prevent any difficulties that might have occurred. I hope you are now pleased. Lord D[ownshire] could have given you every information, as he has been acquainted with all my family.

You say you almost love *him ;* but until your almost comes to a *quite,* I cannot love *you.*

Before I conclude this famous epistle, I will give you a little hint—that is, not to put so many *musts* in your letters—it is beginning *rather too soon ;* and another thing is, that I take the liberty not to mind them much, but I expect you mind me.

You *must* take care of yourself, you *must* think of me, and believe me, yours sincerely

C. C.

And again, she writes, in reply to a letter from Scott, apparently about money affairs, with that admirable French commonsense :

CARLISLE, *November 27th.*

You have made me very triste to-day. Pray never more complain about being poor. Are you not ten times richer than I am ? Depend on yourself and your profession. I have no doubt you will rise very high, and be a *great rich man*; but we should look down to be contented with our lot, and banish all disagreeable thoughts. We shall do very well. I am very sorry to hear you have such a *bad head.* I hope I shall nurse away all your aches. I think you write too much. When I am *mistress,* I shall not allow it. How very angry I should be, if you were to part with *Lenore* (his earliest published work, a translation). Do you really believe I should think it *unnecessary expense* where your health and pleasure can be concerned ? I have a better opinion of you, and I am very glad you don't give up the cavalry, as I love everything that is *stylish.* Don't forget to find a stand for the old carriage, as I shall like to keep it, in case we should go on any journey: it is so much more convenient than the post-chaises, and will do very well till we can keep *our carriage*.

What an idea of yours was that to mention where you wish to have your *bones laid*. If you were married, I should think you were tired of me. A very pretty compliment *before marriage*. I hope sincerely that I shall not live to see that day. If you always have those cheerful thoughts, how very pleasant and gay you must be!

Adieu, my dearest friend. Take care of yourself, if you love me, as I have *no wish* that you should visit that *beautiful* and *romantic* scene, the burying-place. Adieu, once more, and believe that you are loved very sincerely by

C. C.

WILLIAM HAZLITT
(1778–1830)

Hazlitt, the charming essayist, the Shakespearean critic, the true poet, the subtle wit, and the refined philosopher, has been called "the critic's critic," the neglect he suffered from during his life being due to the hostility of his political views and his unfortunate petulance. Fond of the ladies, Miss Windham, Miss Ralston, Miss Sally Shepherd, his large heart had capacity for them all. In the meantime, Mrs. Hazlitt (says J. T. Merydew), whose love was not equally wide, agreed with him to dissolve, as far as possible, a marriage contract which had become a burden to both, on the ground of incompatibility.

It was in 1820, William Hazlitt fell in love at first sight with Miss Sarah Walker, daughter of a tailor, in whose house he lodged. She told him "her affections were engaged," and he called her his Infelice—which she certainly did not understand, "and now" (says her disconsolate lover, a scorned King Cophetua), "without any fault of mine, but too much love, she has vanished from me and I am left to wither." It was all in vain for Sarah to say, " Sir, I told you I could feel no more for you than friendship." Hazlitt continued to wither. At last the common end of all true love arrives—he meets her with another man, a former lodger, a Mr. C——. In the words of the nigger song, " Mary's gone wid a coon."

Thus in these letters, which fringe the ludicrous, if they were not sincere, we see that Love is not a respecter of persons, and that " grave and reverend seigniors " may be fooled by tailors' daughters, on whom wit and knowledge are thrown away, provided they be not spoken by a pretty fellow, who has " engaged her affections." As says Cyrano de Bergerac : " All words are fine, provided the moustache be fine." Let the man of forty remember the old legal doctrine, " Caveat emptor " (The buyer must look out for himself ").

February 1822.

You will scold me for this, and ask me if this is keeping my promise to mind my work. One-half of this was to think of Sarah ; and beside I do not neglect my work either, I assure you. I regularly do ten pages a day, which mounts up to thirty guineas' worth a week, so that you see I should grow rich at that rate, if I could keep on so ; *and I could keep on so*, if I had you with me to encourage me with your sweet smiles, and share my lot. The Berwick smack sails twice a week, and the wind sets fair. When I think of the thousand endearing caresses that have passed between us, I do not wonder at the strong attachment that draws me to you, but I am sorry for my own want of power to please. I hear the wind sigh through the lattice, and keep repeating over and over to myself two lines of Lord Byron's tragedy,

> " So shalt thou find me ever at thy side,
> Here and hereafter, if the last may be,

applying them to thee, my love, and thinking whether I shall ever see thee again. Perhaps not—for some years at least—till both thou and I are old—and then when all else have forsaken thee, I will creep to thee, and die in thine arms.

You once made me believe I was not hated by her I loved; and for that sensation—so delicious was it, though but a mockery and a dream—I owe you more than I can ever pay. I thought to have dried up my tears for ever the day I left you; but as I write this, they stream again. If they did not, I think my heart would burst. I walk out here of an afternoon and hear the notes of the thrush that comes up from a sheltered valley below, welcome in the spring; but they do not melt my heart as they used—it is grown cold and dead. As you say, it will one day be colder.

God forgive what I have written above; I did not intend it; but you were once my little all, and I cannot bear the thought of having lost you for ever, I fear through my own fault.

Has anyone called? Do not send any letters that come. I should like you and your mother (if agreeable) to go and see Mr. Kean in *Othello*, and Miss Stephens in *Love in a Village*. If you will, I will write to Mr. T——, to send you tickets. Has Mr. P—— called? I think I must send to him for the picture to kiss and talk to. Kiss me, my best beloved. Ah! if you can never be mine, still let me be your proud and happy slave,

H.

Miss Sally Walker's reply is written strictly without prejudice.

Sir,—I should not have disregarded your injunction, not to send you any more letters that might come to you, had I not promised the gentleman who left the enclosed to forward it at the earliest opportunity, as he said it was *of consequence*. Mr. Patmore called the day after you left town. My mother and myself are much obliged by your kind offer of tickets to the play, but must decline accepting it. My family send their best respects, in which they are joined by

Yours truly,
S. WALKER.

And as finally to his further impassioned appeals she makes no reply, and Hazlitt discovers her amour with a former lodger, he abjures his false goddess with " bell and book." " She knows what she is," he thus concludes his *Liber Amoris*, " so that my overweening opinion of her must have appeared like irony or direct insult. Besides, she looks but indifferently. She is diminutive in stature. I am afraid she will soon grow common to my imagination, as well as worthless in herself. Her image seems fast 'going into the waste of time,' ' like a weed that the wave bears farther and farther from me.' "

And with this sour-grape philosophy we must be content to let the shade of Hazlitt go and cultivate his garden.

LEIGH HUNT

(1784–1859)

Leigh Hunt takes his place in English poetry as the leader of the " Cockney " school. As a critic he ranks high, but below Lamb, Coleridge, and Hazlitt. It is chiefly as an essayist of the Addisonian order that he claims attention. Unlike the majority of poets, he may be said to be a man of one love. Miss Marianne Kent was a little girl with sparkling black eyes, of about thirteen, Leigh Hunt a romantic scribe of seventeen. They met, saw, she conquered, and they were engaged. He married her in 1809. The high spirits of the budding literary man are seen in the following epistle, written by Harry Hunt from Scaithing Moor, in Nottinghamshire, in 1807, two years before he married her.

(1)

(2)

(3)

(4)

(1) LEIGH HUNT.   (2) SHELLEY.   (3) ROBERT BURNS.
(4) COUNTESS GUICCIOLI (BYRON).

" So Harry Hunt came to Scaithing Moor
To Scaithing Moor came he;
And when he came to merry Scaithing,
He swallowed some cho-co-la-tè."

Well, my dear Marianne, I am now 135 miles from you, and yet I do not find you a jot farther from my heart. . . . I take up my pen to converse with you. Heaven bless the inventor of pens and postmen. I happened to meet in the coach when I set off on Tuesday mornin—— Marianne (lifting up two bright, astonished eyes) : On Tuesday morning, sir ? You must mean Monday morning, sir !

H. Madame, you must excuse me, I mean Tuesday morning.

M. Why, sir, you took leave of us on Monday morning.

H. Yes, madam, and the coach took leave of me.

M. Why, sir, the coach went off at eight ?

H. (with much sorrow). Yes, madam.

M. And lost half your fare ?

H. Yes, madam.

M. A guinea and a half ?

H. Yes, madam.

M. Well, sir, you have only paid a guinea and a half for a lesson in prudence.

H. True, madam. Some pay as much for a lesson on the fiddle. Which is the most useful of the two ?

M. But, my dear sir, why didn't you return to Titchfield Street ?

H. Why, my dear madam, there is something inexpressibly foolish in going twice on the same errand in vain. I took a place at the White Horse in Fetter Lane, so I slept in Gray's Inn to be in time next morning.

M. Well, my dear Henry, all is well that ends well. I was afraid that you had been detained by a worse accident.

H. You are the dearest girl in the world, and if you please I'll go on with my story . . .

JOHN KEATS
(1795–1821)

This humbly born Cockney youth, who had to abandon medicine as a profession owing to ill-health, became in his brief life (a " mature " career of some five years or so) first among latter-day poets as the poet of beauty, the foremost representative of that rarefied and controlled sensuousness which is considered pre-eminently Greek. The sculptor's sense of form, the painter's dream of colour, the musician's rapt ecstasy in perfected sound, are all here.

The following letter, dated July 8th, 1819, is full of thoughtful regard and tender love, and shows how complete his passion was for Fanny Brawne.

MY SWEET GIRL,—Your letter gave me more delight than anything in the world but yourself could do ; indeed, I am almost astonished that any absent one should have that luxurious power over my senses which I feel. Even when I am not thinking of you, I perceive your tenderness and a tenderer nature stealing upon me. All my thoughts, my unhappiest days and nights, have I find not at all cured me of my love of Beauty, but made it so intense that I am miserable that you are not with me ; or rather breathe in that dull sort of patience that cannot be called Life. I never knew before, what such love as you have made me feel, was ; I did not believe in it ; my Fancy was afraid of it, lest it should burn me up. But if you will fully love me, though there may be some fire 'twill not be more than we can bear when moistened and bedewed with Pleasures. You mention " horrid people," and ask me whether it depends upon them whether I see you again. Do understand me, my love, in this. I have so much of you in my heart that I must turn Mentor, when I see a chance of harm befalling you. I would never see anything but Pleasure in your eyes, love on your lips, and Happiness in your steps. I would wish to see you among those amusements suitable to your inclinations and spirits ; so that our love might be a delight in the midst of Pleasures agreeable enough, rather than a resource from vexations and cares. But I doubt much, in case of the worst, whether I shall be philosopher enough to follow my own Lessons ; if I saw my resolution give you a pain I could not. Why may I not speak of your Beauty, since without that I never could have lov'd you ? I cannot conceive of any beginning of such love as I have for you but Beauty. There may be a sort of love for which, without the least sneer at it, I have the highest respect and can admire it in others ; but it has not the richness, the bloom, the full form, the enchantment of love after my own heart. So let me speak of your Beauty, though to my own endangering ; if you could be so cruel to me as to try elsewhere its Power. You say I am afraid I shall think you do not love me— in saying this you make me ache the more to be near you. I am at the diligent use of my faculties here, I do not pass a day without scrawling some blank verse or tagging some rhymes ; and here I must confess that (since I am on the subject) I love you the more in that I believe you have liked me for my own sake and for nothing else. I have met with women whom I really think would like to be married to a Poem and to be given away by a Novel. I have seen your Comet, and only wish it was a sign that poor Rice would get well, whose illness makes him rather a melancholy companion. And the more so as to conquer his feelings and hide them from me, with a forc'd Pun. I kissed your writing over in the hope you had indulged me by leaving a trace of honey. What was your dream ? Tell it me and I will tell you the interpretation thereof. Ever yours, my love !

JOHN KEATS.

SHELLEY (1792–1822) TO MARY GODWIN

Shelley is no longer regarded as the anarchist in literature, the " beautiful, ineffectual angel," the prophet of Atheism and Communism. In the mature years of his brief life, Shelley was the poet of revolt; but this was a reasoned and controlled revolt of the intellect and the spirit against the gross dominion of materialism.

Shelley found an enthusiastic admirer, a kindred soul, and enfranchised thinker in Mary Wollstoncraft Godwin, who became his wife, in 1816, after his first wife, Harriet Westbrook, had committed suicide. Shelley does not write in the enthusiastic strains one would have expected, his correspondence being full of sense and good judgment.

BAGNI DI LUCCA,
Sunday morning, 23rd Aug., 1818.

MY DEAREST MARY,—We arrived here last night at twelve o'clock, and it is now before breakfast the next morning. I can of course tell you nothing of the future, and though I shall not close this letter till post-time, yet I do not know exactly when that is. Yet, if you are very impatient, look along the letter, and you will see another date, when I may have something to relate. . . . Well, but the time presses. I am now going to the banker's to send you money for the journey, which I shall address to you at Florence, Post Office. Pray come instantly to Este, where I shall be waiting in the utmost anxiety for your arrival. You can pack up directly you get this letter, and employ the next day on that . . . I have been obliged to decide on all these questions without you.

I have done for the best—and, my own beloved Mary, you must soon come and scold me, if I have done wrong, and kiss me, if I have done right, for I am sure I don't know which—and it is only the event that can show. We shall at least be saved the trouble of introductions, and have formed acquaintances with a lady who is so good, so beautiful, so angelically mild, that were she as wise too she would be quite a ——. Her eyes are like a reflection of yours. Her manners are like yours when you know and like a person.

Do you know, dearest, how this letter was written ? By scrap and patches and interrupted every minute. The gondola is now coming to take me to the banker's. Este is a little place and the house found without difficulty. I shall count four days for this letter, one day for packing, four for coming here—and the ninth or tenth day we shall meet.

I am too late for the post, but I send an express to overtake it. Enclosed is an order for fifty pounds. If you knew all that I have to do ! Dearest love, be well, be happy, come to me. Confide in your own constant and affectionate

P. B. S.

Kiss the blue-eyed darlings for me, and do not let William forget me. Clara cannot recollect me.

Once more, to quote a further extract :

My greatest content would be utterly to desert all human society. I would rather retire with you and our child to a solitary island in the sea ; would build a boat, and shut upon my retreat the flood-gates of the world. I would read no reviews and talk with no authors. If I dared to trust my imagination, it would tell me there are one or two chosen companions beside yourself whom I should desire.

But to this I would not listen . . . where two or three are gathered together, the devil is among them. And good, far more than evil impulses, love, far more hatred, has been to me, except as you have been its object, the source of all sorts of mischief. So on this plan, I would be *alone*, and would devote either to oblivion, or to future generations, the overflowings of a mind which, timely withdrawn from the contagion, should be kept for no baser object. . . . We must do one thing or the other—for yourself, for our child, for our existence. The calumnies, the sources of which are deeper probably than we perceive, have ultimately, for object, the depriving us of the means of security and subsistence. You will easily perceive the gradations by which calumny proceeds to pretext, pretext to persecution, and persecution to the ban of fire and water. It is for this, and not because this or that fool, or the whole course of fools, curse and rail, that calumny is worth refuting or chastising.

LORD BYRON

(1788–1824)

Byron was one of the great poets and literary forces of the nineteenth century. His many love-affairs are well known. Married to Anne Milbanks in 1816, she left him a year later and returned to her parents. While in Switzerland, Byron met the Shelleys; from thence he passed on to Venice, where in 1819 he became acquainted with the Countess Guiccioli, then only seventeen, and married to a man old enough to be her grandfather. He wrote the following impulsive note at Bologna to her, in her copy of *Corinne*.

My DEAREST TERESA,—I have read this book in your garden. My love, you were absent, or else I could not have read it. It is a favourite book of yours, and the writer was a favourite friend of mine. You will not understand these English words, and others will not understand them . . . which is the reason I have not scrawled them in Italian. But you will recognise the handwriting of him who passionately loved you, and you will divine that, over a book which was yours, he could only think of love.

In that word, beautiful in all languages, but most in yours—*amor mio*—is comprised my existence here and hereafter. I feel I exist here; and I feel I shall exist hereafter, to *what* purpose you will decide; my destiny rests with you, and you are a woman, seventeen years of age, and two out of a convent, I wish you had stayed there, with all my heart, or at least, that I had never met you in your married state. But all this is too late, I love you, and you love me—at least you *say so*, and *act*, as if you *did* so, which last is a great consolation at all events.

But I more than love you and cannot cease to love you. Think of me sometimes, when the Alps and ocean divide us, but they never will, unless you wish it.

BYRON.

ALEXANDER SERGEIEVITCH PUSHKIN

(1799–1837)

PUSHKIN, the Russian poet, dramatist, historian, and
novelist, who perhaps may be called the Russian Byron,
is best known by his poem on modern life, *Onegin*,
which is in the form of a novel. It is the first real
Russian novel; it is as real as Tolstoy, as finished in
workmanship and construction as Turgenev. And it
contains the type of all that is best in the Russian
woman, Tatiana. Tatiana falls in love with Onegin
at first sight. She writes to him and confesses her
love, and in all the love-poetry of the world there is
nothing more simple and touching than this confession. It is perfect. Placed beside any of the great
confessions of love in poetry—Francesca's story in
the Inferno, Romeo and Juliet's leave-taking, Phèdre's
declaration, Don Juan Tenorio's letter—the beauty
of Tatiana's confession would not be diminished. In
1837 came the catastrophe, caused by gossip and
Pushkin's own susceptible and violent temperament. A
guardsman had been flirting with his wife, and Pushkin
being wrongly convinced from an anonymous letter
that he was the author of it, wrote him a violent
letter which made a duel inevitable, in which Pushkin
was mortally wounded. His keen wit and outspoken
criticism is illustrated in the following letter to
his wife :

Pushkin to his Wife

BOLDINO, *October 30th,* 1833.

Yesterday I received both your letters, dear heart;
I thank you. But I must read the Riot Act to you
a little. You seem only to think now of flirting—but
look here; it is not the fashion any more and is
considered as the mark of bad bringing-up. There
is little sense in it. You are pleased that men run
after you—much cause for pleasure! Not only you,
but Praskowja Petrowna could succeed with ease in
getting all the unmarried pack of loafers to run after
her. When the trough is there, the pigs come of
their own accord. Why do you need to receive men
who make love to you in your house? One can never
know what sort of people one may come across. Read
the Ismailov fable of Foma and Kusma. Foma enter-
tains Kusma with caviar and herring. Kusma wished
to drink after that. But Foma gave him nothing;
whereupon the guest gave the host a sound thrashing.
From this the poet draws the moral lesson; You
pretty women! do not give your adorers a herring to
eat, if you have no intention of giving them something
to drink afterwards; for you could easily come across
a Kusma. Do you see? I beg of you, to arrange no
academical dinners in my house. . . .

And now, my angel, I kiss you, as if nothing had
happened, and thank you, that you have elaborately
and sincerely described your entire life of pleasure.
Have a good time, little wife, but do not overdo it
and do not forget me altogether. I can hardly hold
out any longer—so keen am I to see you *coiffée à la
Ninon;* you must look delicious. Why did you not
think before of this old [strumpet?] and copy her
coiffure? Write to me, what successes you have at
balls. . . . And my angel, please, please, do not flirt
too outrageously. I am not jealous, and I know that
you will not overstep the utmost limits, but you know
how I dislike everything which smells of our Moscow
" young ladies," who do not surpass the *il faut,*

who are what one calls in English " vulgar." . . . If
I find on my return, that your dear, simple aristocratic
tone has changed, I shall get a divorce, I swear to you,
and become a soldier out of grief.   You ask me, how
I do, and whether I have become handsomer.   To begin
with, I am growing a beard, whiskers, and moustache
which are an ornament to man ; when I go out into
the street, they call me uncle ; secondly, I wake up
at 7 o'clock, drink coffee, and lie in bed till 3 o'clock.
Lately I started writing, and have scribbled a lot
of stuff ; at 3 o'clock I go riding, at 5 I take a bath,
and then comes my dinner—potatoes and buckwheat.
Till 9 o'clock I read.   Thus the day passes, and every
day is alike.

VICTOR HUGO

(1802–85)

The greatest among French poets, initiator of the
Romantic period in France with his *Hernani*, charming
in his family idyll, *The Art of Being a Grandfather*,
fell in love with his playmate Adèle Foucher, when she
was sixteen and the young poet seventeen.   He recalls
her with her large eyes and long hair, her glowing
dark skin, her red lips, and her rosy cheeks.

" However, it is not more than a year ago that we
ran about together ; we fought together.   I refused
to give her the finest apple in the orchard ; I struck
her on account of a bird's nest.   She cried, I said
' serve you right ' and we went together to complain
to our mothers, who said that we were wrong, and
thought, in their minds, that we were right.   Now
she leans on my arm, and I am so proud and touched.
We walk slowly, we speak low.   She lets her handkerchief drop ; I pick it up for her.   Our trembling hands
meet and touch.   She tells me about the little birds,
the star we can see in the distance, the red sunset
behind the trees, or perhaps about her girl friends
at the pension, about her dress and her finery.   We

(1)

(2)

(3)

(1) VICTOR HUGO AS A YOUNG MAN.   (2) HONORÉ DE BALZAC.
(3) STENDHAL.

talk about innocent things, and we both blush.   The
little girl has become a young lady."

And so we get this charming collection of real love-
letters, when the heart is young and they talk about
love and nothing else.   These letters were written
during the three years and a half of their nascent love
and came to a happy end when they married in 1822.
Their respective families having authorised the
engagement in the spring of 1822, one would imagine
that the young lovers had nothing more to say to
each other, that could not be said much better by
word of mouth.   But no !   The young poet is anxious
for her to realise the extent of his love, the kind of love
he wants her to love him with.   Just as he loves her,
profoundly, uniquely, inordinately, jealously. And then
all other obstacles having cleared away, there must be
lovers' quarrels, misunderstandings about airy nothings,
because she said " Yes " when she ought to have said
" No," and because she said " No " when she ought
to have said " Yes."   She is forgetful, she has glanced
at another man, she has been gay when he has been
sad, she is not concerned when he is in low spirits.
A thousand trivial reasons for tribulations and heart-
ache.

" Lover's letters ! " as writes in melancholy reminiscence the old poet himself, in his *Autumn Leaves*,
on re-reading these outpourings of his impetuous
youth.

> " O, time of dreams, of force, and of gracefulness,
>   Waiting at nights to see a passing dress,
>   To kiss a fallen glove,
>   Asking from life her all—love, glory, power,
>   To be pure, proud, sublime, believing every hour
>   In the purity of Love ! "
>
>   (Original translation.)

1822, Friday night, March 15th.

After the two ravishing evenings of yesterday and
the day before, I shall certainly not go out this evening ;
I shall write to you.   And Adèle, my adorable Adèle,

what have I not to say to you! O Dieu! since two days I am asking myself every moment if so much love is not a dream; it seems to be that what I feel is not of this earth, I could not realise a more beautiful heaven. Adèle! What follies, what delirium, did not your Victor give way to during these eight eternal days!

At one moment I was for accepting the offer of your adorable love [Adèle had offered to run away with him, in case his parents opposed the marriage.— Ed.]. Driven to the last extremity by a letter from my father, I was going to get some money, then carry you off, thou, my fiancée, my companion, my wife, from everybody who should try to separate us; I would have traversed France, your husband in name, to go to some foreign country, where I could rightfully achieve it; in the daytime, we would travel in the same carriage, at night we would sleep under the same roof. But do not believe, my noble Adèle, that I would have taken advantage of so much happiness; is it not true that you would not affront me by believing it? You would have been more respectable and respected than ever by your Victor; you would have been able to sleep in the same room with him without fear of a touch, nor even of a look. Only, I would have slept or watched, on a chair or on the ground by the side of your bed, as the guardian of your repose, the protector of your sleep. The right to defend you and to protect you would have been, of all the rights of your husband, the only one that your slave would have claimed, until a priest had given him all the others. . . .

Adèle, oh, do not hate me, do not despise me for having been so weak and so downcast when you were so strong and so sublime.

Think of my loneliness, my isolation, of what I had to expect from my father; think, that since eight days I had to look forward to losing you, and do not be amazed at the excess of my despair. Thou, a young girl, thou art admirable, and in truth I think it would flatter an angel to compare him to you. Thou hast received everything from thy privileged nature, thou hast energy and tears !

O Adèle, do not take these words for blind enthusiasm ; this enthusiasm has already lasted all my life and has done nothing but increase day by day. All my soul is yours. If all my existence had not been yours, the inmost harmony of my being would have been broken, and I would have died, yes, died irrevocably.

These were my meditations, Adèle, when the letter, containing my destiny arrived. If you love me, you know what joy was mine. I will not depict to you what you must have divined.

My Adèle, why do we merely call that joy ? Are there no expressions in the human language to express so much Happiness ?

This sudden passing from gloomy resignation to an immense felicity has unsettled my soul for a long time. I am still in a dazed condition, and sometimes I tremble lest I should be brusquely awakened from this beautiful divine dream. Oh, thus thou art mine ! Thus thou art mine ! Soon, in some months maybe, this angel will sleep in my arms, will wake, will live in my arms. All her thoughts, all her moments, all her looks will be mine ; all my thoughts, all my moments, all my looks will be hers ! Mon Adèle ! . . .

Thus therefore thou wilt belong to me. Thus I am destined to enjoy on earth a heavenly felicity. I see thee, young wife, then young mother, and always the same, always my Adèle, as tender, as adored in the chastity of marriage as she will have been in the virginity of a first love. Chère amie, tell me, answer me, canst thou conceive this happiness, an immortal love in an eternal union. Well, such will be ours !

Meanwhile, after relating how he had answered his father, and besieged the various Government offices, where he was seeking for a permanent appointment, sufficient to enable them to marry on, the letter finishes thus :

Mon Adèle, now I may say that no obstacle will dishearten me, neither in my work, nor in my applications [for a position]. Every step that I am taking on these two roads will bring me nearer to you. How should they seem painful to me ? Do not wrong me by thinking that, I beg of you. What matters a little trouble, to acquire so much happiness ? Have I not a thousand times offered Heaven to redeem it with my blood ? Oh, how happy I am, I shall be !

Adieu ! my angelical and well-beloved Adèle, Adieu ! I shall kiss your locks and then go to bed, still far away from you, but yet dreaming of you. Soon, maybe, I will be at your side. Adieu ! Forgive such delirium of your husband's, who embraces you and adores you for this life and the next.

Thy portrait ?

STENDHAL

(1783–1842)

Marie Henri Beyle, the French author, known under the pseudonym of " Stendhal " (from Stendal, the home of Winkelmann, whom he greatly admired), was the first of the French fiction writers to break away from the romantic conception into the realism of an accurate, unimpassioned, detailed examination of actual life, as laid down in his remarkable novel *Le Rouge et le Noir*. Even in his love-letters one discovers that sober regard for remorseless truth mingled with the disenchantment of cynicism, which characterised his fiction. His affairs of the heart were always under the control of his affairs of the head.

Stendhal to the Countess Clémentine Curial

PARIS, *June 24th*, 1824, *midday*.

You cannot imagine what sombre thoughts your silence has created. I thought you would have found time last night before your departure to write me a few lines, which you could have put in the box at L——. As I did not, however, see a letter from you yesterday, I hoped for one this morning. I said to myself, that during the change of horses in S——, she will have asked for a sheet of writing paper. But no. Solely and only occupied with her little daughter, she forgets him who does nothing else but think of her.

With closed window-shutters I dream, seated at my writing-table, and amuse myself in the gloom of my anxiety by composing the following letter, which you perhaps will soon be sending to me. What else could have prevented you, to write me a few words ?

Here then is the letter, which I shall sooner or later be called upon sorrowfully to peruse.

" My dear Henri,—You have made me promise to be sincere. This preamble to my letter will enable you to foresee, what still remains to be added. Do not take it too much to heart, my friend ; remember that in the absence of livelier feelings, there will always be the bond of sincere friendship between us, which will assure you of the tenderest sympathy in everything that befalls you. From the tone of my letter you will gather, dear friend, that the most absolute confidence has taken the place of feelings of another nature. I cherish the hope that you will justify it, that I shall never have to regret what I have been to you.

" Farewell, dear friend ! Let us both be reasonable. Accept the friendship, the tenderest friendship, which I offer you, and do not fail to visit me on my return to Paris.

" Farewell, my friend.

" Menta."

Stendhal to Guiditta Pasta (the celebrated Italian opera-singer)

PARIS, *August 21st,* 1825.

MADAME,—I have the feeling that my enterprise is ridiculous. Since more than two months, day by

12

day, I argue with myself, how ridiculous, yes, how improper it would be, if I, unknown individual, dared to write to a celebrated woman, who without doubt is in touch with everything bright and amiable in France. I personally am an unknown, simple cavalry lieutenant of the Guards, recently transferred here, dependent upon my paternal remittance. I am no Adonis, although not an ugly man. Before I had the good fortune to know you, before my rebirth, which took place on that day, on which you sang the " Viago à Reims," I fancied I was well built, respectable and distinguished to look upon. Since then I have entirely lost that good opinion of myself. Everything about me seems banal, with the exception of the flaming passion, which you have set alight in me. For what reason do I tell you all this ? I feel too well that my undertaking is ridiculous ! You will show my letter to people, who will crack their jokes at my expense. Oh, what pain beyond measure ! Jokes about my passion for Signora Pasta ! and yet I swear to you, Signora, the danger of making myself ridiculous in your eyes is not in itself that which makes me timid. For you I would face dangers immeasurably greater. But I would die of grief, if I heard strangers talk about my love for you. This love is my life. I take music lessons, I learn Italian, I read the papers which I never even used to glance at, in the hope to discover your name therein. I only peruse page after page for the big P, with which your name begins, and my heart beats, when I find one, even though followed by an indifferent word.

But why do I relate to you all my follies ? How will that help me ? How could I become acquainted with you ? How could I be presented to you ? I am only introduced in a few old-fashioned salons, which have no relations with you. I frequent the Duke of ——, do you go there ? I am very unhappy, Signora. You cannot understand my immeasurable grief ! For twenty years I was devoured by the longing to come to Paris, I was crazy about horses ;

a soldier in body and soul.   All that has now become
distasteful to me.

How could I become acquainted with you ?   Whenever you were staying in Paris, I got into a cab, as if
expecting someone, and gazed at your windows.   But
you are in the country, so I hear, and I cannot get the
porter to tell me the name of the place.   I believe
I am afraid of the man.   Oh, I detest myself ! and
if I should have the good fortune to be presented to
you, you too would be afraid of me.

I have had to break off my letter. I was too unhappy.

I am twenty-six years old, dark, fairly tall ; one
can see that I am a soldier, as the people say ; but
after the incident with your porter, I have had my
whiskers trimmed as much as possible.   Had it not
been contrary to regimental regulations, I would have
had them taken off altogether.   Oh, if only you would
not be afraid of my distressed appearance, if I ever
should have the good fortune to be presented to you !
Have no fear, Signora, I am not at all importunate.
I shall never speak to you of my unhappy passion.   I
am content to become acquainted with you.   I shall
say nothing but, " I am Charency."

Fool that I am !   They will pronounce my name
quite loud enough, when I am presented to you.

But I will go on telling you about myself.   I come
of a good family from Lorraine.   I shall have a comfortable income to fall back upon.   I have received
an excellent education.   The pity is that nobody
ever hit on the idea to let me go to Italy, or I should
understand Italian and, above all, music.   Perhaps—
but that seems to me impossible—I should love you
more passionately, if I were to appreciate the heavenly
melodies which you sing, as a connoisseur, but, no, no,
that seems to me impossible !

Farewell, Signora, my letter is much too long already.
And besides, what is the good of my writing to you ?

With the greatest esteem, Signora, I am your devoted
and most obedient servant

EDMOND DE CHARENCY.

HONORÉ DE BALZAC
(1799–1850)

Success came to Balzac, after some years of penury in Paris, when, in his thirtieth year, he published, under his own name, *Les derniers Chouans*, after which he continued to send out a prodigious number of novels, some historical, but mainly illustrative of French contemporaneous life and manners, afterwards grouped under the collective title of " La Comédie Humaine."

Few have excelled the power and vividness with which he presents contemporary life and manners, linked with the keenest analysis of the human heart. For many years he loved and corresponded with the Polish Countess Hanska, who lived in the Ukraine, and when he finally married her, his death occurred three months after his return from his wedding-trip. All his life he seems to have been loaded down with debt, which he struggled to wipe out by his ceaseless toil.

Balzac to Countess Hanska (returning from a visit to her)

DRESDEN, *October* 21st, 1843.

I leave to-morrow, my seat is reserved, and I am going to finish my letter, because I have to put it in the post myself ; my head is like an empty pumpkin, and I am in a state which disquiets me more than I can say. If I am thus in Paris, I shall have to return. I have no feeling for anything, I have no desire to live, I have no longer got the slightest energy, I seem to have no will-power left. . . . I will write to you from Mayence, if I am better ; but, for the moment, I can only paint my situation like Fontenelle, the centenarian, explained his, as a *difficulty of existing*. I have not smiled since I left you. This is translated in English by the word " spleen " ; but this is the spleen of the heart, and it is far more serious, for it is a double spleen.

Adieu, dear star, a thousand times blessed ! There

will perhaps come a moment when I shall be able to
express to you the thoughts which oppress me. To-day
I can only say that I love you too much for my repose,
because after this August and September, I feel that
I can only live near to you, and that your absence, is
death—— Ah! how happy I would be to walk and
talk with you, in that little garden raised so daintily
at the end of the bridge of Troisk, and where there
are nothing yet but broomsticks, under the pretext that
one day they will put trees in their place. For me,
it is the most beautiful garden in Europe, meaning,
of course, when you were there. There are instants
I see again perfectly the least little objects which surround you ; I look at the cushion bordered with a
design in shape of black lace, upon which you rest,
and I count the points of it. . . . What a power and
what happiness there is in these returns to a past
which one thus sees anew ; in those moments it is
more than life, for it has held an entire life in that hour,
torn from the real existence, to the benefit of the
remembrances which inundate my soul in torrents.
What sweetness and what force is there not in the
simple thought of certain material objects, which have
hardly attracted the attention in the happy days of
the past ; and how happy I feel myself at having this
feeling. Adieu! I am going to take my letter to
the post. A thousand tendernesses to your child a
thousand times blessed ; my friendly greetings to
Lirette, and to you everything that is in my heart,
my soul, and my brain. . . .

(In going to put this one in the post.) If you knew
what emotion seizes me when I throw one of these
packets in the box.

My soul flies towards you with these papers ; I
say to them like a crazy man, a thousand things ; like
a crazy man I think that they go towards you to repeat
them to you ; it is impossible for me to understand
how these papers impregnated by me will be, in eleven
days, in your hands, and why I remain here. . . .

Oh yes, dear star, far and near, count on me like on yourself ; neither I nor my devotion will fail you any more than life will fail your body. One can believe, dear fraternal soul, what one says of life at my age ; well, believe me that there is no other life for me than yours. My task is done. If misfortune were to happen to you, I would go and bury myself in an obscure corner and ignored by everybody, without seeing anybody in the world ; *allez*, this is not an empty word. If happiness for a woman is to know herself unique in a heart, alone, filling it in an indispensable manner, sure to shine in the intelligence of a man as his light, sure to be his blood, to animate each heart-beat, to live in his thought as the substance itself of that thought, and having the certainty that it would be always and always so ; *eh bien*, dear sovereign of my soul, you can call yourself happy, and happy *senza brama*, for so I shall be for you till death. One can feel satiety for human things, there is none for divine things, and this word alone can explain what you are for me. Never has any letter made me experience more enjoyment than that I have just read ; it is full of that dear *esprit* so delicate, so gracious and of that infinite goodness and without the slightest triviality. This forehead of a man of genius which I have so much admired, is to be found always and everywhere.

And in a letter, written to the Countess in 1842, eight years before his marriage and death, he describes his attitude towards women, in explanation to a party of gentlemen who taxed him with being a professional lady-killer. Asked about his facile successes, Balzac replied, " I never had any."

Balzac's Explanation of the Artist's Position in Love

" Sir," I said to him, " I have written this year twelve volumes and ten acts, that is, I have not slept for three hundred nights out of the three hundred and sixty-five, which God has made. Well, then, the year 1841 resembles in every point the ten previous ones. I do not deny that many women have fallen in love with a Monsieur de Balzac who only existed in their imaginations, but they never got near to that fat, chubby-cheeked warrior who has the honour to answer your inquiry. Every one of the ladies desired (the highest and the lowest, duchess as well as grisette) that they should monopolise one entirely. A man whose mind is engrossed in the highest things, they could not stand for ten days, without recriminations. That is why all women love fools. The fool gives up his whole time to them, and proves to them thereby, that he devotes himself to them alone, that they are being loved. Even though a man of genius should give them his heart, his possessions, his blood, but does not sacrifice his time, then even the noblest of women does not believe that he loves her. I, who have to pay off 200,000 francs of debts by my pen, who pass sleepless nights, who have no bread in February if I do not work in January —I have not, in ten years, known ten days' constant love. The certainty of having no rival is not sufficient, and as soon as a woman has a lover, who is morally chained, she discards him. *I have been loved only once*, for I have not the confidence to count on the present, as the woman whom I love is not aware of the feelings she inspires me with."

GUSTAVE FLAUBERT

(1821-80)

Flaubert, one of the most painstaking of French authors, originated the naturalistic school (followed by the Goncourts, Zola, etc.), in his celebrated *Madame Bovary*. His literary work caused him intense labour, page by page, which is reflected in the half-morose, half-satirical attitude he takes towards life in his letters to Louise Colet, an authoress, to whom he addressed his voluminous correspondence of love-letters (of a sort) from his lonely retreat at Croisset, near Rouen, whither he retired, suffering as he did from epileptic attacks.   But the lady refuses eventually his advances.   She wishes to be something more than an " amie," and their relations come to an end.

CROISSET, *night of Thursday*, 1 *o'clock.*

Yes, I would that you did not love me and that you had never known me, and in that I believe I express a regret touching your happiness.   How I would wish not to be loved by my mother, not to love either her nor anybody in the world ; I would wish that there were nothing that issued from my heart to affect others, and nothing that issued from the heart of others to affect mine ; the more one lives, the more one suffers.   To tolerate existence, has one not invented, since the world exists, imaginary worlds, and opium, and tobacco, and strong liqueurs, and ether ?   Blessed be he who discovered chloroform : doctors object that one can die from it ; what has that got to do with it ? the fact is that you have not sufficient hatred of life and of everything attached to it ; you would understand me better if you were in my skin, and in the place of a gratuitous hardness, you would see an emotional commiseration, something of tenderness and generosity, it seems to me.   You believe me to be bad or egotistical, at least, only think-ing of myself, only loving myself.   Not more than the others, come, less perhaps, if one were allowed to praise oneself.   You will in any case accord me the merit of being sincere.   I feel perhaps more than I say, for I have eliminated all emphasis from my style.

Nobody can do anything but within his limits.   It is not a man, aged like me in all the excesses of solitude, nervous up to fainting point, troubled with repressed passions, full of doubt from inside and outside—it is not that man whom you should have loved.   I love you as well as I can, badly, not enough, I know it, I know it.   Mon Dieu, whose fault is that ?   That of

Chance! that old ironical fatality, which always brings things together for the greatest harmony of the ensemble and the greatest disagreement of the parties ; one only meets to knock up against each other, and everyone, carrying in his hands his torn entrails, accuses the other, who gathers up his own.

Take life from a higher standpoint, mount upon a tower (even if the base were to crack, believe it to be solid), then you will see nothing else but the blue ether all round you. If it be not blue, it will be foggy ; what matters it if everything disappears, drowned in a still vapour ? One must esteem a woman to write such things to her.

I torment myself ; I scratch myself ; my novel has difficulty in getting under weigh. I have accesses of style and the phrase itches me without coming. What a heavy oar is not a pen, and what an arduous current is the idea, when one has to plunge into the stream with it ! I am so downhearted about it that it amuses me very much. Thus I have passed an entire day : the window open, with the sun on the river and the greatest serenity of the world ; I have written a page, and sketched out three others. I hope in a fortnight to be furiously at work, but the colour into which I dip, is so new for me, that it makes me open astonished eyes.

My cold is about to disappear—that is well. At the middle of the next month I shall go to Paris to pass two or three days there. Work, think of me, not too sombrely, and if my image come back to you, let it bring bright remembrances, one must laugh in spite of everything. *Vive la joie !*

CROISSET, *night of Saturday,* 1 *o'clock.*

You say to me very tender things, dear Muse. *Eh bien,* receive in exchange all those still more tender things than you could imagine. Your love ends by penetrating me like a lukewarm rain, and I feel myself soaked in it down to the very bottom of my heart. Hast thou not everything needful for me to love thee—

body, mind, tenderness ? You are simple of soul and strong of head, very little poetical, and extremely a poet ; there is nothing but good in you, and you are entirely like your bosom, white and soft to the touch. Those I have known *va*, were not equal to you, and I doubt whether those that I have desired were your equal. I try sometimes to imagine to myself your face when you are old, and it seems to me that I shall love you as much, perhaps more. I am, in my actions of body and of mind, like the dromedaries with whom one has great trouble, as much in getting them to start as in getting them to stop. The continuity of rest and of motion is what suits me. At bottom, nothing more variegated than my person.

How afraid I am of becoming stupid ! You esteem me to such a point that you must be wrong and end by dazzling yourself. There are few people who have been so belauded as I have. Ah, Muse, if I were to avow to you all my weaknesses, if I were to say to you all the time that I love in *dreaming* of my little *appartement* of next year ! How I see ourselves in it ! But one must never think of happiness, that allures the devil, for it is he who has invented that idea to render the human race furious. The conception of Paradise is at bottom more infernal than that of Hell. The hypothesis of a perfect felicity creates more despair than that of a torment without cease, since we are destined never to attain it ; fortunately it is absolutely inconceivable ; that is what consoles one.

Since it seems we shall never quaff nectar, it increases one's satisfaction to sip chambertin. Adieu ! What a pity that it is so late ! I have no desire for sleep, and I had still many things to say to you, to speak to you of your drama, etc. Tuesday do not speak of Du Camp to Gautier ; let him come to it if you want to make a friend. I believe that Bouilhet is a subject which amuses him very little. What a poor opinion one must have of oneself to be envious of anybody else. A thousand tendernesses. Do you know that father Hugo begins to take on the aspect of a very good man ;

this long tenderness for Juliette touches me ; I love long passions which traverse patiently and in a straight line all the currents of life like good swimmers without deviating.

Aphorisms of Flaubert, culled from his letters

I am in a great literary heat. The good of these states is, that they reinvigorate you and infuse into your pen a younger blood.

One has in one's head all sorts of spring flowerings, which last no longer than the lilac, which fades in a night, but which smells so good.

Have you felt sometimes like a great sun which came from the inmost depth of yourself, and which dazzled you ?

One can judge of the weight of a burden by the drops of sweat it causes you.

If one wants to take the measure of what public esteem is worth, and what a fine thing it is to " be finger-pointed at," as says the Latin poet, one must go out in Paris, in the streets, the day of Shrove Tuesday. Shakespeare, Goethe, Michel-Angelo have never had four hundred thousand spectators at the same time, as has this ox; what draws him closer to the remaining genius, is that they cut him into little pieces afterwards.

Life, for me, has never been short of cushions, to make myself comfortable in corners, and forget the others.

May the devil take me if I do not feel as sympathetic to the fleas which bite a beggar as to the beggar.

It is not because an idiot has two feet like mine instead of having four like an ass that I consider myself forced to love him, or at the very least, to say that I love him and that he interests me.

I believe that later on one will recognise that the love of humanity is something as paltry as the love of God, one will love the just in itself for itself, the beautiful for the beautiful; the height of civilisation will be not to need any good feeling as it is called. Sacrifices will be useless, but one will still have to have a few policemen.

The idea of the people is as played-out as that of the king.

The better a work, the more it attracts the critics; it is like fleas which precipitate themselves on white linen.

In the measure that I seem to approach to the masters, the art of writing in itself seems to me more impracticable, and I am more and more disgusted with everything that I produce. Oh! the word of Goethe! " I would perhaps have been a great poet if the language had not shown itself so indomitable." . . . And that was Goethe!

Two years passed in the complete absorption of a *happy* love seem to me a mediocre thing. Stomachs which find in human grub their satiety are not great; if it were only grief, good. But joy—no, no, it is long to pass two years without the desire to go out from here, without forging a phrase, without turning towards the Muse. At what shall one employ one's hours when the lips are idle? to love? to love? These intoxications are beyond me, and there is in it a capacity for happiness and idleness, something so *satisfied* which disgusts me.

(*About a recent poet*): *Life* is rather wanting in his verse, his heart does not get beyond his flannel vest, and remaining entirely in his breast, does not heat his style.

The real poet for me is a priest. When he is consecrated he must abjure his family.

To conduct a pen with a valiant arm, one must do like the Amazons, one must burn one entire side of one's heart.

O makers of elegies, it is not on ruins that you should lean your elbows, but on the bosom of gay women.

I only have one objection to prostitution, namely that it is a myth; the kept woman has ousted the fast woman, as the journalist has ousted poetry; we are drowning in half-shades. The courtesan exists no more than the saint; there are supper-girls and " lorettes," which in itself is still more fetid than the " grisette."

I think of what I should feel if thou wert to die, my poor Muse, if I had you no more ; no, we are not good, but this faculty to assimilate all the sorrows and to suppose oneself having them is perhaps the true human charity.

I hope to make tears to flow from others with these tears of a single individual, filtering them through the chemistry of style.

Nobody is original in the strict sense of the word, talent as well as life transmits itself by infusion, and one must live in a noble environment, adopt the " social spirit " of the masters.

I need, in order to write, the *impossibility* (even if I wanted it) of being disturbed.

Whence comes the prodigious success of the romances of Dumas ? It is because, in order to read them one needs no initiation ; their action is amusing, thus one is diverted while reading them ; then, when the book is closed, as no impression is left and as all that has passed like running water, *one returns* to one's business.

The artist must raise everything, he is like a pump, he has in himself a big pipe which goes down into the entrails of things, in the deep layers ; he draws up and pours into the sunlight in gigantic jets that which was flattened out underground and one could not see.

What a discovery would not be, for example, an axiom like this one. Such a people being given, virtue is to force as three is to four ; therefore as long as you are at one point, you will not go to the other. Another mathematical law to discover : how many idiots must one know in the world to give one the inclination to kill oneself ? etc.

I give to humanity what it gives me, *indifference.*

One believes a trifle too generally that the sun has no other object here below than to make the cabbages grow ; one must replace from time to time " le bon Dieu " on His pedestal, therefore He sees to it to remind us in sending us now and again some pest, cholera, unexpected catastrophe, and other manifestations of the rule, that is to say, the evil.

If our bodies are far away, our souls touch. Mine is often with thine ; *va*, it is only in old affections that this penetration happens. One enters thus into each other through the force of pressing against each other. Have you noticed that the physique even feels it ? Old married people end by resembling each other. Have not all the people of the same profession the same appearance ?

What an artist one would be if one had never read anything but the beautiful, seen but the beautiful, loved but the beautiful ! if some guardian angel of the purity of our pen had kept away from us, from the beginning, all the bad acquaintances, if one had never come into contact with idiots, nor read the papers !

The individuality of the human race has changed since Homer. The belly of Sancho Panza would burst the girdle of Venus.

One can judge of the excellence of a book by the vigour of the first-blows which it has given you and by the length of time it takes one to recover from it afterwards.

I believe that the greatest character of genius is before everything *Force ;* therefore what I detest most of all in the arts, what sets me on edge, is *ingeniousness, esprit.*

But *l'esprit,* on the contrary, is incompatible with real poetry. Who had more *esprit* than Voltaire and who was less of a poet ? Now in this charming country of France, the public does not admit poetry excepting in disguise ; if one gives it them entirely crude they object ; therefore one must treat them like the horses of Abbas Pacha, in order to make which vigorous they give them balls of meat wrapped in flour. That is art. Know how to make wrappers for your books ; have no fear ; offer this flour to keen tasters ; they will rush for it from twenty paces off, recognising the smell.

What vices I should have, if I did not write. The pipe and the pen are the two safeguards of my morality, a virtue which resolves itself into smoke by the two safety-valves.

As for *Bovary,* impossible to think of it ; I must be *chez moi* in order to write, my liberty of mind depends on a thousand accessory circumstances, very miserable ones, but very important. . . . Everything one invents is true, be sure of that. Poesy is a thing as precise as geometry ; induction has the same value as deduction ; and then, arrived at a certain place, one makes no more mistakes with regard to everything that is of the soul. My poor Bovary without doubt suffers and weeps in twenty villages of France together, even at the same hour.

Apropos of *Industry,* have you reflected sometimes on the quantity of stupid professions which it engenders and on the mass of stupidity which eventually must come from it. That would be a frightful statistic to draw up. What can one expect of a population like that of Manchester, which passes its life in making pins ? and the manufacture of a pin demands five or

six different specialities ! The work subdividing itself,
there are formed therefore side by side with the
machines a number of men-machines. What a job
that is of pointsman on a railway ! of folding wrappers
in a printing establishment !

Yes, I maintain (and this for me must be a practical
dogma in the life of an artist) that one must make two
parts of one existence ; to live like a bourgeois and
to think like a half-god. The satisfaction of the body
and the head have nothing in common.

THE VICTORIAN ERA

PRINCE PUECKLER-MUSKAU TO HIS WIFE
(1785–1871)

PRINCE PUECKLER-MUSKAU is known as the most important exponent of the art of landscape gardening in Germany, having studied the same under W. Kent in England, and adapted his knowledge to his feudal castles in Muskau and other places. Married in 1817 to the widowed Countess of Pappenheim, from whom he was divorced in 1826 by mutual consent, he went to England in search of an heiress to restore his shattered fortunes. However, not having found her, the Prince returns to his first and only love, his divorced wife, with whom he continued to live happily, without re-marriage.

In his correspondence Prince Pueckler-Muskau displays the charming wit and easy superficiality of nineteenth-century high life, his letters being not unlike those of eighteenth-century Horace Walpole, especially as they deal mostly with events in English society. As such, they may be of interest, as sidelights on social history of the nineteenth century.

Prince Pueckler-Muskau to his Wife

BRIGHTON, *January 19th*, 1828.

When I think of the good God, I think also as a rule of you, because just then love fills my soul. Whether and how He exists, I poor man, really do not know, but that my *Schnucke* [*Schnucke*, term of endearment, untranslateable, *vide* notes on Kleist] lives, that I know, and that whatever kindliness I can show her, God receives as well, I also know, and nothing is more beautiful in the teachings of Christ than this saying. He surely was a divine man, and even if He did not exist, the man did whose poetic fiction He was.

In the evening I went, at the incoming tide of the ocean as it foamed and thundered, to my home ; the stars looked down sparkling and clear, eternal rest above and wild booming and motion below, Heaven and Earth in their true characters ! How splendid, how agreeable, how terrible, how awe-inspiring, is the world ! The world—which never began, which never ends—whose space nowhere has a limit—in the endless pursuit of which, phantasy itself sinks to earth, hiding its head with a shudder.

Oh, my *Schnucke*, you understand me. Love only feels an outlet out of this labyrinth, where every other power of the mind sees itself destroyed.

April 27th, 1828.

To-day I was asked to dinner by the Duchess of St. Albans " to meet the Duke of Cumberland and Sussex," but could not go there, as I had been previously invited by Buelow " to meet Mademoiselle Sontag," whom I only met by chance here in society. You can imagine the ecstasy of that ever complimentary Frau von Laemmers. She found I had become not only younger and more handsome, but assured me she had seen nothing so fine in England as Muskau. But what put me in a good temper with her, nevertheless, were her exaltations of praise of your condescension for her, which she really appreciated more gratefully than we deserve. *À tout prendre*, her presence, as reminiscence of something lovable and bygone, does me good ! The Sontag was delightful and went to some *frais*[1] for me—it is a charming creature, and certainly exceedingly captivating for people who are either quite fresh in the world or have

---

[1] *Frais*, effort to please.

no worries nor anything else to do than to follow their
desires.   The little coquette had at once noticed my
weak point and spoke with her soft looks of nothing
but the happiness of home comforts and a life in the
country, and how unhappy she felt leading an empty
life of vanity, and, in spite of all seeming brilliance, of
dissatisfaction, and often humiliation.

In the evening I met her again at St. Albans, where
she sang in German from the *Freischuetz* (according
to my taste, with less expression than the Seidler).
I escorted her to her carriage, and she invited me to
go with her to-morrow to the play, for which the
Duke of Devonshire had presented her with his box ;
for as something new and celebrated, she is just now
in the highest *Fashion* and has all the *Grandees* at
her feet, which, however, does not seem in the slightest
to have turned her head.

Do you know, *Schnucke*, that I am in love—only
guess with whom ?   With your portrait, which I kiss
every time early and late, with which it always seems
to appear very content.   Well, heaven will not desert
us both, I imagine, and we shall still taste of joy once
more, which has become such a stranger to us for
such a long, long time.

May 27th, 1828.

To-day I was present at a wedding and a breakfast.
The same person of whom I once wrote you that I
had got to know her too late.   After the breakfast
the happy pair drove off in a fine carriage, harnessed
with four fast horses, to spend the honeymoon in
Italy :   a very pretty fashion—they leave newly-
married people a while quite alone and to their own
devices.   But I have yet to speak of yesterday's dinner
and ball.   At Rothschild's they dined off golden
vaisselle,[1] whose value would be sufficient to make us
rich people.   At the King's, everything was equally
" *magnifik*," a select company, noble building, and

[1] *Vaisselle*, plate.

excellent attendance. His Majesty spoke to me; I was quite well dressed; they treated me with consideration, and I would have been quite satisfied if it had been possible.

Besides this a small star of hope has spun into view; whether it will again become a will-o'-the-wisp? but the circumstances seem to be particularly favourable here.

(In the evening.)

I went to a big dinner at Lady P.'s, where the Duke of Cumberland was also to have been, but did not come. She is a good, old, distinguished woman, eats enormously, and whose conquest I have made, inasmuch as I sat next to her at several dinners and procured her two portions of every dish. Her own dinner was excellent, and no old woman has a better knowledge of kitchen and cellar. From the dinner I drove with Admiral Beresford to the opera *Semiramis*, a leading role of Mme. Pasta, and then to a ball, where, owing to the terrible heat, I felt so unwell that I arrived home with a splitting sick-headache. I found your letter here, which unfortunately continues to contain very uncertain and unsatisfactory news. But enough of that—you love me and are well, that is the chief thing. I have bitten off the head of the snake of pain, which was lacerating my heart, and my wounds heal slowly, but the scars will always remain and smart with each change of the weather of the soul!

ROBERT SOUTHEY

(1774–1843)

Southey, Englishman of letters and Poet Laureate, best known by his *Life of Nelson*, in 1797, secretly married Edith Fricker, and in second marriage, more than forty years afterwards, Caroline Bowles. It was his wish that his correspondence with his second wife should be published. " Our earthly life, dear Caro-

(1) CHARLES DICKENS.　　(2) TOM HOOD.　　(3) ROBERT SOUTHEY.

line," he wrote, " lasts longer than in the hearts of those we love ; it endures in the hearts of those whom we have never known, and who learn to love us after our work on earth is done. They who live on earth, in their good works continue to make friends there as long as their works survive; and it may be one of the pleasures of another state to meet those friends when they seek us in Heaven. I often feel that this will and must be so when, reading a good old book, my heart yearns towards the author."

As early as 1818, more than twenty years before they were finally united, Caroline Bowles is already writing to Southey. In 1824, she writes from Buckland :

You are almost the only living creature in whom I have never found myself mistaken or disappointed, and you do not shun me because I am in sorrow, as is the world's way, and as I have bitterly experienced in times past from some who had sought and caressed me in my happier days.

Well, one friend of all weathers would compensate for the unkindness of fifty such worlds ; and if I have found you late, it is not too late for, as you say, we shall meet " surely and lastingly hereafter."

God grant we may here, and I do not despair of it, because, though hopeless of the physical regeneration you speak of, mine is not a disease that very quickly accomplishes its work. . . . God bless you, dear friend, bless and preserve you.

CAROLINE A. BOWLES.

P.S.—You wrote to me on your birthday. I shall not forget that day if I live till its next anniversary. If I live till the 6th of next December, I shall then complete my thirty-seventh or thirty-eighth year—I am not certain which. The next 6th of December will be doubly a wintry day for me, for it will be the first in the remembrance that will bring with it no tribute of affection.

My dear *bonne*, according to the custom of her country, used always to buy me a nosegay on that morning; yes, flowers even on that wintry day, and I believe if we had dwelt on the Great St. Bernard, she would have contrived to find some among its eternal snows. No voice, no kiss, no flowers now. It will be all winter.

And Southey writes to Caroline Bowles, from Keswick in 1829, on January 1st:

If there were sky-packets to the other world, dear Caroline, as perhaps there would have been if Sin and Death had not entered this, and may be hereafter when the victory over them shall be completed; if there were such packets, I would not wish you many happy returns of a new year, for I should rather take counsel with you about making a party, and setting off for one of those lovely stars, which one can hardly look at without fancying that in some of them there will be a resting-place for us.

But things being as they are, I pray God to give you better health, fewer vexations, more comforts, and life long enough to enjoy the fruits of the reputation you deserve, and cannot fail to obtain.

You have sent me a precious drawing and a pleasant letter. Your letters indeed are always pleasant, except when they tell me you have been suffering sickness, molestation, or such mishap as this late one [the sinking of a wall of her house], which might have been so much more serious in its consequences. . . . Dear friend, God bless you.

ROBERT SOUTHEY.

HUGH MILLER

(1802–56)

The Scottish geologist and man of letters had a fascinating personality, which caused his future wife, Lydia Fraser, to prefer him, though then only a

stonemason and ten years older than herself. It
was a grand moment for him that Lydia's mother
relented and permitted the acquaintanceship to ripen,
for it opened up to him new hopes and ambitions,
whereby he was stimulated to gird up his loins for
the race of life.

Hitherto " he professed just what he felt, to be
content with a table, a chair, and a pot, with a little
fire in his grate, and a little meal to cook on it." But
now such a humble idea no longer satisfied him, for
he longed to give his wife the home and position of
a lady, so he writes from Cromarty to his lady-love :

I am afraid you are still unwell. Your window was
shut till ten this morning, and as I saw no light from
it last evening, I must conclude you went early to bed.
How very inefficient, my L——, are the friendships
of this earth.

My heart is bound up in you, and yet I can only
wish and regret and—yes, pray. Well, that is something. I cannot regulate your pulses, nor dissipate
your pains, nor give elasticity to your spirits ; but I
can implore on your behalf of the great Being who
can. My mother, as you are aware has a very small
garden behind her house. . . . Some eight years ago
I intended building a little house for myself in this
garden. I was to cover it outside with ivy, and to
line it inside with books ; and here was I to read and
write and think all my life long—not altogether so
independent of the world as Diogenes in his tub, or
the savage in the recess of the forest, but quite as much
as is possible for man in his social state. Here was I
to attain to wealth, not by increasing my goods but
by moderating my desires.

Of the thirst after wealth I had none. I could live
on half a crown per week and be content ; nor yet
was I desirous of power—I sought not to be any man's
master, and I had spirit enough to preserve me from
being any man's slave. . . .

Love, I could have nothing to fear from. I knew

myself to be naturally of a cool temperament; and then, were not my attachments to my friends so many safety-valves! Besides, no woman of taste could ever love me, for I was ugly and awkward; and as I could only love the woman of taste, I could never submit to wed one to whom I was indifferent, my being ugly and awkward was as an iron wall to me. No, no, I had nothing to fear from love. My dear L——, only see how much good philosophy you have spoiled. I am not now indifferent to wealth or power or place in the world's eye. I would fain be rich, that I might render you comfortable; powerful, that I might raise you to those high places of society which you are so fitted to adorn; celebrated, that the world might justify your choice. I never think now of building the little house or of being happiest in solitude; and if my life is to be one of celibacy, it must be one of sorrow also—of heart-wasting sorrow, for——but I must not think of that.

It is sad to think of the end of this man of such lofty ideals and simple life. In his last days his reason failed and he shot himself.

THOMAS HOOD

(1799–1845)

Always to be remembered as the author of " The Song of the Shirt," which he wrote in *Punch*, his wit and humour were more lucrative to this brave struggler than the qualities with which they were inseparably blended. In him " the strings attuned to mirth had their chords in melancholy," and his quaintest extravagances cover a fine moral sincerity. Married to the sister of John Hamilton Reynolds, whom he assisted in the editorship of the *London Magazine*, he addresses some very tender letters to his brave and sweet-tempered wife from the Rhine, where, through pressure of debt, he was obliged to live for five years.

(1)

(2)

(3)

(1) ELIZABETH BARRETT BROWNING.   (2) ROBERT BROWNING.
(3) THOMAS CARLYLE.

My own dearest and best Love,— . . . I do hope you will soon be able to come, and in the meantime I will do everything I can think of to facilitate your progress. . . .

I saw a vision of you, dearest, to-day, and felt you leaning on me, and looking over the Moselle at the blue mountains and the vineyards. I long but to get to work with you and the pigeon pair by my side, and then I shall not sigh for the past. . . . Get yourselves strong, there is still a happy future; fix your eyes forward on our meeting, my best and dearest.

Our little home, though homely, will be happy for us, and we do not bid England a very long good night. Good night, too, my dearest wife, my pride and comfort.

A further illustration of the high regard he had for his wife may be gathered from the following extract:

I never was anything, dearest, till I knew you; and I have been a better, happier, and more prosperous man ever since.

Lay by that truth in sweet lavender, sweetest, and remind me of it, when I fail. I am writing warmly and fondly, but not without good cause. First, your own affectionate letter, lately received; next, the remembrance of our dear children; then a delicious impulse to pour out the overflowings of my heart into yours; and last, not least, the knowledge that your dear eyes will read what my hand is now writing.

THE BROWNINGS: ROBERT BROWNING (1812–89); ELIZABETH BARRETT (1806–61)

It is difficult to select specific letters from the two big volumes written during the close-on two years of their courtship, from 1845 to 1846. Do poets have more time to write private letters, outpourings of the soul, than ordinary folks? or do they, as Goethe did in *Werther* and George Sand in *Elle et Lui*, make literary capital out of their own soul-turmoil, and find it a good investment to plot clinical temperature-charts of their personal passions ? One can hardly believe that such sordid reasons dwelt in either of the Brownings, he " looking for the highest " in his ethical message, incomprehensible though it was to the millions, and she, Elizabeth Barrett (her sonnets from the Portuguese mark the highest and finest expression, in English or any other literature, of a woman's love for man), whose frail life was prolonged to the fifty-sixth year by the power of love and happiness. Whether the Brownings indited ideal love-letters may be a matter of opinion, but there is no doubt that this fortunate marriage, which lasted sixteen happy years, belongs to the ideal things in life, for the two great poets knew a perfect union, in their home at Florence, where they lived till Mrs. Browning died in 1861.

The correspondence, commencing with Robert Browning's complimenting Miss Barrett about her poems on January 10th, 1845, does not reach its culmination of declared love till September 13th of that year, when the " dearest friend " has become, for good and all, " dearest," and finally " dearest Ba."

R. Browning to Elizabeth Barrett

Saturday morning, September 13th, 1845 (postmark.)

Now, dearest, I will try and write the little I shall be able, in reply to your letter of last week—and first of all I have to entreat you, now more than ever, to help me and understand from the few words the feelings behind them (I should *speak* rather more easily I think, but I dare not run the risk ; and I know, after all, you will be just and kind where you can). I have read your letter again and again. I will tell you —no, not *you*, but any imaginary other person who should hear what I am going to avow ; I would tell that person most sincerely there is not a particle of fatuity, shall I call it, in that avowal ; cannot be, seeing

that from the beginning and at this moment I never
dreamed of winning your *love*. I can hardly write
this word, so incongruous and impossible does it seem ;
such a change of our places does it imply—nor, next
to that, though long after, *would I*, if I *could* supplant
one of any of the affections that I know to have taken
root in you—*that* great and solemn one, for instance.
I feel that if I could get myself *remade*, as if turned
to gold, I WOULD not even then desire to become
more than the mere setting to *that* diamond you must
always wear. The regard and esteem you now give
me, in this letter, and which I press to my heart and
bow my head upon, is all I can take and all too embarrassing, using *all* my gratitude. And yet, with
that contented pride in being infinitely your debtor
as it is, bound to you for ever as it is ; when I read
your letter with all the determination to be just to
both of us ; I dare not so far withstand the light I am
master of, as to refuse seeing that whatever is recorded
as an objection to your disposing of that life of mine
I would give you, has reference to some supposed
good in that life which your accepting it would destroy
(of which fancy I shall speak presently)—I say, wonder
as I may at this, I cannot but find it there, surely there.
I could no more " bind *you* by words " than you have
bound me, as you say—but if I misunderstand you,
one assurance to that effect will be but too intelligible
to me—but, as it *is*, I have difficulty in imagining
that while one of so many reasons, which I am not
obliged to repeat to myself, but which anyone easily
conceives ; while *any one* of those reasons would impose
silence on me *for ever* (for, as I observed, I love you as
you are now, and *would* not remove one affection
that is already part of you)—*would* you, being able
to speak *so*, only say, *that you* desire not to put
" more sadness than I was born to " into my life ?—
that you " could give me only what it were ungenerous to give ? "

Have I your meaning here ? In so many words, is
it on my account that you bid me " leave this subject? "

I think if it were so, I would for once call my advantages round me. I am not what your generous, self-forgetting appreciation would sometimes make me out—but it is not since yesterday, nor ten or twenty years before, that I began to look into my own life, and study its end, and requirements, what would turn to its good or its loss—and *I know*, if one may know anything, that to make that life yours and increase it by union with yours would render me *supremely happy*, as I said, and say, and feel. My whole suit to you is, in that sense, *selfish*—not that I am ignorant that *your* nature would most surely attain happiness in being conscious that it made another happy, but *that best, best end of all* would, like the rest, come from yourself, be a reflection of your own gift.

Dearest, I will end here—words, persuasion, arguments, if they were at my service I would not use them —I believe in you, altogether have faith in you—in you. I will not think of insulting by trying to reassure you on one point which certain phrases in your letter might at first glance seem to imply—you do not understand me to be living and labouring and writing (and *not* writing) in order to be successful in the world's sense ? I even convinced the people *here* what was my true, "honourable position in society," etc., etc., therefore I shall not have to inform *you* that I desire to be very rich, very great ; but not in reading Law gratis with dear foolish old Basil Montagu, as he ever and anon bothers me to do ; much less—enough of this nonsense.

"Tell me what I have a claim to hear " ; I can hear it and be as grateful as I was before and am now —your friendship is my pride and happiness. If you told me your love was bestowed elsewhere, and that it was in my power to serve you *there*, to serve you there would still be my pride and happiness. I look on and on over the prospect of my love, it is all *on*wards —and all possible forms of unkindness—I quite laugh to think how they are *behind*—cannot be encountered in the route we are travelling ! I submit to you and will obey you implicitly—obey what I am able to conceive of your least desire, much more of your expressed wish. But it was necessary to make this avowal, among other reasons, for one which the world would recognise too. My whole scheme of life (with its wants, material wants at least closely cut down) was long ago calculated, and it supposed *you*, the finding such a one as you, utterly impossible—because in calculating one goes upon *chances*, not providence—how could I expect you ? So for my own future way in the world I have always refused to care—anyone who can live a couple of years and more on bread and potatoes as I did once on a time, and who prefers a blouse and a blue shirt (such as I now write in) to all manner of dress and gentlemanly appointment, and who can, if necessary, groom a horse not so badly or at all events would rather do it all day long than succeed Mr. Fitzroy Kelly in the Solicitor-Generalship —such a one need not very much concern himself beyond considering the lilies how they grow. But now I see you near this life, all changes—and at a word, I will do all that ought to be done, that everyone used to say could be done, and let " all my powers find sweet employ," as Dr. Watts sings, in getting whatever is to be got—not very much surely. I would print these things, get them away, and do this now, and go to you at Pisa with the news—at Pisa where one may live for some £100 a year—while, lo, I seem to remember, I *do* remember that Charles Kean offered to give me 500 of those pounds for any play that might suit him —to say nothing of Mr. Colbourn saying confidentially that he wanted more than his dinner, a novel on the subject of *Napoleon !*

So may one make money, if one does not live in a house in a row, and feel impelled to take the Princess's theatre for a laudable development and exhibition of one's faculty.

Take the sense of all this, I beseech you, dearest— all you shall say will be best—I am yours.

Yes, yours ever. God bless you, for all you have been

and are, and will certainly be to me, come what He shall please !

                                                    R. B.

A thousand words or more to ask her to be his !   At least, that seems to be the gist of the letter, picking it out from the flood of reservations, contentions, digressions, repetitions, hesitations, psycho-analytical self-examinations, in italics, caps, dashes, commas, exclamation and quotation marks, brackets, and notes of interrogation, " to make that life yours and increase it by union with yours, would render me *supremely happy*."   A characteristically obscure letter by the poet of "Sordello," which Mrs. Carlyle (a word-spinner too) was said by her husband to have read, " without being able to make out whether Sordello was a man, a city, or a book."

Elizabeth Barrett, in her replies, had the same habit of dilating or diluting her meaning.   But then, she had the excuse of having to spend most of her life on a sofa.

Elizabeth Barrett Browning to Robert Browning

Thursday evening (postmark, *December 20th*, 1845).

DEAREST,—You know how to say what makes me happiest, you who never think, you say, of making me happy !   For my part I do not think of it either ;   I simply understand that you *are* my happiness and that therefore you could not make another happiness for me, such as would be worth having—not even *you*.   Why, how could you ?   *That* was in my mind to speak yesterday, but I could not speak it— to write it, is easier.

Talking of happiness—shall I tell you ?   Promise not to be angry and I will tell you.   I have thought sometimes that if I considered myself wholly, I should choose to die this winter—now—before I had disappointed you in anything.   But because you are better and dearer and more to be considered than I, I do *not* choose it.   I *cannot* choose to give you any

pain, even on the chance of its being a less pain, a less
evil, than what may follow perhaps (who can say ?)
if I should prove the burden of your life.

For if you make me happy with some words, you
frighten me with others—as with the extravagance
yesterday—and seriously—*too* seriously, when the
moment for smiling at them is past—I am frightened, I
tremble ! When you come to know me as well as
I know myself, what can save me, do you think, from
disappointing and displeasing you ? I ask the question
and find no answer.

It is a poor answer to say that I can do one thing
well—that I have one capacity largely. On points
of the general affections, I have in thought applied
to myself the words of Mme. de Staël, not fretfully, I
hope, not complainingly, I am sure (I can thank God
for most affectionate friends !) not complainingly, yet
mournfully and in profound conviction—those words
—" jamais je n'ai pas été aimée comme j'aime."
The capacity of loving is the largest of my powers, I
think—I thought so before knowing you—and one form
of feeling. And although any woman might love you
—*every* woman—with understanding enough to dis-
cern you by—(oh, do not fancy that I am unduly
magnifying mine office)—yet I persist in persuading
myself that ! Because I have the capacity, as I said—
and besides I owe more to you than others could, it
seems to me ; let me boast of it. To many, you might
be better than all things while one of all things ; to
me you are instead of all—to many, a crowning happiness—to me, the happiness itself. From out of the
deep dark pits men see the stars more gloriously—
and *de profundis amavi!*

It is a very poor answer ! almost as poor an answer
as yours could be if I were to ask you to teach me to
please you always ; or rather how not to displease you,
disappoint you, vex you—what if all those things were
in my fate ?

And—(to begin !) . . . *I* am disappointed to-night.
I expected a letter which does not come—and I had

felt so sure of having a letter to-night—unreasonably sure perhaps, which means doubly sure.

And after some business transactions with Mr. Kenyon follows this charming digression on Bad Temper, which might have come from the pen of the author of the *Essays of Elia* :

As your letter does not come it is a good opportunity for asking what sort of ill-humour, or (to be more correct) bad temper, you most particularly admire—sulkiness ?—the divine gift of sitting aloof in a cloud like any god for three weeks together perhaps—pettishness ?—which will get you up in a storm about a crooked pin or a straight one either ? obstinacy ?—which is an agreeable form of temper, I can assure you, and describes itself—or the good open passion which lies on the floor and kicks, like one of my cousins ? —Certainly I prefer the last, and should, I think, prefer it (as an evil), even if it were not the born weakness of my own nature—though I humbly confess (to *you*, who seem to think differently of these things) that never since I was a child have I upset all the chairs and tables and thrown the books about the room in a fury—I am afraid I do not even " kick " like my cousin now. Those demonstrations were done by the " light of other days "—not a very full light, I used to be accustomed to think ; but *you*—*you* think otherwise, *you* take a fury to be the opposite of " indifference," as if there could be no such thing as self-control !

Now, for my part, I do believe that the worst-tempered persons in the world are less so through sensibility than selfishness—they spare nobody's heart, on the ground of being themselves pricked by a straw. Now see if it isn't so ? What, after all, is a good temper but generosity in trifles—and what, without it, is the happiness of life ? We have only to look around us. I *saw* a woman, once, burst into tears, because her husband cut the bread and butter too thick. I saw *that* with my own eyes. Was it *sensibility* I wonder! They were at least real tears and ran down her cheeks. " You *always* do it," she said.

Why, how you must sympathise with the heroes and heroines of the French romances (*do* you sympathise with them very much ?) when at the slightest provocation, they break up the tables and chairs (a degree beyond the deeds of my childhood !—*I* only used to upset them) break up the tables and chairs and chiffoniers, and dash the china to atoms. The men *do* the furniture and the women the porcelain ; and pray observe that they always set about this as a matter of course! When they have broken everything in the room, they sink down quite (and very naturally) *abattus*. I remember a particular case of a hero of Frederic Soulié's, who, in the course of an " emotion " takes up a chair *unconsciously*, and breaks it into very small pieces, and then proceeds with his soliloquy. Well—! the clearest idea this excites in *me*, is of the low condition in Paris, of moral government and of upholstery. Because—just consider for yourself— how *you* would succeed in breaking to pieces even a three-legged stool if it were properly put together— as stools are in England, just yourself, without a hammer and a screw! You might work at it *comme quatre*, and find it hard to finish, I imagine. And then as a demonstration, a child of six years old might demonstrate just so (in his sphere) and be whipped accordingly.

How I go on writing !—and you, who do not write at all !—two extremes, one set against the other.

But I may say, though in ever such an ill temper (which you know is just the time to select for writing a panegyric upon good temper) that I am glad you do not despise my own right name too much, because I never was called Elizabeth by any one who loved me at all, and I accept the omen. So little it seems my name that if a voice said suddenly " Elizabeth," I should as soon turn round as my sisters would—no sooner. Only, my own right name has been complained of for want of euphony. *Ba* . . . Now and

14

then it has—and Mr. Boyd makes a compromise and calls me *Elibet*, because nothing could induce him to desecrate his organs, accustomed to Attic harmonies with a *Ba*. So I am glad and accept the omen.

But I give you no credit for not thinking that I may forget you—I! As if you did not see the difference! Why, *I* could not even forget to *write* to *you*, observe!

Whenever you write, say how you are. Were you wet on Wednesday?

Your own——

THOMAS CARLYLE

(1795–1881)

Evidently the people of the nineteenth century had more time to write letters than we of to-day, for it may be doubted whether there are many readers brave enough to-day to wade through the two thick volumes of Carlyle's love-letters to Jane Welsh, let alone write them.

Perhaps that is the reason too that, when married, Mr. and Mrs. Carlyle's relations turned out so unhappily. They had told each other every compliment they knew or could think of beforehand. People of such exaggerated nervous susceptibility need an *alter ego* that is made of more impervious stuff, to serve as a kind of buffer to ward off the slings and arrows of butcher, baker, and landlord. The letters, of course, are delightful, *qua* literature, and that on both sides; but, as all history shows, love's happiest time is when it is speechless. A madrigal to your mistress's eyebrow is only the next best thing. It is not till the one hundred and eleventh letter of their correspondence that, to use an ultra-slang expression, Carlyle "cuts the cackle and comes to the 'osses." All his letters are impregnated with that Teutonic diffuseness, discussing with professorial tiresomeness the metaphysical reasons of his most insignificant thoughts, feelings,

and actions. But, of course, the Victorians, with
whom time ambled withal, liked that sort of thing.
They were the lineal descendants of Lady Mary
Wortley Montagu, who would start a conversation by
saying, " And now, let us talk about the soul."

LETTER III

T. Carlyle to Miss Welsh, Haddington

PENTONVILLE, 9th January, 1825.

MY DEAREST,—I trust that the same cheerful spirit
of affection which breathes in every line of your last
charming Letter, still animates you, and disposes you
kindly towards me.

I have somewhat to propose to you ; which it may
require all your love of me to make you look upon with
favour. If you are not the best woman in this world,
it may prove a sorry business for both of us.

You bid me tell you how I have decided ; what
I mean to do. My Dearest ! it is you that must
decide : I will endeavour to explain to you what I
wish ; it must rest with you to say whether it can
ever be attained. You tell me. " *You* have land
which needs improvement ; why not work on that ? "
In one word then : will you go with me, will you be
my own for ever ; and I embrace the project with
my whole heart ? Say, Yes ! And I send my brother
Alick over to rent that Nithsdale Farm [Craigenputtock.
—ED.] for me without delay ; I proceed to it, the
moment I am freed from my engagements here ; I
labour in arranging it, and fitting everything for your
reception ; and the instant it is ready, I take you home
to my hearth, and my bosom, never more to part
from me, whatever fate betide us !

I fear you think this scheme a baseless vision : and
yet it is the sober best among the many I have medi-
tated ; the best for me, and I think also, as far as I
can judge of it, for yourself. If it take effect and be
well conducted, I look upon the recovery of my health

and equanimity, and with these, of regular profitable and natural habits of activity, as things which are no longer doubtful. I have lost them by departing from Nature. I must find them by returning to her. A stern experience has taught me this; and I am a fool if I do not profit by the lesson. Depend on it, Jane, this literature, which both of us are so bent on pursuing, will *not* constitute the sole nourishment of any true human spirit. No truth has been forced upon me, after more resistance, or with more invincible impressiveness, than this. I feel it in myself, I see it daily in others. Literature is the *wine* of life; it will not, cannot be its *food*. What is it that makes Blue-stockings of women, Magazine-hacks of men? They neglect household and social duties, they have no household and social enjoyments. Life is no longer with them a verdant field but a *hortus siccus* (parched garden); they exist pent up in noisome streets, amid feverish excitements; they despise or overlook the common blessedness which Providence has laid out for *all* his creatures, and try to substitute for it a distilled quintessence prepared in the alembic of Painters and Rhymers and sweet Singers. What is the result? This *ardent spirit* parches up their nature; they become discontented and despicable, or wretched and dangerous. Byron and all strong souls go the latter way; Campbell and all weak souls the former. "Hinaus," as the Devil says to Faust, "Hinaus ins frey Feld" (out into the free field!). There is no soul in these vapid "articles" of yours: Away! Be men, before attempting to be *writers*!

You, too, my Darling, are unhappy; and I see the reason. You have a deep, earnest, vehement spirit, and no earnest task has ever been assigned to it. You despise and ridicule the meanness of the things about you: to the things you honour you can only pay a fervent adoration, which issues in no practical effect. O that I saw you the mistress of a house; diffusing over human souls that loved you those clear faculties of order, judgement, elegance, which you are now reduced to spend on pictures and portfolios ; blessing living hearts with that enthusiastic love which you must now direct to the distant and dimly seen ! All this is in you, Jane ! you have a heart and an intellect and a resolute decision, which might make you the model of wives, however widely your thoughts and your experience have hitherto wandered from that highest destination of even the noblest woman. I too, have wandered wide and far ! let us return, my Dearest ! Let us return *together !* Let us learn thro' one another what it is to live ; let us become citizens of this world ; let us set our minds and habitudes in order, and grow under the peaceful sunshine of Nature, that whatever fruit or flowers have been implanted in our spirits may ripen wholesomely and be distributed in due season ! what is genius but the last perfection of true manhood ? The pure reflexion of a spirit in union with itself, discharging all common duties with more than common excellence, extracting from the many-coloured scenes of life in which it mingles, the beautifying principle which more or less pervades them all ? The rose in its full-blown fragrance is the glory of the fields ; but there must be a soil and stem and leaves, or there will be no rose. Your mind and my own *have* in them many capabilities ; but the first of all their duties is to provide for their own regulation and contentment : if there *be* an overplus to consecrate to higher ends, it will not fail to show itself ; if there be none, it is better that it never should attempt to show itself.

But I must leave these generalities, and avoid romance ; for it is an earnest practical affair we are engaged in, and requires sense and calculation, not poetics and enthusiasm. " Where then," you ask me, " are the *means* of realising these results, of mastering the difficulties and deficiencies that beset us both ? " . . . The first, the lowest but a most essential point, is that of funds. . . . In my present state my income tho' small might to reasonable wishes be sufficient ; were my health and faculty restored, it *might* become abundant. Shall I confess to you, my Dearest, this is a difficulty, which I imagine we are apt to overrate. The essentials of even elegant comfort are not difficult to procure : it is only vanity that is insatiable in consuming. To my taste, cleanliness and order are far beyond gilding and grandeur, which without them are an abomination ; and for displays, for festivals and " parties," I believe you are as indisposed as myself. Your Mother's house is truly the *best* I have ever seen ; tho' in my travels I have looked at some where *thirty* times the money was expended. After all, what is the use of this same vanity ? Where is the good of being its slaves ? If thou and I love one another, if we discharge our duties faithfully and steadfastly, one labouring with honest manful zeal to provide, the other with noble wife-like prudence in dispensing, have we not done all *we can ;* are we not acquitted at the bar of our own conscience ? and what is it to us, whether this or that Squire or Bailie be richer or poorer than we ?

Two laws I have laid down to myself : that I must and will recover health, without which to think or even to live is burdensome or unprofitable ; and that I will *not* degenerate into the wretched thing which calls itself an Author in our Capitals, and scribbles for the sake of filthy lucre in the periodicals of the day. Thank Heaven ! there are other means of living ; if there were not, I for one should beg to be excused. My projects I will give you in detail *when we meet.* That translation of *Schiller,* I think, will *not* take effect ; that of the *Lives* has brightened up in me again, and I think, *will.* Perhaps, it is better for me ; I ought to thank the timorousness of Booksellers for driving me back on it. Failing both, there are other schemes, schemes unconnected with writing altogether. But here is not an inch of space for speaking of them.

On the whole I begin to entertain a certain degree of contempt for the Destiny, which has so long persecuted me. I will be a man in spite of it ! Yet it lies with you, my Dearest, whether I

shall be a *right* man, or only a hard bitter Stoic.   What
say you, Jane ? Decide for yourself and me ! Consent,
if you dare trust me ! Consent and come to my faithful
breast, and let us live and die together !   Yet fear
not to deny me, if your judgement so determine.   It
will be a sharp pang that tears away from me for ever
the hope, which now for years has been the solace of
my existence : but better to endure it and all its
consequences, than to witness and to cause the forfeit
of your happiness.   At times, I confess, when I hear
you speak of your gay Cousins, and contrast with their
brilliant equipments my own simple exterior, and
scanty prospects, and humble but to me most dear
and honourable-minded kinsmen, whom I were the
veriest dog if I ever ceased to love and venerate and
cherish for their true affection, and the rugged sterling
[worth] of their characters ; when I think of all this,
I could almost counsel you to cast me utterly away,
and connect yourself with one whose friends and station
were more analogous to your own.   But anon, in
some moment of self-love, I say proudly, There is
a spirit in *me*, which is worthy of this noble maiden,
which shall be worthy of her ! I will take her. to
my heart, careladen but ever true to her ; I will teach
her, I will guide her, I will make her happy ! together
we will share the joys and sorrows of existence ; I
will bear her in my arms thro' all its vicissitudes,
and Fate itself shall not divide us.

Speak then, my Angel ! How say you ? Will you
be mine, mine ? Or am I a fool for having hoped it ?
Think well ; of me, of yourself, of our circumstances ;
and determine. Or have you not already thought ?

You love me do you not ? Dare you trust me ;
dare you trust your fate with me, as I trust mine with
you ? Say, Yes ! and I see you in February, and take
" sweet counsel " with you about all our hopes and
plans and future life, thenceforward to be one and
indivisible. Say No ! and—— But you will not
say no, if you can help it ; for you *do* love me, deny it
as you will ; and your spirit longs to be mingled with

mine, as mine with yours, that we may be *one* in the sight of God and man forever and ever !

Now judge if I wait your answer with impatience ! I know you will not keep me waiting—Of course it will be necessary to explain all things to your Mother, and take her serious advice respecting them. For your other " friends " it is not worth consulting one of them. I know not that there is one among them that would give you as disinterested an advice as even I, judging in my own cause. May God bless you, and direct you, my Dearest ! decide as you will, I am yours for ever,

T. Carlyle.

In letter 112, in reply to Carlyle's impassioned appeal, Jane Welsh does not approve of his scheme. She would not spend a month at Craigenputtock with an Angel. She has told him a hundred times, she loves him, but is not *in love* with him, meaning thereby that her passion does not overcloud her judgment. This letter is hardly a love-letter, but is an indication of a considerable fund of sound, canny common-sense. However, everything comes to the man who waits, and finally, after sixty-odd more letters have passed between them, Carlyle finally receives Jane Welsh's " last speech and marrying words," as Carlyle calls it in his reply.

LETTER 175

Miss Welsh to T. Carlyle, Scotsbrig

Templand, *Tuesday*, 3. *Oct.* 1826.

Unkind that you are ever to suffer me to be cast down, when it is so easy a thing for you to lift me to the Seventh Heaven ! my soul was darker than midnight when your pen said " Let there be light," and there *was* light as at the bidding of the Word. And now I am resolved in spirit and even joyful, joyful even in the face of the dreaded ceremony, of *starvation*, and every possible fate.

Oh, my dearest Friend! be always *so* good to me, and I shall make the best and happiest Wife. When I read in your looks and words that you love me, I feel it in the deepest part of my soul; then I care not one jot for the whole Universe beside; but when you fly from my caresses to—smoke tobacco, or speak of me as a new *circumstance* of your lot, then indeed my " heart is troubled about many things."

My Mother is not come yet, but is expected this week; the week following must be given to her to take a last look at her Child; and then Dearest, God willing, I am your own for ever and ever. . . .

[Then follow some details about the marriage ceremony.]

Oh mercy! What I would give to be sitting in our doll's house married for a week! . . . [And referring to his sister Jane coming to stay with them] . . . and give her a kiss in my name.

I may well return *one* out of *twenty*. But indeed, Dear, these kisses on paper are scarce worth keeping. You gave me one on my neck that night you were in such good-humour, and one on my lips on some forgotten occasion, that I would not part with for a hundred thousand paper ones. Perhaps some day or other, I shall get none of either sort; *sic transit gloria mundi* [" so passes the glory of the world "] . . . . And then not my will be done, but thine. I am going to be really a very meek-tempered Wife; indeed, I am begun to be meek-tempered already. My Aunt tells me, she could live for ever with *me*, without quarrelling—I am so reasonable and equal in my humour. There is something to gladden your heart withal! and more than this; my Grandfather observed while I was supping my porridge last night, that " she was really a douce peaceable body that *Pen.*" So you perceive, my good Sir, the fault will be wholly your own, if we do not get on most harmoniously together. . . . But I must stop. And this is my last Letter. What a thought! How terrible and yet full of bliss. You will love me for ever, will you not, my own Husband ? and I will always be your true and affectionate

JANE WELSH.

They were married on October 17th, 1826, his wife dying in 1866, and his whole after-life was saddened by the discovery, from her letters and journals, how unhappy her life had been.

CHARLES DICKENS

(1812–70)

Dickens's fault, if it be a fault, was an over-abundance of energy and overflow of life, which is sufficiently evident in his letters to his wife, whom as Catherine Hogarth, he married in 1836, when still an unknown reporter on the *Morning Chronicle*, the first number of *The Pickwick Papers* being published in March 1836.

The letters can hardly be called love-letters proper. They are not in the clouds, and do not deal in oh's ! and ah's ! and seraphic raptures, but display good honest sentiment, and much detailed discussion about the subjects nearest to his heart, the work he is engaged on.

Charles Dickens to Catherine Hogarth

FURNIVAL'S INN, *Wednesday evening*, 1835.

MY DEAREST KATE,—The House is up, but I am very sorry to say that I must stay at home. I have had a visit from the publishers this morning, and the story cannot be any longer delayed ; it must be done to-morrow, as there are more important considerations too than the mere payment for the story involved. I must exercise a little self-denial, and set to work. They [Chapman & Hall] have made me an offer of fourteen pounds a month, to write and edit a new publication they contemplate, entirely by myself, to be published monthly, and each number to contain four woodcuts. I am to make my estimate and calculation, and to give them a decisive answer on Friday morning. The work will be no joke, but the emolument is too tempting to resist. . . .

The story of the inception of *The Pickwick Papers* is well known. Cockney sporting designs by Seymour needed letterpress. Of sport Dickens knew as little as an Englishman can. Seymour died; the sporting element was dropped, and Dickens had a free hand.

Sunday evening.

. . . I have at this moment got Pickwick and his friends on the Rochester coach, and they are going on swimmingly, in company with a very different character from any I have yet described, who I flatter myself will make a decided hit. [This was " Jingle."—Ed.] I want to get them from the ball to the inn before I go to bed ; and I think that will take me until one or two o'clock at the earliest. The publishers will be here in the morning, so you will readily suppose I have no alternative but to stick to my desk. . . .

NICOLAS LENAU

(1802–50)

THE Hungarian poet Nicolas Lenau (whose real name was Niembsch von Strehlenau) was of that fiery yet melancholy nature which imbues the denizens of the endless Hungarian pusztas. The whole gamut of feeling lies in his lyric and lyric-epical poems, eventually overclouded by his ever-increasing melancholy, ending by his death in a madhouse. The secrecy of his overwhelming passion for the wife of his friend Loewenthal gnawed at his vitals and undermined his short life. Amongst his love-letters may be cited the following, full of poetical and melancholy charm.

VIENNA, *June* 10th, 1837.

. . . Dost thou really believe, I pay no heed to the running sands of time ? I should like to hold fast to each moment and caress it with the prayer, not to pass by so quickly from our happiness. But time is a cold, soulless thing ; otherwise it would be stayed at our happiness, and lost in joy would stand still. But it flies, you go to rest, blow out your light and shut your eyes, which only an hour ago, gazed at me so beautifully and tenderly. Why must it pass so quickly ? Eternity must be very beautiful and splendid, otherwise it is really not worth while for us to be hurried towards it so speedily, away from such pleasures as we have enjoyed to-day. But for the nonce, I cannot conceive of Heaven otherwise, than that there will be safe and lasting, what is unstable and fleeting here below. I like to depict it to myself,

MOZART.

as it were ; my atmosphere your breath, my light your eye, my drink your word, my food your kiss, my resting-place your heart, my footway the Kingdom of God with you, with you, dear Sophie !

I shall write to you in Stuttgart daily ; since it pleases you so, you shall receive a real packet of my gossip. Everything I do and experience you shall have. I shall devote my time unstintingly to be back with you soon. Were I only there again ! Good night, my heart, sleep well.

Good morning ! I wait at my window, to see you pass by on your way to church. How did you sleep ? My clocks have stopped, I do not know the time, but a girl in the street says it is half-past six, and so you have still to pass. But I just notice breakfast being taken in to my neighbour Panovski, and almost think that it is, must be, later. Or should the hunger of my neighbour be an earlier riser than your devotions ? Breakfast with me to-day, dear little heart ! When you pass by, come in.

MOZART TO CONSTANZE WEBER

(1756–91)

Mozart, the Viennese wonder-child, of sparkling, precocious genius, married, in 1782, the pianist and singer Constanze Weber, a sister of his boyish love, Aloysia Weber, thereby increasing his financial difficulties and bringing upon him the wrath of his father. The kind-hearted, childlike simplicity of his character is as visible in the melodious charm of his music as in the joyous and sparkling youthfulness of his letters.

VIENNA, *April 29th*, 1782.

DEAREST, BESTE FREUNDIN,—This name I am sure you will allow me to call you by ? I am sure that you will not hate me to that extent that I may no longer be your Freund and you no longer will be my Freundin? and—even if you do not want to be so any more, yet you cannot forbid me to think well of you, my Freun-din, as I have always been accustomed to. Consider well, what you have said to me to-day. You have (in spite of all my prayers) three times refused to marry me [Germ. allocution, *den Korb gegeben*, " given me the basket," " given me the rebuff "] and have told me, straight to my face, that you do not wish to have anything more to do with me. I, to whom it is not so indifferent as it is to you, to lose the beloved object, am not so hot-headed, ill-advised, and un-reasonable, as to accept the rebuff. For this, I love you too much. I beg you therefore once more, to consider well the cause of this annoyance, and to remember, what it was that I had taken objection to, namely that you had been of such shameless levity, to tell your sisters N.B. (*nota bene*—be it noted) in my presence, that you had allowed a Chapeau to measure your calves. No woman does that, who respects her honour. The maxim to do what the company does, is quite a good one. But one has to consider in doing so many contingencies ; whether there are present only good friends and acquaintances ? whether I am a child or a girl ripe for *marriage* ? but particularly, whether I am a promised bride ? but above all, whether only people of my standing or beneath me, but particularly, whether people of superior station, are present ?—Though really the Baroness herself may have let him do it, that is quite a different thing, seeing that she is already an elderly woman (who cannot possibly attract any more), and has besides, a predilection for the etceteras. I trust, liebste Freundin, that you will never desire to lead such a life as she does, even if you do not want to be my wife. If you really felt impelled to do as the others—although it does not always befit even a male to follow my leader, let alone a female—and felt it impossible to withstand, you should, in Gottes Namen, have taken the tape and have measured your own calves (just as *all women of honour* have done in my presence in similar cases) and not by a Chapeau (I—I—would

never have done this to you in the presence of others),
I would have handed you the tape, much less therefore
by a stranger, who is nothing to me.—But that is over,
and a small confession of your, on that occasion, somewhat ill-considered performance, would have propi-
tiated and—if you do not take it in bad part, liebste
Freundin—would still conciliate everybody. I *do not
flare up as you do*—I reflect—I consider and I feel.
If *you feel, if you have feeling*, then I am convinced,
that before the day is out I shall be able to say without
hesitation : Constanze is the virtuous, honour-loving,
reasonable, and faithful love of upright and thinking-
well-of-you,

MOZART.

DRESDEN, *the* 13*th April,* 1789,
7 *o'clock in the morning.*

DEAREST LITTLE WIFE,—If only I had a letter of
yours too ! If I were to tell you everything, what I
do with your dear portrait, you would laugh a good
deal. For instance, whenever I take it out of its
confinement, I say " Gruess dich Gott, Stanzerl !
—Gruess dich Gott, Spitzbub—Krallerballer—Spit-
zignas—Bagatellerl—schluck und druck." [*Ed. note.*—
These are practically nicknames of affection hard to
render in English, as who might say, " Cheerio, Cossy
(dim. of Constanze)—Cheerio, Rogue, Rowdy-dowdy
—Snub-nose—Good-for-nothing—Tip and run.] And
when I put it back, I let it slip down by degrees, and
say at the same time—Nu—Nu—Nu—Nu ! but with
a certain emphasis which this word of so many meanings
requires, and finally quickly, " Good night, mousey,
sleep soundly ! " Now, really I believe I have written
down something quite too stupid (for the world at
least) ; but for us, who love each other so very dearly,
it is not stupid at all. . . . To-day is the sixth day
that I am away from you, and bei Gott, it seems to
me a year ago. . . . You will, I am sure, often be at
pains to read my letter, because I write in haste, and

therefore somewhat badly. Adieu, love, one and only,—the carriage is there—I cannot say, good luck; and the carriage is really there—but *male*. . . . Fare well and love me always, as I do you! I kiss you a million times most tenderly, and remain eternally your tender loving husband,

W. A. MOZART.

FRANKFURT, *a.m. the 29th September*, 1790.

DEAREST, BEST LITTLE WIFE OF MY HEART,—This moment we arrive—that is at one o'clock p.m.—so we have only taken six days. We could have done the journey quicker still, if we had not taken a little rest three times of nights. We are staying meanwhile in the suburb Sachsenhausen at an inn, delighted beyond measure that we have been able to snap up a room. Now we still remain ignorant of our disposal, whether we stay together or are to be separated;— if I can't get a room for nothing somewhere and provided I don't find the inns too dear, I shall certainly stay. I hope you will have safely received my epistle from Efferding; I could not write you any further while on the road, because we rarely stopped and only long enough to take a rest. The journey was very pleasant; excepting one day, the weather was fine— and this one day caused us no inconvenience, because my carriage (*I* should like to kiss it) is magnificent. In Regensburg, we dined sumptuously at middle day, had a divine table music, angelical entertainment, and a magnificent Mosler wine. In Nürnberg we break- fasted—an ugly town; at Würzburg we fortified our expensive stomachs with coffee—a handsome sump- tuous town. The meals were everywhere very pass- able, only at two-and-a-half posting distances from here, in Aschaffenburg, the herr host deigned to overcharge us most contemptibly. I await with longing your news, about your health, about our circumstances I.I [prima-prima ?—possibly A1]. Now I am firmly resolved to do my business here as well as possible, and then look forward with pleasure to

be back with you. What a magnificent life we shall
lead—I shall work—work so, in order not, through
unforeseen accidents, to get into such an embarrassing
situation again. . . . I should wish for you to send
for * * * through Stadler about all this. His last
offer was, that somebody would lend the money
only on Hoffmeister's signature—1,000 florins down
and the rest in cloth ; with that everything could be
paid and something over, and I should be at liberty
on my return to devote myself exclusively to work.
By a charta bianca from me through a friend the whole
thing could be disposed of.

Adieu, I kiss you a thousand times.

Eternally yours,

Mozart.

LUDWIG V. BEETHOVEN

(1770–1827)

The life of Beethoven, one of the greatest of musical
composers, was rendered unhappy by his passionate
and ungovernable temper, complicated by the deaf-
ness which arose, when twenty-eight years old ; later,
abdominal ailments brought about hypochondria, so
that he was more and more dependent upon his own
internal soul-life up to his death at fifty-seven. The
three letters found amongst his papers were presumably
never sent off to the " Immortal Beloved." Was it
the Countess Brunswick or Countess Guicciardini, or
perhaps one of the aristocratic ladies whose idol he
was in Vienna ? They resemble the movements of
his pathetic symphonies, in the rise and fall of their
passionate yearnings, in the harmonies of their majestic
chords mingled with jarring discords and appeals
for love and sympathy. He never married. He
was one of the great lonely ones, who lived alone
with his gigantic genius.

Ludwig v. Beethoven to the "Immortal Beloved"

July 6th, morning.

My angel my all, my own self—only a few words to-day, and that too with pencil (with yours)—only till to-morrow is my lodging definitely fixed. What abominable waste of time in such things—why this deep grief, where necessity speaks? Can our love persist otherwise than through sacrifices, than by not demanding everything? Canst thou change it, that thou are not entirely mine, I not entirely thine? Ach, Gott, look into beautiful Nature and compose your mind to the inevitable. Love demands everything and is quite right, so it is *for me with you*, for *you with me*—only you forget so easily, that I must live *for you and for me*—were we quite united, you would notice this painful feeling as little as I should. My journey was terrible. I only arrived here yesterday at four o'clock in the morning; as they were short of horses, the post-chaise went by another travel-route, but what a terrible one; at the station, one before last, I was warned about driving by night, was told to fear a wood, but that only tempted me—and I was wrong, the carriage could not avoid breaking down on this terrible road, bottomless, an ordinary country path; without such postilions, as I had, I would have been thrown out there on the road.

Esterhazy had on the other ordinary road to bear the same fate with eight horses, that I had with four. However, I felt somewhat pleased, as always, when I survive something luckily. Now quickly, to the inner from the outer; we shall probably soon meet, even to-day I cannot communicate my remarks to you, which during these days I made about my life—were our hearts close together, I should probably not make any d.g. [*der gleichen*, "of that kind"]. My bosom is full, to tell you much—ach! there are moments when I find that speech is nothing at all. Brighten up—remain my true and only treasure, my all, as

I to you. The rest the gods must send, what must
be for us and shall.

Your faithful
LUDWIG.

Monday evening, July 6th.

You suffer, you, my dearest creature. Just now I
perceive that letters must be posted first thing early.
Mondays—Thursdays—the only days, when the post
goes from here to K. You suffer—ach! where I am,
you are with me, with me and you, I shall arrange that
I may live with you. What a Life! so! without you—
pursued by the kindness of the people here and there,
whom I mean—to desire to earn just as little as they
earn—humility of man towards men—it pains me—
and when I regard myself in connection with the
Universe, what I am, and what he is—whom one calls
the greatest—and yet—there lies herein again the
godlike of man. I weep when I think that you will
probably only receive on Saturday the first news from
me—as you too love—yet I love you stronger—but
never hide yourself from me. Good night—as I am
taking the waters, I must go to bed. Ach Gott—
so near! so far! Is it not a real building of heaven,
our Love—but as firm, too, as the citadel of heaven.

Good morning, on July 7th.

Even in bed my ideas yearn towards you, my Immortal Beloved, here and there joyfully, then again
sadly, awaiting from Fate, whether it will listen to us.
I can only live, either altogether with you or not
at all. Yes, I have determined to wander about for
so long far away, until I can fly into your arms and
call myself quite at home with you, can send my soul
enveloped by yours into the realm of spirits—yes,
I regret, it must be. You will get over it all the more
as you know my faithfulness to you; never another
one can own my heart, never—never! O Gott, why
must one go away from what one loves so, and yet

my life in W. as it is now is a miserable life. Your Love made me the Happiest and Unhappiest at the same time. At my actual age I should need some continuity, sameness of life—can that exist under our circumstances ? Angel, I just hear that the post goes out every day—and must close therefore, so that you get the L. at once. Be calm—love me—to-day—yesterday.

What longing in tears for you—You—my Life—my All—farewell. Oh, go on loving me—never doubt the faithfullest heart

of your beloved L——.

Eternally Yours.
Eternally Mine.
Eternally Ours.

CARL MARIA VON WEBER
(1786–1826)

The founder of German romantic opera, Carl Maria von Weber is best known to us by his opera *Der Freischuetz*. Having married in 1817, after many peregrinations, the opera-singer Karoline Brandt, and constituted a home, he went to London in 1826 to produce his opera *Oberon ;* but the English climate affected his already delicate lungs, and he died in London, after a short three months' stay, in June 1826.

His letters to his wife describe his experiences both in Vienna and London.

Carl Maria von Weber to his Wife Karoline

VIENNA, *September 26th, 1823.*

Now the *Mukkin* [motherkin ?] will be sitting at tea as well and sending her thoughts hither just as I send mine thither. Max will demand " papp papp " and will be naughty from sheer health, and I hope perform *Rupse-crupse* and *Bauz !* [baby-talk ?]. You cannot imagine how much interest I now take

in children, particularly if I can discover a likeness to
Max. And besides, they all like me, because I know
how to get on with them. The whole day yesterday
I was prevented from chatting with you, for I drove
to Schoenbrunn in order to deliver the letter from
Princess Karolina to the Princess of Salerno. There
I saw a little princess, just sixteen months' old as well,
such a speaking likeness to our Princess Karolina, that
I gave a regular start—a dear, dear child, who gave me
her pat-hand at once, and was so friendly and affectionate to me, that everybody was surprised. That
affected me so, that I had trouble to keep my eyes
dry. I was received very kindly, and had to tell them
much news. They had already taken very particular
notice of me at the theatre, and knew when I occupied
a different box from the usual one. This drive to
Schoenbrunn lost me a whole day, as I could not speak
to the Archduchess till later. I therefore at the same
time visited the magnificent pleasure-gardens, which
are truly grand and imposing. You must really take
an opportunity to run over here in a few years' time.

Finally, the evening before last I heard *Semiramis*.
Of the music I can say no more than that it is by
Rossini, but of the performance ! ! ! Of course, when
they sing and act like that, everything *must* tell ! The
Fodor and *Lablache* were unsurpassed. You know,
when a peculiar shiver runs down one's back, then it
is the real thing. A duet in particular, which the two
sang, something after the style (only *slightly* different)
of " Search thy black heart," was quite splendid, and
had to be repeated. I had to promise her to come to
Naples, and to write for her, which I did conditionally,
and yesterday morning she departed with Barbaja.

Surely a letter will come to-day ? Oh, of course, I
know, dear *Mukkin*, that you can have no subject to
write about, for as much as one may have *to tell each
other*, it cannot be written down, therefore I will have
to take patience ; why I should even consider it as
a *good* sign, that nothing extra has happened. Well then
adieu meanwhile, till this evening. Good appetite. . .

LONDON, *Wednesday, April 12th*, 1826,
at night, ¾ to 12 o'clock.

MY TENDERLY BELOVED LINA,—By God's grace and assistance I have this evening *again had such a complete success as perhaps never before*. The brilliance and emotion of such a complete and unalloyed triumph cannot be described. *To God alone be the honour!*

When I entered the orchestra, the whole overflowing house rose, and an incredible ovation awaited me, with shouting of " Vivat " and " Hurrah," waving of hats and fluttering of handkerchiefs, and could with difficulty be repressed again. The overture had to be repeated. Every musical number interrupted twice and three times with the greatest enthusiasm. Brahms's aria *da capo*. The finale they also wanted to have twice, but it could not be done on account of the scenery. In the third Act, Fatima's ballad *da capo*, at the finish they called for me with tumultuous impetuosity, an honour which has never before been accorded to a composer in England, and the whole thing, I must say, went superbly, and all about me were all delighted. Thus much for to-day, my beloved life, from your heartily tired *Muks*, who would, however, not have been able to sleep had he not at once informed you of the fresh dispensation of heaven. Good, good night. If you could only have had an inkling to-day of the fortunate result !

(*The* 13*th*.) Good morning, good heart ! I have slept very sweetly, although I needed a short while before I could get to rest. Was naturally too excited, and this morning I am so truly tired through and through, but well. After such a triumph a certain beneficial composure results, that a great step into the world has once more been surmounted. In any case, I was placed here with *Oberon* on a much more uncertain foundation than in all my earlier works. The jealousy of the theatres, the highly-excitable public, which is always accustomed to opposition, and enjoys it, and the events of the previous day, which had made me uncertain about the outcome of the performance, all that made the success doubly brilliant and appreciated. There was not even the smallest opposition in the inordinate applause. Nothing but pure enthusiasm. But let me tell you, how my star always resumes its ascendancy. After I had sent off to you No. 18 on the 11th, I had at twelve o'clock a rehearsal of the overture and those pieces which had been the least practised, then I dined with the music publisher Hawes, and at seven o'clock there took place the dress rehearsal which I announced to you. A brilliant and elect audience filled the boxes. The first act went off well, with the exception of some details. In Act 2, when after the storm Rezia and Huon should enter, nobody appears. The stage stands empty for a while; finally enters Fawcett and announces that a piece of scenery has fallen on Miss Paton's head, that he would request any doctor who happens to be present to come upon the stage, but that Miss Paton hopes, after a short recuperation, to be able to continue the performance. But she did not recuperate. After waiting a long time, we had to continue the rehearsal without her, leaving out her principal aria. Thus so far the rehearsal ended fairly luckily, and the applause and the hope of a furore the next day were universal. Another rehearsal was called for Miss Paton for twelve o'clock yesterday; but she did not turn up, and sent word she must reserve herself for the evening. So we rehearsed some minor parts. I dined at home at four o'clock with Smart, and drove at six in a somewhat anxious mood to the theatre. But—everything went excellently!

The Paton sang magnificently, and the performance was conducted with great enthusiasm and good will, such as you well know, my music has the good fortune to inspire in people. How many times did I not think during all this of you; *lieber Gott*, you would, at the very least, have been prostrated with anxiety!

But is not that peculiar about my star! But I rely on him from experience, and know that he will not leave me in the lurch now. I should like to describe to you in detail many other things, but I cannot do so and must leave that over till we meet face to face in Holsterwitz. The splendour and perfection of the settings surpasses all description, and I do not suppose I shall ever see anything like it again. They say that the opera cost about 7,000 pounds sterling, somewhere near 49,000 Thalers. The performances now take place daily for as long as the singers can hold out. I have undertaken to direct the first twelve performances. Then I am sure to have had enough of it, and I already shudder at the idea that they will want to see the opera in Dresden as well. Fortunately we cannot find the cast, and as to putting it on myself at any other place, ten horses will not drag me to it. Adieu, for now I have to write a good many more letters. What would I not give to be a witness of your joy when you open this letter. That I must wait such a long, long time before I hear anything, almost a month, is very depressing. I embrace you tenderly. Adieu, adieu for to-day.

ROBERT SCHUMANN
(1810–56)

Robert Schumann may be considered, by the side of Mendelssohn, as the foremost representative of the romantic movement in German music of the thirties. The tender, simple feeling displayed in his songs makes him as popular in English homes as in German ones. Broken down by excessive work, he tried to drown himself in 1854, and spent the last two years of his life in an asylum. The charm of his feeling is well rendered in the following letter to his future wife, Clara Wieck, from whose father he encountered great opposition to their marriage.

LEIPZIG, 1834.

MY DEAR AND REVERED CLARA,—There are haters of
beauty, who maintain that swans were really geese
of a larger kind—one might say with equal justification
that distance is only a close-up that has been pushed
apart.   And so indeed it is, for I speak with you daily
(yes, even more softly than I usually do), and yet I
know that you understand me.   In the beginning I
had various plans with regard to our correspondence.
I wanted, for instance, to start a public one with you
in the musical journal; then I wanted to fill my
air-balloon (you know that I own one) with ideas for
letters, and arrange an ascent in a favourable wind with
a suitable destination. . . . I wanted to catch butter-
flies as letter-carriers to you.   I wanted to send my
letters first to Paris, so that you should open them
with great curiosity, and then, more than surprised,
would believe me in Paris.   In short, I had many
witty dreams in my head, from which only to-day the
horn of the postilion has awakened me.   Postilions,
my dear Clara, have, by the way, as magical an effect
on me as the most excellent champagne.   One seems
to have no head, one has such a delightfully light heart,
when one hears them trumpeting so joyously out
into the world.   They are real waltzes of yearning to
me, these trumpet-blasts, which remind us of something that we do not possess.   As I said, the postilion
blew me out of my old dreams into new ones. . . .

And in answer to her letter with the restrictions
her father places upon their intercourse :

September 18th, 1837.

The interview with your father was terrible. . . .
Such frigidness, such disingenuousness, such devious-
ness, such contradictions—he has a new manner of
destruction, he stabs you to the heart with the handle
of the knife. . . .
What now then, my dear Clara ?   I do not know

what to do now—*not in the slightest*. My wits are
going to pieces here, and in such a frame of mind
one can assuredly not come to terms with your father.
What now then, what now then ? Above all, prepare
yourself, and do *not once allow yourself to be sold*. . . I
trust you, oh, *from all my heart*, and that is what
upholds me. . . . But you will have to be very *strong*,
more than you dream of. Did not your father say
those terrible words to me, that nothing can move *him* ?
Fear everything from him ; he will *compel you by force*,
if he fails in stratagem. Be afraid of everything !

I am to-day so dead, so *humiliated*, that I can hardly
conceive a beautiful, good idea. So disheartened as
to give you up I have not yet become ; but so embittered, so hurt in my holiest feelings, so locked in a
frame of the most ordinary commonplace.

If I only had a word from you ! You must tell me
what I am to do. Otherwise my being will turn to
scorn and a byword, and I shall be off and away.

Not even to be allowed to see you ! We could do
so, he said, but in a neutral spot, in the presence of
all, a regular show for everybody. How chilling all
that is—how it rankles ! We might even correspond,
when you are on a journey !—that was all that he
would consent to. . . .

Give me consolation, *lieber Gott*, that he may not
let me perish in despair. I am torn up by the roots
of my life.

RICHARD WAGNER TO MATHILDE WESEN-
DONK (1813-83)

Wagner, dramatist and musician, had married in
1837, as musical director in Koenigsberg, the actress
Minna Planer—an unhappy union, he living separated
from her for many years, until, after her death in 1866,
Wagner married Cosima von Buelow, a daughter of
Liszt. A morbidly sensitive, vain man, self-centred,
he was puffed up with his importance as a musician

WAGNER.

and a genius ; perhaps he was most sincere and natural in his love-affair with Mathilde Wesendonk.

ZURICH, *August*, 1858, *Tuesday morning.*

I am sure you do not expect me to leave your beautiful, splendid letter unanswered. Or should I be obliged to renounce the beautiful right of reply to the noblest word ? But how could I answer you, except as worthy of you ? . . .

The enormous conflicts which we have endured, how could they end but with the victory over every wish and desire ? Did we not know in the most ardent moments of approachment that this was our goal ?

Certainly ! Only because it was so unheard-of and difficult it was only to be reached after the hardest fights. But have we not now fought to a finish all battles ? or what others could still be awaiting us ? . . . Truly, I feel it deeply, they are at an end ! . . .

When I proclaimed my decision a month ago, to break off the personal intercourse with you and yours I had—given you up. But in that I was not quite sincere. I only felt that only a complete union of our love could safeguard us from the terrible contacts which we had seen them exposed to latterly. Thus there stood out against the feeling for the necessity of our separation, the contemplated—even though not desired—possibility of a reunion. But herein there lay a spasmodic tension, which we both of us could not support. I came to you, and clearly and definitely it stood before us, that such other possibility implied a sin, which was not even to be thought of.

. . . Never have I felt before so deeply and terribly, as in the recent months that have passed. All earlier impressions were without substance compared to these last. Commotions such as I suffered in that catastrophe would necessarily dig their traces deeply, and could there be anything to heighten the grave seriousness of my sentiment, it was the condition of my wife. During two months I anticipated every day the possibility of news of her sudden death ; for this possibility the doctor had been obliged to warn me. Everything around me, breathed the air of death ; all my glances forward and backward fell on representations of death, and life—as such—lost its last charm for me. Impelled to the utmost consideration of the unfortunate woman, I was obliged nevertheless to decide to destroy our newly founded recent hearth and home, and, finally inform her of it, to her greatest dismay. . .

With what feelings, do you think, I surveyed in this beautiful summertime this delightful asylum, which answers so entirely to my wishes and endeavours of yore, as I wandered in the mornings through the dear little garden, and gazed on the flowering blooms, surprised the grass-gnat, which was building its nest in the little rose-tree ? Ask yourself who, you who know my mind so intimately as no one else, what this tearing asunder from the last anchor meant to me !

Did I once fly from the world, can you imagine I could now return to it ? Now that everything in me has become tender and susceptible to the utmost through the continually increasing detachment from all contact with her ? Even my last meeting with the Grand Duke of Weimar showed me more clearly than ever that I can only thrive in the most clearly defined independence, so that I must repudiate every possibility of any contractual responsibility from my innermost being, even towards this really not unamiable prince. I cannot—cannot turn towards the world again ; to make a home permanently in a great city is unthinkable for me ; and—shall I again think of founding a new asylum, a new hearth, after having had to destroy behind me this one, scarcely enjoyed, which friendship and noblest love had founded for me in this delightful paradise ? Oh no—to go away from here is the same thing for me as to—perish ! Now, with these wounds in my heart, I cannot try to found another home !

My child, I can think of only one salvation, and this can only issue from the inmost depth of the heart,

but not from any exterior arrangement, that is:
Rest! rest from longing! quiescence of every desire!
noble, dignified restraint! to live for others—as a
consolation for ourselves! . . .

You know now the whole serious, decisive sentiment
of my soul; it has reference to my entire philosophy
of life, to the future, to everything which is near to
me—and thus also to you, who are dearest to me. Let
me now—in the ruins of this world of longing—make
you happy!

Look, never in my life, under any circumstances,
did I ever push myself forward, but have always been
of an almost excessive sensitiveness. Now for the
first time I am going to appear forward to you and
beg you to allow your mind to dwell on me in absolute
peace. I shall often visit you, for you shall only see
me in future, when I am sure to show you a bright
and tranquil face. Once on a time I used to seek your
house in suffering and longing; thither, from whence
I sought for consolation, I brought unrest and suffering.
That shall be so no longer. When, therefore, you
do not see me for a long time, then, pray for me—
secretly! for then you will know that I suffer! But
when I do come, then be sure that I bring you a pleasant gift of myself into your house, a gift which perhaps
it is only given to me to confer, to me who suffered
so much and so gladly. . . .

Perchance, yes—certainly, shortly, I surmise, at
the beginning of the winter already, the time will
come, when I must leave Zurich entirely for a lengthy
period; the amnesty I am soon to expect will reopen
Germany to me anew, whither I periodically return,
in order to satisfy my desire for the only thing which
I could not arrange for here. Then I shall often not
see you for a long time. But then to return again
to the asylum which has become so familiar, in order
to rest from worry and unavoidable annoyance, to
breathe pure air and to gain new zest to the old labour,
for which nature it seems has selected me—that will
always be, if you will allow it, the soft perspective of

light, which upholds me there, the sweet consolation that beckons to me here. . . .

My child, the last months have turned the hair at my temples visibly grey ; there is a voice in me which calls me with longing to rest—to that rest which I made my " Flying Dutchman " long for, years ago. It was the longing for the " home "—not for a sensuous love-enjoyment. A loyal, splendid woman was the only one who could have conferred this home on him. Let us sanctify this beautiful death, which comprises and calms all our longing and desires. Let us fade away in blessedness, with composed and resigned look, and the holy smile of beautiful self-denial ! and—none shall then *lose*, when we—*conquer* !

Farewell, my dear, holy angel !

[In English] " It must be so ! " R. W.

LUDWIG I OF BAVARIA AND LOLA MONTEZ
(1786–1868)

LUDWIG I of Bavaria, in his love for the arts, lost his throne in the revolutionary year of '48, through his infatuation for the Spanish dancer and adventuress Lola Montez, who was really of Scotch origin, and whose conflicts with the German and Russian police and the numerous duels fought on her account gave her so much notoriety that she practically had been expelled everywhere, until in 1846 she was able to attract the King of Bavaria by her dancing. But her unruly behaviour and the aggressive demeanour by which she sought to interfere in the governing of the country brought about her banishment and, eventually, Ludwig's deposition. She died in destitution in New York in 1853, after having had three more husbands.

Ludwig of Bavaria to Lola Montez

Oh, my Lolita! a ray of sunshine at the break of day! As a stream of light in an obscure night. Hope causes chords long forgotten to resound, and life became once again as brilliant as of yore. Such. were the feelings which I felt during this night of happiness, when, owing to you alone, everything was joy. Thy spirit lifted up mine out of its sadness; never did an intoxication equal mine.

Thou hast lost thy gaiety, persecution has stripped you of it; it has deprived you of your health; the happiness of your life is already disturbed.   But more and more solidly are you attached to me ; one will never be able to separate me from you ; you have suffered because you love me.

HEINRICH HEINE

(1797–1856)

Heine's outstanding contributions to literature are his love-lyrics, in which only Goethe had equalled him.   In Germany he was unpopular on account of his French sympathies, yet wherever Germans are gathered together, they sing the ballad of the " Loreley."   His *Buch der Lieder* contains the majority of his finest lyrics, which have been set to music many times.   They are mainly inspired by his unhappy love for his cousin Amalie Heine and later her sister Thérèse.   Married in Paris in 1841 to his mistress, a pretty, but superficial and uneducated spendthrift Frenchwoman, Eugénie Mirat, he found himself, through the death of his uncle Salomon Heine, in continual financial difficulties which brought on a paralytic stroke in 1845, chaining him from 1848 to his death in 1856 to a " mattress grave," though it left the vigour of his mind unimpaired, as witness his " Romancero " poems in 1851.   The last months of his life were cheered by Camille Selden, the lady whom he called Mouche, or his " beautiful angel of death."   The bulk of his works show a strange vacillation between pathos and coarseness, attributable, no doubt, to the weakness of his character, owing to some extent to his continual decrepitude and consequent financial trouble.   Heine writes to his wife in Paris from Hamburg, whither he had gone to see his uncle Salomon Heine, and to confer with his publisher, Campe.   " Nonotte" was the pet name Heine gave his wife.

HAMBURG, *November 2nd,* 1843.

MOST BEAUTIFUL TREASURE! BELOVED NONOTTE!—
I hope that you are well; I am well. Only my dis-
gusting head suffers somewhat of that nervous ailment
which you know of. Yesterday I dined at my uncle's,
who was very much upset; the poor man undergoes
terrible sufferings. But I succeeded in making him
laugh. To-day I dine at my sister's with the young
married couple and my old mother. The weather
is fine and mild, so that I only wear my little over-
coat. . . .

I think only of you, my dear Nonotte. It is a serious
decision, to have left you alone in Paris, in that terrible
abyss! Do not forget that my eye is always upon you;
I know everything that you do, and what I do not
know now, I shall find out later.

I hope that you have not omitted to take lessons
from a pupil of Favarget, and that you are well
employing your actual leisure.

I am convinced that you have at this moment not
a "sou" left in your purse. Next week I shall send
you the necessary receipt, so that you can collect in
my name my monthly pension from Fould, and I shall
let you know at the same time how I propose to dispose
of this sum.

I have received no letter from you; if you have not
yet written, I beg of you not to delay writing any
longer, to "Herrn H.H. Adr. Hoffman and Campe,
Booksellers in Hamburg."

HAMBURG, *November 5th,* 1843.

DEAREST NONOTTE,—I have not had any news from
you yet, and I am already beginning to become very
anxious about it. I beg of you urgently, to write to
me as soon as possible, under the address of Herren
Hoffman and Campe, in Hamburg, which I have
already given you. I shall probably remain here
another fourteen days, and when I leave, shall take
precautionary steps, in order that your letters may be

sent back to Paris, in case they should arrive too late. I am being spoilt by everybody here. My mother is happy, my sisters are beside themselves with delight, and my uncle finds in me all imaginable good qualities. And I really am very amiable. What a hard task! I have to please the most uninteresting people! On my return I shall be as sour-faced as possible, in order to recuperate from the efforts of my amiability.

I think continually of you, and cannot quiet down. Undefined and dull cares torture me day and night. You are the only joy of my life—do not make me unhappy!

All my relatives reproach me for not having brought you with me to Hamburg. I have, however, done well, to study the ground a little before coming in your company. Probably we shall spend the spring and summer here. I hope that you will be sufficiently rewarded for your actual ennui. I shall do all I can to make up to you for it. Adieu, my angel, my dearest, my poor child, my good wife!

Do not forget to convey a thousand amiabilities from me to Madame Darte. I hope that you are on the best terms with the good Aurecia [proprietress of the *pension*].

I implore you to visit no people with whom I am on bad terms and who would betray you any day, when you had quarrelled with them. To-morrow or the day after I shall send you the necessary papers, for you to collect my pension.

My God! my God! since fourteen days I have not heard your chirping. And I am so far from you! It is a real exile. I kiss you on the little dimple of your right cheek.

HENRI HEINE.

Heinrich Heine to Camille Selden

In the Summer of 1855.

DEAREST, FINEST MOUCHE,—Or shall I take no notice of your seal-ring, and name you after the perfume of your letter? In that case I should have to call you "most graceful of musk-cats."

I have received your letter yesterday—the *pattes de mouche* are persistently hopping about in my head, perhaps even in my heart. My liveliest thanks for all the sympathy that you show me. The translation of the poems is very beautiful, and I repeat what I have told you before your departure. And I also am delighted to see you again soon, and to be able to *poser une empreinte vivante* [a favourite expression of the lady's.—ED.; "to place a living imprint"] upon the dear *Schwaben-gesicht* ["Suabian face," for the lady came from that part of Germany]. Ach! this sentence would gain a less platonic meaning if I were still a man! But I am no longer anything but a spirit; that may suit *you* perhaps very well, but I am satisfied with it only so-so.

The French edition of my poems is just appearing and creates sensation. But it may yet take another two or three months before the so far unpublished poems, z. B.[1] the "New Spring," will appear in one of the last volumes of the French edition. You see, you have not missed much.

Yes, I am looking forward with pleasure to seeing you again, charming Mouche of my soul! the most graceful of the musk-cats and yet at the same time as charming as an Angora cat, just that kind that I like.

Formerly I loved for a long time the tiger-cats, but that kind is too dangerous, and the *empreintes vivantes*, which they sometimes left on my face were very unpleasant.

My condition is still very bad; continual unpleasantness, attacks of rage—rage at my desperate condition. I am a dead man, who thirsts for the most burning enjoyments that life affords! It is awful.

Good-bye! may the waters bring you strength and health. Sincere greetings from your friend,

HEINRICH HEINE.

---

[1] z. B. ᜸ *zum Beispiel*, for instance.

And then follow some few short scraps of notes, just before his death.

DEAREST FRIEND,—I am still very ill, and cannot see you to-day, but hope you will come to-morrow, Tuesday. Write me a word, whether you could not come before Wednesday.

Your poor friend,

NEBUCHADNEZZAR II,

for I am as mad as the King of Babylon and only eat chopped-up herbs, which nourishment my cook calls spinach.

DEAREST, MOST GRACEFUL OF CATS,—I do not wish to see you to-morrow, Wednesday, for the reason that I feel a migraine coming on ; but if you could spend a few moments with me on Friday afternoon, that would compensate me, in that I have not been able to see you for so long. From Friday on every day will suit me, and the oftener you come, the more joy for me.

My good, charming, delightful Mouche, come and buzz round my nose with your little wings ! I know a song of Mendelssohn's with the refrain " Come soon ! " This melody is singing continuously in my head—" Come soon." I kiss both the dear little paws, not once, but one after the other, farewell

HEINRICH HEINE.

FERDINAND LASSALLE

(1825–64)

Ferdinand Lassalle, the son of a rich Jewish merchant Lassal, the most brilliant and picturesque of German Socialists, was foremost amongst the founders, jointly with Karl Marx, of the Social Democratic party in Germany. He was much more than an agitator. He was a scholar, a man of fashion, and a gallant. As such he had successfully vindicated the Countess

Sophie Hatzfeldt's honour, whose action for divorce
against her husband he carried through successfully,
though accused of the theft of important documents
to win his case.   In 1864 he fell in love, in Switzerland,
with Helene von Doenniges, the beautiful but flighty
daughter of a Bavarian diplomat, and was killed in a
duel by her fiancé, after Helene had been forced by
her parents to repudiate Lassalle.

The Reproachful Love-letter

Here is a type of love-letter which is fortunately
rare—namely, that of broken love-pledges, of wild
recriminations, of aching hearts and tragic issues.
Reproaches are pitifully ineffectual things against
human fickleness.   Spoken they are forgotten, written
they remain, in danger of being read in the divorce
courts.   So our modern lovers are wise in not writing
them, perhaps for the reason that they do not love
so fiercely nor so engrossingly as their forbears in the
spacious times before the haste and change of railways,
telegrams, and flying machines, frittered away the
constancy of true affection.   To swear eternal fidelity
is a rare thing in our days of kinema passions of the
switchback order.   The egotisms of material comforts
have blunted the rhapsodies of *la grande passion*.
Our young ladies like to read about them in novels,
but do not write them.   Are they too proud to re-
criminate ? or are they merely indifferent ?

Helene von Doenniges to Ferdinand Lassalle

GENEVA, *Wednesday, August 3rd*, 1864.

MY DEAR HEART, MY BEAUTIFUL, SPLENDID EAGLE,—
Not yet an hour in our parental house, I can already
tell you news—but only sad news.   I arrived here
and found my little sister Margarete the affianced
bride of Count Kayserlingk—the happiness and the
high joy thereat of my people cannot be described.
Ach, Ferdinand, it hurts me to think how differently
my happiness will affect them.   But it is all the same

to me; *in Joy and in Sadness your true wife, only devoted to you.*

I made use of this moment of joy to announce to Mama your visit, but—well, the poor, poor little woman could only think of my beautiful Ferdinand as a scapegrace. When I met with such definite opposition founded really on such stupid reasons, which are too petty to touch you in the slightest, I felt myself impelled to resort to heroic measures; so I said to her, " Listen, Mama, I want to speak with you very seriously. I am saying to-day for the first time— *I will.* And as true as I stand here before you, I tell you, I shall carry out my will." Here I related to her shortly our meeting again, and continued, " I am exceedingly sorry to have to grieve you so—for I see that you are beside yourself; but I cannot act otherwise. If you are reasonable and consent—well, you will get to know him and to love him, and everything will terminate quietly and smoothly; if not, well then, I shall be very sorry too, and God knows what suffering this causes me; but I must protect myself by law, in order to obtain my rights and my happiness."

I terminated my speech, during which she had listened to me with childlike kindness, and had not interrupted me once, although the tears moistened her eyes; I terminated, I say, with a few more kisses and assurances of affection, and said to her once more, " *Only in him is my Happiness, and that is my Fate.*"

She wept silently and left my room, and I, the child, became your real Brünnhilde; I did not cry, I did not even tremble, I looked at your picture and beseeched you in a low voice, " Come, my high, my proud, my imperial eagle, give me power and strength with your splendid eagle's glance." Thus I beseeched, and my belief in you has helped me. I thank you, my strong Siegfried !

After a little while my poor mother came back and said she must inform Papa of the whole matter, otherwise there would be a terrible scandal. Thereupon I said that was the only thing I demanded for my confidence, and you did not desire that Papa should come to know you with his mind set either *for* or *against*— in short, you wanted to enter the house unbiassed and to be judged similarly; but there she remained inflexible and said, " Papa will now and never accept him. I must go to him and tell him how matters lie." Then I asked her, " What objection has he to Lassalle ? What can he say against him ? *car enfin*, his political position is not sufficient reason not to receive him when he calls." Mama : " Not his political, but his *social* position—the story of the cash-box [his connection with the Countess Hatzfeldt] and many other things besides." I only replied to that, that I asked them for nothing else but to receive you and to make your acquaintance; upon which she said to me, " You cannot demand of Papa, particularly at the same time, *when one daughter is engaged to the Count Kayserlingk,* to receive a man into the family *about whom all the world says such things.*" I : " You are not taking him into the family; you only give your consent for me to leave the family. If you desire it, well then, I will, as much as it hurts me, and God be my judge, that my heart is almost breaking, I will give you my promise, never again to cross your threshold ! "

Now it is 6½ o'clock, and *thou, my Master and my God, art already here.* Oh! this thought gives me back my strength and power—for I must feel the neighbourhood and omnipotence of my *Master and Ruler*, in order not to yield, not to be towards others as to you—*the Child.* But I feel you and your love —and so I fear nothing else and am now and for ever *your wife, your child, your thing which adores you !* Oh, if only the Countess were here ! . . . Tell me on a scrap of paper, that you love me ! for I, Ferdinand, *I love you so much !*

It has happened—they have spoken—my father has declared I am his daughter no longer ! and what will happen now—God knows; he insists I shall not leave his house until I am your wife !

I can . . .

Lassalle to Helene von Doenniges

MUNICH, *August 20th.*

Helene! I write to you, death in my heart. Ruestow's telegram has given me a deadly stroke. You, you betray me!—it is impossible. Yet, yet I cannot believe in so much felony, such horrible betrayal. They have bent your will perhaps for the moment, they have estranged you from yourself; but it is not credible that this can be your true, your permanent will. You cannot have cast from you all shame, all love, all fidelity, all truth to this utmost degree! You would have made yourself discreditable and have dishonoured everything that bears a human face— every better feeling would be a lie; and if you have lied, if you are capable of having reached this lowest degree of depravity, to break such holy oaths and to destroy the truest heart—beneath the sun there would be nothing left in which a human being could believe!

You have imbued me with the determination to struggle for your possession. You have requested me to exhaust first of all every conventional method, instead of eloping with you from Wabern; you have sworn the holiest of oaths to me both verbally and in writing; you have declared, even in your last letter, that you are nothing, nothing but my loving, wife, and no power on earth shall prevent you from carrying out this undertaking; and after you have irresistibly drawn to you this faithful heart, which, once it has surrendered, has surrendered for always, you thrust me, with the battle hardly begun, after a fortnight, with scornful laughter down into the abyss, you betray me and destroy me? Yes, you would have achieved that which fate has attempted in vain, to break, to destroy the hardest man, who has withstood all outward storms without flinching. . . .

Helene! my fate lies in your hands! But if you break me through this villainous betrayal, which I cannot endure, may my lot recoil on you and my curse pursue you to the grave! it is the curse of the truest

(1)

(2)

(3)

(1) NAPOLEON_ III.   (2) MAUPASSANT.   (3) GEORGE SAND.

heart, treacherously broken by you, a heart with which you have trifled most disgracefully. It will strike home. . . . Once more I will and must speak to you personally and alone. I will and must hear my death-sentence from your own lips. Only thus shall I believe that which appears otherwise impossible. I am now taking further steps, to gain you from here, and shall then come to Geneva !

May my fate be on your head, Helene !

F. LASSALLE.

LOUIS NAPOLEON (NAPOLEON III)
(1808–73)

The son of Louis Bonaparte, brother of Napoleon I, and of Hortense Beauharnais, daughter of Joséphine, had become the head and hope of the Napoleonic party at the death of the Duc de Reichstadt in 1832. From the fortress of Ham, where he was imprisoned after making his second premature attempt to regain the French throne, he writes the following love-letters in 1845, shortly before his escape.

Louis Napoleon to a Frenchwoman living in Italy

HAM, *November 2nd,* 1845.

Madame, it is eight days since I had the pleasure of being with you. Your apparition has been for me like a happy dream, but only like a dream ; for your visit was so short, that I had hardly the time to recover in your presence from the emotion which it had produced in me ; and when I had recovered my equanimity sufficiently to enjoy it, you were already gone.

LONDON, *March 24th,* 1845.

. . . Do not believe, madam, that I have ever failed to appreciate you ; to think that would be to wrong me ; for it would imply that you thought that I know neither how to love nor to appreciate that which

is beautiful, devoted and noble. No, I have never
failed to appreciate you ; but when I wrote to you
for the last time, I had taken a decision born of despair
and which would have caused me despair to-day if it
had been carried out. . . .

NAPOLEON LOUIS B.

GIUSEPPE GARIBALDI
(1807–82)

Italian patriot and guerrilla leader, he early became
implicated in Mazzini's movement for Italian liberty
and had in consequence to flee the country. After
serving revolt in South America, he led volunteers
in Italy in 1848, and, dreaming of a united Italy,
undertook various expeditions in 1860, finally unsuc-
cessful. His mistress, Anita, a Brazilian, was separated
from him in the war of '48, and died in 1849.

A soldier, an adventurer, a man of deeds, not words,
he writes the following letter to her, during his
campaign.

Garibaldi to Anita Riveiro di Sylva

SUBIACO, *April 19th,* 1849.

DEAREST ANITA,—I write to inform you that I am
all right and am marching with Colonna upon Anagni,
which I shall probably reach to-morrow; how long I
shall stay there, I cannot tell you as yet. In Anagni
I shall receive the rifles and the rest of the outfit
for the troops. My mind will not be at rest until
I receive a letter from you, confirming that you have
arrived safely in Nice. Write to me immediately, I
must have news from you, my dearest Anita; let
me know your impressions of the events in Genoa and
Toscana. You stalwart and heroic woman! How
contemptuously you must look down upon this effemi-
nate race of Italians, upon these, my countrymen, whom
I have so often tried to imbue with greatness of soul,
and who do not deserve it! It is true that treachery

has lamed every courageous uprising. But however that may be, we are dishonoured ; the Italian name has become scorn and derision in the world. I am indignant that I belong to a family with so many cowards ; but do not think that this has caused me to lose courage and to despair of the future of my country ; on the contrary, I have more hope than ever. Unpunished, one can dishonour an individual, but one cannot dishonour unpunished a nation. The traitors are now known. Italy's heart still beats, and though it may not be quite whole, yet it can throw off the elements of disease, which are the cause of its malady.

The Reaction has succeeded in intimidating the people by treachery and villainy, but the people will never forget the treachery and the villainy of the Reaction ! As soon as it has recovered from its fright, it will uprise with terrible vehemence, and then destroy the coward who caused its abasement. Write to me, I beg of you once again, I must have news from you, from my mother and the children. You need not have an anxiety about me, I am in better health than ever and consider myself and my twelve hundred armed followers insuperable. Rome affords now an imposing picture. All the brave men are in its vicinity, and God will assist us ! Farewell.

Your

GIUSEPPE.

COUNT HELMUTH VON MOLTKE TO HIS BRIDE

(1800–91)

Helmuth von Moltke, born in Mecklenburg in Germany, left the Danish to enter the Prussian army in 1822. All his intellectual life was led retired away from the world, whose publicity he hated. Although nicknamed " the Great Silent One," in his letters to his wife (the stepdaughter of his sister) Marie von Burt, he becomes garrulous, instructing the young bride of sixteen of her duties in her future surroundings.

BERLIN, *Sunday evening, February 13th, 1842.*

MY MARIECHEN,—Your dear letter of the 10th arrived yesterday and pleased me very much, for you seem bright and happy and have probably ample to do with your furnishing. There are still ten weeks from now, then you will be my own, dear little wife. Last night I visited one of my comrades, the squadron commander Oelrichs, of the General Staff, who has also recently got married. He is not younger than I, and his wife is only two years older than you, and also very pretty. These people are sure to please you very much. They send their compliments, although not known to you, and offer advice and assistance, when you need it. I yearn for the coming of the time when we too shall be able to live side by side so sociably. May God give His blessing to it. Let us only be always honest with each other and never sulk. Rather let us quarrel, or better still, let us be quite agreed. . . . I suppose you have noticed that I am sometimes uneven of temper; then let me have my head, I shall always return to you. But I will see to it that I get better. . . . From you I wish for friendly and even, if possible, bright temper [sic], give way in little things, have order in the housekeeping, neatness in attire, and above all, that you love me. Of course you enter quite young into a totally new circle of surroundings, but your quick intelligence and above all the excellence of your mind will soon teach you the right measure in intercourse with other people. Take this from me, my good Marie, that friendliness towards everyone is the first rule of life, which can save us many a grievance, and that even towards those who do not please you you can be amiable without being insincere and untrue. True politeness and the most refined society manners are the inborn friendliness of a kindly heart. In me a bad bringing-up and a youth full of privations had often stifled this feeling, often too has repressed the expression of it, and thus I am left with that acquired cold and supercilious politeness which rarely draws people to you. You, however, are young and pretty, and, as God wills it, shall not know any privations, everyone meets you in friendliness ; then do not omit to respond to people with the same friendliness and to gain them for you. . . . Of course this will necessitate conversation on your part. It is not material for you to say witty things, but if possible something amiable, and if not, to make people feel anyhow, that you would like to say something amiable. . . .Affectation and untruth-fulness is foreign to you, it makes an immediate, tire-some impression, for nothing but truth can awaken sympathy. Real discretion and lack of presumption are the true protection against the slights and set-backs of the great world ; yes, I should like to assert that with these qualities a foolish and constrained de-meanour are incompatible. If we do not wish to appear other than we are, do not desire to usurp a higher position than our due, neither rank nor birth nor crowds and glitter can greatly disturb our equa-nimity. But he who does not draw from himself a feeling of his dignity, but must look for it in the opinion of others, is continually reading in the eyes of other people, like a man who wears a wig and looks in every mirror to see that it has not gone awry. Let me admit, my good Marie, that I abstract these fine lessons from my own self. My entire bearing is only one of embarrassment, veneered over with assurance and usage *du monde*. The oppression of many years, in which I was brought up, has injured my character incurably, has depressed my feeling and broken my good and noble pride. Only late I have begun to rebuild again from my inmost self what was torn down. May you help me in future to better my-self. . . . But you I would like to see nobler and better, and that means the same as happier and more contented, than I can be. Be therefore modest and unassuming, and you will be quiet and uncon-strained.

With pleasure I shall look forward to many people

paying you their addresses ; nor have I any objection to your flirting a little. The more you are amiable towards everybody, the less people will be able to say that you have preferences for individuals. That you must guard against, for men seek to please, primarily, in order to please, and then in order to be able to boast about it, and you will find in society far more wit than kindness. It cannot possibly fail for me very often to cut an inferior figure in comparison with other men, whom you will see here. At every ball you will find some who dance better, make a more elegant toilet, at every party those who have a livelier speech and are of better temper than I. But even when you find it so, that does not prevent your preferring me to all of them in so far as you only realise that I feel for you far more deeply than any of these. Only in case there is something that you cannot tell me you must thereby take warning from yourself and through yourself. And now give me a kiss and I will stop lecturing you. I am pleased to hear that Ernestinchin is recovered, and that little Henry is getting on. Hearty greetings to Papa and Mama !

One thing more, dear Marie, when you write, do re-read the letter, which you are answering, once more. There are not only the questions that have to be answered, but it is well to touch on all the subjects which are contained in it. Otherwise the exchange of letters will continue to dwindle, the mutual relations will disappear, and one ends eventually by only wanting to communicate matters of moment. Now life altogether consists in only little and rarely important things. The small events of the day, on the other hand, are linked into hours, weeks and months, and end by making up the sum of life with its good and bad luck. Therefore a conversation by word of mouth is much better than a written one, because one tells each other the unimportant things and finds a little worth while writing about.

Now it is midnight, you are no doubt asleep, if not

chatting with Jeannette, to whom I send heartiest greetings. Good night, dear, sweet soul,

Cordially yours,

HELMUTH.

PRINCE BISMARCK TO HIS BRIDE, JOHANNA VON PUTTKAMER

(1815–98)

Otto von Bismarck, the Iron Chancellor, who had inherited from his Pomeranian Junker ancestors that magnificent constitution and colossal stature, which enabled him to fight twenty-seven duels as a student and consume untold quantities of food, tobacco, beer and other liquids, right up to his old age, was in his private life, a man of warm affections, a staunch friend, and a bitter enemy. Though imperious in character, and sometimes unscrupulous and vindictive, he was cast in a large mould, while both he and his future wife held strong religious tenets. He married in 1847 Johanna von Puttkamer, who throughout his long life was a devoted wife, to whom he described in his lengthy correspondence many of the moving and picturesque incidents of his career both in the early days of the Berlin Revolution of '48 and later, when, as Chancellor of the North German Conferation, he was present at the capitulation of Sedan and the fall of Napoleon III. A man of massive and somewhat ruthless intellect, his letters are lightened up by much humour of the Prussian sort, and an unwavering affection for his Johanna, who remained content all her life to defer to the wishes and look after the health of the great statesman, much undermined by his grosser appetites.

When corresponding with his bride (to whom he did not pay his open addresses until he had reassured her father as to the soundness of his evangelical faith) he was captain and warden of dykes (Deich-Hauptmann) on the Lower Elbe, his care being to supervise the clearing away of the yearly winter ice, and preventing perilous inundations by maintenance of the dykes.

The following letter is an interesting picture of the life and daily duties of a Prussian Junker.

SCHOENHAUSEN, *February 1st*, 1847.

I had only waited for the light, in order to write to you, my *mein theures Herz* [my dearest heart], and with the light there came also your little green spirit-lamp, to bring my lukewarm water to the boil, but found it this time almost ready to boil over. Your pity for my restless nights is premature as yet; but still I will place it to your credit. The Elbe lies as yet muddy and creaking in her bonds of ice; the call of the spring to burst them is not yet loud enough. I say to the weather, " Ach! that you were either cold or warm, but you stand continuously at 0, and so the matter may be drawn out; my business consists at the present in sending out from my warm place at the writing-table all sorts of formulated incantations into the world, through whose spell masses of faggots, boards, push-carts, and manure [sic] from the interior of the country move towards the Elbe, in order to withstand, as prosaic dam, the poetic foaming of the flood. After having spent the afternoon with these more useful than agreeable correspondences, my resolve was to chat through the evening with you comfortably, " beloved one " [sic, in English.—ED.], as if we were seated arm in arm on the sofa of the red drawing-room, and in sympathetic deference the post has held over for me your letter just for this hour of chat, which I should by rights have received yesterday. . . .

In Stettin I found drinking, card-playing friends. Wilhelm Ramin said, after a casual remark about reading the Bible, " Well, in Reinfeld [Johanna's home.—ED.] I would have said the same thing in your place; but that you think you can get your oldest acquaintance to take that in, is a scream." My sister I found well, and full of joy about you and me; she has, I believe, written to you before she had received your letter. Arnim is full of foreboding that I

might become " pious "; his look rested serious
and thoughtful, with pitying solicitude, the whole
time upon me, as if on a dear friend whom one would
like to save, and yet almost thinks lost; seldom, I
have seen him so gentle. Surely there are curious
ways of looking at things among very clever people.
In the evening in the Hotel de Rome (I hope you were
not writing as late as that) I drunk your health with
half-a-dozen Silesian Grafen, Schaffgotch, etc., in
the foaming juice of the grape of Sillery; and on
Friday morning convinced myself that the Elbe-ice
still bore my horse, and that, with regard to the high-
water I might be even to-day at your blue or black
side [the blue or green side, the left side.—Ed.]
had not other daily service-duties laid claim to me
likewise. To-day the whole day snow fell very
busily, and the country is white again, without frost.
When I arrived, this side of Brandenburg everything
was free of snow, the air warm and the people plough-
ing; it was as if I had travelled from winter into the
beginning of spring, and yet in me the short spring
had become winter; the nearer I came to Schoenhausen, the heavier weighed upon me the thought of
heavens knows how long I was stepping into the old
solitude. The pictures of a turbulent past arose in
front of me, as if they tried to push you away from me.
I was almost in the mood for tears as I used to be
when, after the holidays, I caught sight of the towers
of Berlin from the post-coach. The comparison of
my condition with that in which on the 10th I travelled
on the same road in the opposite direction, the conviction that my solitude, to tell the real truth, was a
voluntary one, which I could make an end to by a
resolve somewhat contrary to my duty, it is true, and
a forty hours' journey, brought me again to recognise
that my heart is an ungrateful one, discouraged and
stubborn, for soon I said to myself, " with the satisfaction of the bridegroom," that I am no longer lonely
here and was happy in the consciousness of being
loved by you, *mein Engel*, and on the other hand to

17

be yours, not only in body but to the innermost of my heart. When driving into the village I felt, never perhaps so clearly, how beautiful it is to have a homeland and a homeland with which one is intertwined by birth, memory, and love! The sun shone bright on the substantial farms and their prosperous inhabitants with the long coats, and the women in bright colours with the short ones greeted me much friendlier even than usual; on every face there seemed to be an aspect of congratulations which in me developed always and every time in a thanks to you.

B.'s inspector in Schoenhausen, Bellins, fat greyhead, smiled round about, and, honest old soul, the tears ran down as he patted me on the shoulder in a fatherly way and expressed his satisfaction; his wife naturally wept copiously; even Odin was more boisterous than usual, and his paw upon my coat-collar proved undeniably that the weather was thawing. Half an hour later Miss Breeze galloped with me to the Elbe, clearly proud to carry your fiancé, for never before did she spurn the ground so contemptuously with her hoofs. Fortunately you cannot judge, *mein Herz*, with what a hopeless apathy I used to enter my house after a journey, what a depression took possession of me, when the door of my room yawned at me, and the dumb furnishments in the noiseless room stood in front of me, as tired as I was. Never was the emptiness of my existence as evident as in such moments, until eventually I picked up a book, of which none seemed to me but dull enough, or attended mechanically to any daily task. By preference I used to come home of nights, in order to go to bed at once. Compare the enclosed, in which I often found my innermost expression. [Refers to Bismarck's note, at end of letter.] "Now never any more" [the last sentence in English.—ED.]. Ach! Gott, and now? How I regard everything with other eyes; not only what concerns you and because it concerns you as well (although for two days I am torturing myself as to where your writing-table shall stand), but my entire outlook on life is a new one, and even dyke and police duties I attend to with good temper and interest. This change, this new life, next to God, I have to thank you for, *ma très chère, mon adorée Jeanneton*, who do not cook in me occasionally as a spirit flame, but influence my heart as a heating fire. . . .

Leb Wohl, my treasure, my heart, comfort of my eyes, thy faithful

BISMARCK.

And in the enclosed are verses from English poems, of which the following are extracts :

" And dost thou ask what secret woe
I bear corroding joy and youth ?
And wilt thou vainly seek to know
A pang even thou must fail to soothe ?

" It is not love, it is not hate
Nor low-ambition's honours lost
That bids me loathe my present state
And fly all I prized the most.

" It is that weariness which springs
From all I meet or hear or see :
To me no pleasure beauty brings ;
Thine eyes have scarce a charm for me.

" It is that settled, ceaseless gloom
The fabled Hebrew wanderer bore
That will not look beyond the tombe
But cannot hope for rest before," etc. (BYRON.)

" What is the worst ?   Nay, do not ask,
In pity from the search forbear ;
Smile on—nor venture to unmask
Man's heart, and view the hell that's there."

Another picture, description of a storm in the Alps, which arrests my attention, attracts me as I open the book and pleases me much.

" And this is in the night—most glorious night !
Thou wert not sent for slumber ! let me be
A sharer in thy fierce and fair delight—
A portion of the tempest and of thee ! "

To me the thought is uncommonly near in such a night, to wish to be " a sharer in the delight, a portion of the tempest " [quoted in English], to fall, on a runaway horse, over the cliffs into the rushing of the Rhine-falls or something similar, a pleasure of this kind unfortunately one can only provide for oneself once in a lifetime. There lies something intoxicating in storms at night-time. Thy nights, " dearest," [sic], I hope you consider as " sent for slumber, not for writing " [sic]. I see with sorrow that I write English more unreadably even than I do German, once again, *leb wohl mein Herz*. To-morrow midday, I am invited to Frau von Brauchitch, probably in order to be cross-examined thoroughly about you and yours. I shall tell them as much as pleases me. *Je t'embrasse mille fois*, your own

B.

The correspondence of Bismarck continues from all parts of Europe, to which he was sent as representative of Prussia, and describes principally the picturesque events he sees amongst kings and courts, and the customs of different peoples. Of historical interest is his letter to his wife (now Countess of Bismarck), after the battle of Sedan :

VENDRESS, *September 3rd*, 1870.

MY DEAR HEART,—The day before yesterday before break of day I left my quarters here, return thither to-day, and have, in the meantime, witnessed the great battle of Sedan, on the 1st, on which we have made about 30,000 prisoners, and have thrown the remainder of the French army, which we have been chasing since Bar-le-Duc, into the fortress, where they had to surrender as prisoners of war with their Emperor. Yesterday morning early at five o'clock, after I had been negotiating up to one o'clock in the morning with Moltke and the French Generals about the capitulation to be completed, I was woke by General Reille, whom I know, in order to tell me that Napoleon wished to speak to me. I rode unwashed and unbreakfasted towards Sedan, found the Emperor in an open carriage with three adjutants and three on horseback by his side, stopping on the country road before Sedan. I got off, saluted him just as politely as in the Tuileries, and asked for his commands. He wished to see the King; I told him, in keeping with the truth, that H.M. had his quarters three miles away, at the place where I now write. Upon N.'s question, whither he should now direct himself, I offered him, as I did not know the neighbourhood, my quarters at Donchéry, a small place on the Maas close to Sedan; he accepted, and drove, accompanied by his six Frenchmen, by me, and by Carl, who had meanwhile ridden after me, through the lonely morning, towards our side. In front of the place he regretted it, owing to the possibly great crowds of people, and he asked me whether he could get down at a lonely workman's house on the wayside; I had it examined by Carl, who reported that it was poor and not clean. "*N'importe*," said N., and climbed with him up a broken-down narrow staircase. In a room of 10 feet square, with a table of pine and two rush-covered chairs, we sat for an hour; the others were downstairs. A mighty contrast to our last interview, '67, in the Tuileries. Our conversation was difficult, if I did not wish to touch on things, which must painfully affect the man thrown down by God's powerful hand. Through Carl I had sent to fetch officers from the town, and to beg Moltke to come. Then we sent one of them to reconnoitre, and discovered half a mile from there in Fresnois, a small château with a park. Thither I conducted him with an escort of the Life-Cuirassiers Regiment, which had meanwhile been brought up, and there we completed the capitulation with the French commanding General Wimpfen, by power of which, 40,000 to 60,000 Frenchmen, the exact numbers I do not yet know, with everything they have, became our prisoners. The day before and yesterday cost France 100,000 men and an Emperor. To-day early the latter departed with all his courtiers, horses, and carriages to Wilhelmshoehe, near Cassel.

It is a world-historical event, a victory for which we will thank God the Lord in humility, and which decides the war, even though we must still carry on the latter against Emperor-less France.

I must close. With sincere pleasure, I see from yours and Marie's letters that Herbert has arrived at yours. I spoke to Bill yesterday, as I already wired, and embraced him in the presence of H.M. from my horse, whilst he stood at attention in the ranks. He is very well and merry. Hans and Fritz Carl I saw, both Buelows at the 2 G. Dr.[1] well and bright. *Leb wohl mein Herz*, greet the children. Your

v. B.

FIELD-MARSHAL LOUIS VON BENEDEK
(1804–81)

Austrian General, who commanded the Austrian armies in 1866, when defeated by the Prussians at Sadowa. A victim of circumstances, he was forced against his will to undertake the leadership of the Austrian armies, and when disaster ensued, was overwhelmed with universal obloquy, and placed before a council of war, and retired in disgrace. The letter here given is a touching instance of a husband's appeal to his wife's clemency, who, siding with his accusers, had reproached him in her letters. Many people would not call this a love-letter, but they must remember that love, with life, contains many trials, and that real affection is that which bravely takes its share, not only of the sunshine but of the shadow. The solid gold of pure love can only be tested in the crucible of adversity, and the bitterest drop in the cup of the old Field-Marshal's sorrow, was to find his wife not on his side, when all the rest of the world was against him.

---

[1] G. Dr. ▬ Dragoon Guards.

Field-Marshal Benedek to his Wife, Julie

VIENNA, NEUSTADT, *August 4th*, 1866.

I just received your partly good, partly unjust letter of the 2nd.

You say, towards you I was always severe, yes, hard ! This I shall leave undiscussed, unanswered.

When all the world about you talks evil and accuses loud and openly everywhere, then the wife of Field-Marshal Benedek should mourn with quiet and dignity the misfortune which has fallen on Austria and her husband, she should weigh her words, in order that the evil tongues, the envious, and the enemies of her husband, and perhaps her own too, may not find an opportunity to interpret any violent expression of the wife of Field-Marshal Benedek in an evil sense.

Finally, and that is the chief thing, you know very well, and you ought to know it, that real, painful, deep, and permanent hurt has only come to me through you, and can only come through you. All the world, high and low, great and small, relations and strangers— in short, nothing in the world is capable to touch the inmost fibres of my heart and my mind, only you have that power over me.

Is it asking too much, if I beg you, if I demand, that you shall spare my heart and my mind ? Is it a necessity to you to blurt out every time or to put in writing what passes through your overheated little head ; what venom and vindictiveness and passion inspires you, or what malicious or stupid gossip of stupid and malicious people à la Reichel, etc., etc., has been put about ? Why do you not spare me such reflections, which my position and my misfortune cannot change. Be satisfied, dear Julie, that I bear in such a dignified manner what destiny and my submission as soldier and subject have forced me to accept. It surely does me more honour than if I were to say out loud what I think. The time will yet come which will justify me. And even if it did not come, it suffices me so far, that I have a clean sheet towards myself, towards my conscience, and towards my God. I have the keen desire, and know but one happiness, that is, to end my days with you, dear Julie, in peace and harmony. Whether I love you, whether I honour and respect you, my letters during the campaign must have proved, and really you ought to have known that a long time ago. If that does not suffice, if you feel the need to lacerate my wounded heart and mind, if you cannot treat my misfortune as sacred, then it is better that I remain away and bear it alone and end alone in no matter which corner of the world.

I say all this with an equable reason, with a clear mind, with a warm heart, and with great resignation ; there arises in me not a breath of passion, emotion, or vindictiveness. I am complete master of my nerves, and only, when I think of you, does my eye become dim and there is a pain at my heart. Since months I have been wonderfully well, only this morning early, when I went out for a ride, I slipped and fell on the polished stair and am still much shaken. Fortunately there were no broken bones. 'Twill soon be all right again.

It looks as if I shall have to await the end of the inquiry here in Neustadt. Perhaps they will call me to appear once more at the end of it, and after recapitulating the evidence of others, will again examine me, to which I shall again reply, that I wish to strike nobody in the face, and as my memory has suffered, cannot—will not speak or answer.

To-day writing is very difficult to me. I only answer you by return of post because I always like to defer to your wishes, even if I can only do so partly.

When, at some future date, railway travelling will be feasible for everybody in the usual way, I will give you a rendezvous in Bruck, if that suits you. That is my idea at the present. To Neustadt you cannot and shall not come. Furthermore, in a few days I shall know more about my own position. True, I am here for nothing at all, but you understand that for nothing in the world would I put a request to anybody. For Heaven's sake, what is this about your heart-spasms ? Keep in good health, my dear Julie, for only you can in this world give me pleasure, and make me very unhappy. I'm done up.

With very hearty kisses from your
                                                        Louis.

LÉON GAMBETTA

(1838–82)

When the French Empire fell, after the Franco-Prussian War, Gambetta, the extreme Republican, was an important factor in averting a bloody revolution. When MacMahon fell, in 1876, and with him the danger of a royalistic régime, Gambetta, as President of the Chamber of Deputies, became the mainstay of the Republic and the most powerful man in France. He is the representative of " La Révanche," of per-petual protestation against the German seizure of Alsace and Lorraine, with his historic phrase, " Pen-sons-y toujours, et n'en parlons jamais." His love-romance was that with Léonie Léon, a beautiful unknown, whom he had noticed listening to his speeches in the Strangers' Gallery of the French Chamber of Deputies, and with whom he eventually lived, in strictest seclusion, up to his sudden and dramatic death, subsequent to an accident with a pistol, which lent itself to the persistent rumours of his having been shot by her as the result of a discussion. His love-letters date through the ten years from 1872 to his death, as the secrecy of their liaison forced Gambetta to be frequently absent, and she had refused to marry him, in order not to hurt his career. He was carried off a few days before the date at which she had consented to become his official wife. Gambetta was practically a self-taught man, whose great strength lay in his fierce and overwhelming oratory, his uncom-promising patriotism, and personal courage, and the charm of his southern fire and handsome personality.

His letters do not show proof of great culture, are of
the declamatory type of the people's tribune, but
possess the real accents of unalterable and passionate
love.

November 22nd, 1876.

If I had the pen of Pope ?   I would write a little
poem on the lost-ear-ring, and I would take the opportunity to tell the most remote posterity, the mysteries
of our love.   But, alas ! I can repeat after the greatest
of our masters : I know not how to read nor to write,
and am only a stranger in the chorus of poets and artists.
It is really a pity, because I have seen and known sub-
limities ignored by other mortals, and one must go
back to the pre-historic ages, to find goddesses so
generous as to communicate themselves to men. The
good Homer sleeps an eternal sleep, and it is not our
adventures which will awaken him. Let us be contented to live our poem ; let us place our pride in
loving each other, and let us snap our fingers at posterity ; it will always know enough to envy us, without
being able to imitate us.

Friday evening, May 23rd, 1879,
written at the distance of a kiss.

DEAR LITTLE ADORED WOMAN,—Hast thou ever
penetrated to the bottom of my soul like to-day ?
and in spite of the most vivid impressions of our most
adorable encounters, have you the reminiscence of
a sweeter and more voluptuous day ? I am quite
sure that I have to-day possessed the full and entire
essence of your nature. I have lived in your life
and not in mine. I would lose with pleasure the
sentiment of my personality to pass into yours. The
dream is accomplished, the revelation is complete,
I respire in the azure which you inhabit, and it is
fitting to say again with the prophet-king, I feel as
if I were a god, and I am that, because the property,
the gift of the divinity, is Love. It is in you that I
lose myself for all eternity, and I have no further

desires beyond this, beyond this ineffable communion.
To thee, then, in thee and for thee.

PARIS, August 3rd, 1881.

CHÈRE FEMME ADORÉE,—Hast thou not felt, my
bien-aimée, that in speaking of these compensations
of an orator's life, I thought before all of the infallible
consolation of your love which fortune, become
hostile, would be powerless to tear from me. It was
the supreme cry of defiance which burst from my soul
towards you to affirm louder than ever that thou wert
the rest, the hope, the support of my whole life. No,
nothing can ever throw itself between us, I do not
say to separate us, but even to cause us to stumble.
Voilà, now long years during which I have gained
conscience and possession of myself, and in which
caprice, fantasy, have given way to the irrevocable,
to the unalterable religion of your heart.

The world might crumble around me ; as long as
there should remain to me a glimmer of reason, an
atom of force, I feel myself eternally bound to the
woman three times blessed who cherished me and
saved me from myself. I love thee with my head,
with my heart, and my senses, I love thee to infinity.
Till Friday, till always. I will send you a short word
from Tours, a flower from the garden of France
" Terra elicta," said Dante.

ALFRED DE MUSSET (1810–57) AND GEORGE SAND (1804–76)

When Alfred de Musset, one of France's great
lyrical poets, declared his love to George Sand, the
authoress—an expert in the passions of the heart—
in 1833, he was twenty-three and she was twenty-nine.
After she had been divorced from her husband Dude-
vant in 1831, he made her acquaintance by letter,
apropos of her novel *Lelia*, based on her life-story,
namely, that of a noble woman unequally yoked to

an irresponsive husband. The two authors conceived a passion for each other which culminated in the visit they paid together to Italy in 1834.

After Musset's death, his health undermined by intemperance, in his forty-seventh year, Madame Sand tells the story of their melancholy episode in *Elle et Lui*.

Although written about the same time as the youth-- ful love-letters of Victor Hugo to his fiancée, what an abyss there lies between those frank outpourings of an innocent heart, and these morbid confessions between an *enfant du siècle*, after excesses of sensuality, and a woman who studies human passions as a literary theme, while livening them with inimitable *esprit*!—But love ? Is this not the very travesty of Love masquerading in the rags of cast-off passions ?

Alfred de Musset to George Sand

1833.

MY DEAR GEORGE,—I have something stupid [*bête*] and ridiculous to tell you. I am foolishly writing you instead of having told you this, I do not know why, when returning from that walk. To-night I shall be annoyed at having done so. You will laugh in my face, will take me for a maker of phrases in all my rela- tions with you hitherto. You will show me the door and you will think I am lying. I am in love with you. I have been thus since the first day I called on you. I thought I should cure myself in seeing you quite simply as a friend. There are many things in your character which could cure me ; I have tried to convince myself of that as much as I could. But I pay too dearly for the moments I pass with you. I prefer to tell you and I have done well, because I shall suffer much less if I am cured by your showing me the door now. This night during which . . . [*Note.* —Madame Sand, who re-edited these letters herself for publication, crossed out with a pen the last two words, and cut out the line following with scissors.— ED.] I had decided to let you know that I was out

(1) GARIBALDI.   (2) ALFRED DE MUSSET.

of town, but I do not want to make a mystery of it nor have the appearance of quarrelling without a reason. Now George, you will say : " Another fellow, who is about to become a nuisance," as you say. If I am not quite the firstcomer for you, tell me, as you would have told me yesterday in speaking of somebody else, what I ought to do. But I beg of you, if you intend to say that you doubt the truth of what I am writing, then I had rather you did not answer me at all. I know how you think of me, and I have nothing to hope for in telling you this. I can only foresee losing a friend and the only agreeable hours I have passed for a month. But I know that you are kind, that you have loved, and I put my trust in you, not as a mistress, but as a frank and loyal comrade. George, I am an idiot to deprive myself of the pleasure of seeing you the short time you have still to spend in Paris, before your departure for Italy, where we would have spent such beautiful nights together, if I had the strength. But the truth is that I suffer, and that my strength is wanting.

ALFRED DE MUSSET.

Poor de Musset. He was born too late to be a romantic poet, and inherited nothing but disenchantment, disbelief, and disgust of his world and his fellowmen. " My cup is not large," he said, " but I drink in my cup." The pity was that he drank it to the dregs.

Musset's Letter to Sand

Whose fault is that ? [He had been reproaching himself for having two sides to his character, a frivolous and a serious one.] Mine ! Pity my sorry nature which has accustomed itself to live in a sealed coffin, and hate the people who have forced me to it. Here is a prison wall; you said yesterday, everything would break against it. Yes, George, here is a wall; you have only forgotten one thing, that there is a prisoner behind it.

That is my entire history, my past life, my future life. Much it would have helped me, towards happiness, if I had scrawled bad rhymes on the walls of my cell. A pretty calculation, a fine arrangement it would be, not to unburden oneself in the presence of the being who can understand you, in order to store one's sufferings in a sacred hoard and then to empty it in all the sewers, all the gutters, at six francs a copy. Pouah !

Pity me, do not despise me.   Since I have not been able to speak out to your face, I will die without having spoken.   If my name is inscribed in a corner of your heart, however faint, however faded be the impression, do not efface it.   I may dare embrace a filthy and dead-drunken trollop, but I dare not embrace my mother.

Love those who possess the art of loving.   I have only learnt how to suffer.   There are days when I could kill myself ; but I shed tears or burst into laughter instead, though not to-day, *par example*. Adieu, George ; I love you like a child.

The pity was that De Musset and Sand deceived themselves as to the value of lovers' oaths, and went on that unhappy journey to Italy together, from which De Musset returns a broken and disappointed man, though followed by a flood of self-accusing letters by George Sand.

George Sand replies to Musset

April 15–17th, 1834.

I was in a state of shocking anxiety, my dear angel, I did not receive any letter from Antonio [who was to have given her news of Musset's state of health].   I had been at Vicenza, on purpose to learn how you had passed this first night.   I only heard that you had passed through the town in the morning.   Thus the sole news I had about you were the two lines you wrote to me from Padua, and I did not know what to think.   Pagello [her and his Italian doctor] told

me that certainly, if you were ill, Antonio would
have written us; but I know that letters get lost or
remain six weeks on the way in this country. I was
in despair. At last I got your letter from Geneva.
Oh, how I thank you for it, my child! How kind
it is and how it cheered me up! Is it really true
that you are not ill, that you are strong, that you do
not suffer? I fear all the time that out of affection
you are exaggerating your good health. Oh, may
God give it you and preserve you, my *cher petit*. That
is as necessary for my life henceforth as your friendship.
Without the one or the other, I cannot hope for a
single good day for me.

Do not believe, do not believe, Alfred, that I could
be happy with the thought of having lost your heart.
That I have been your mistress or your mother, what
does it matter? That I have inspired you with
love or with friendship—that I have been happy or
unhappy with you, all that changes nothing in the
state of my mind, at present. I know that I love you
and that is all. [Here three lines are erased.] To
watch over you, to preserve you from all ill, from all
contrariety, to surround you with distractions and
pleasures, that is the need and the regret which
I feel since I have lost you. Why has so sweet a
task and one which I should have performed with
such joy become, little by little, so bitter, and then,
all at once, impossible? What fatality has changed
to poison the remedies that I proffered? How is it
that I, who would have offered up all my blood to give
you a night's rest and peace, have become for you a
torment, a scourge, a spectre? When these atrocious
memories besiege me (and at what hour do they leave
me in peace?), I almost go mad. I moisten my pillow
with tears. I hear your voice calling to me in the
silence of the night. Who will call me now? Who
will have need of my watching? How shall I use
up my strength that I had accumulated for you, and
that now turns against me? Oh, my child, my child!
How much do I not need your tenderness and your

pardon! Never ask me for mine, never say that you have done me wrong. How I do know? I don't remember anything, except that we have been very unhappy and that we have parted. But I know, I feel that we shall love each other all our lives from our heart, from our intelligence, that we shall endeavour, by a sacred affection [here a word is erased] to cure ourselves mutually from the ills we have suffered for each other.

Alas, no! it was not our fault. We obeyed our destiny, for our characters, more impulsive than others', prevented us from acquiescing in the life of ordinary lovers. But we were born to know and to love each other, be sure of that. Had it not been for thy youth and the weakness which thy tears caused me, one morning, we should have remained brother and sister. [She goes on to justify their liaison, in spite of everything and concludes as follows :] Thou art right, our embraces were an incest, but we did not know it. We threw ourselves innocently and sincerely into each other's arms. Well, then, have we had a single souvenir of these embraces which was not chaste and holy? Thou hast reproached me, on a day of fever and delirium, that I never made you feel the pleasures of love. I shed tears at that, and now I am well content that there has been something true in that speech. I am well content that these pleasures have been more austere, more veiled than those you will find elsewhere. At least you will not be reminded of me in the arms of other women. But when you are alone, when you feel the need to pray and to shed tears, you will think of your George, of your true comrade, of your sick-nurse, of your friend, of something better than that. For the sentiment which unites us is combined of so many things, that it can compare to none other. The world will never understand it at all. So much the better. We love each other, and we can snap our fingers at it.

[A description of her life at Venice follows, and of the artful little starling that Pagello had given her.]

Adieu, adieu, my dear little child. Write me very often, I beg of you. Oh that I knew you arrived in Paris safe and sound!

Remember that you have promised me to take care of yourself. Adieu, my Alfred, love your George. [And then, from pathos into bathos, she asks him to attend to numerous little errands for her, books and other small fribbles. The ensuing lines, following on immediately without any postscriptum after her poetic flight to the empyrean, from soul-turmoil into soul-peace, could only have been written by a woman, by a Frenchwoman, and by George Sand.] *Send me, I beg of you, twelve pairs of glacé gloves, six yellow and six of colour.* Send me, above all, the verses you have made. All, I have not a single one!

(After that, as the French say, "On peut tirer l'échelle": one can let down the curtain.)

GUY DE MAUPASSANT (1850–93) AND MARIE BASHKIRTSEFF (1860–84)

We have here the clash of two different civilisations, Maupassant, writer of brilliant and mordant short stories, representing the blasé Parisian, tired of the boulevard life that he has tasted to the dregs, and Marie Bashkirtseff, typical of the Slav character, full of primeval *morbidezza* and elemental passion, thinly veneered over by French art, music, and romantic literature. It tickles the fancy of this child of whim and genius to enter into an anonymous literary flirtation with the most celebrated novelist of the day, whose sparkling Gallic wit is seen at its best in these desultory passages of arms with an unknown, whom he guesses to be a woman.

Love, to both of these Bohemians, neither of whom took the other seriously, was a pastime, a theme to be philandered with, between four and six at the "five-o'clock," an agreeable *apéritif* to open the appetite, or a post-prandial *pousse-café* to pour oil upon the troubled waters of undisciplined emotions.

Neither of these abnormal beings knew love in any other sense, but the way they bandy it about and play battledore and shuttlecock with their *concetti* is inimitable fooling. However, the pupil of Flaubert takes care to throw cold water on the tentative notes of passion of the Russian *demi-vierge*. A shadow of tragedy and the sadness of unfulfilled longing lies in the fact that they never met.

It was no doubt for the best. What their fate might have been, we can see, *mutatis mutandis*, in what happened to George Sand and Alfred de Musset.

Marie opens the ball by writing to Maupassant anonymously, passing herself off as a pretty young Englishwoman.

Marie Bashkirtseff to Guy de Maupassant

MONSIEUR,—The perusal of your books affords me almost unalloyed happiness. As an ardent admirer of the realities of Nature, you love to surprise her grand poetic moods, and yet you move us to the core with those truly human touches, which we hail as our own, and love you for them, as we love ourselves. Empty words ? Well, let them go ; I mean most of what I say.

Of course, I needn't tell you how delighted I should be if I could put all this into highflown and impressive language, but really, at such short notice, it's beyond me. I am all the more sorry, for I know you to be big enough to deserve someone into whose ear you could pour the confessions of that beautiful soul of yours, assuming, for the sake of argument, that your soul is beautiful. If your soul be not beautiful and "you are not to be taken in by soft-soap," it would grieve me, more for you than for me, and besides, I should put you down as a potboiling hack, and let it go at that.

A whole year I have been on the point of writing to you, but—now and again, I considered that I exaggerated your importance and that it wasn't worth while.

Then suddenly, two days ago, I read in the *Gaulois* that someone had honoured you with a gracious epistle and you had inquired the address of this good person, in order to reply. That immediately aroused my jealousy; your literary merits dazzled me afresh; and here I be.

Now lay this to heart : you will never know who I am (I mean it, really), nor do I even hanker to get a glimpse of you, from a distance. Goodness knows, I might not like the looks of you. I only know that you are young and unmarried; that's enough to go on with, even when one is up in the clouds.

But you may as well know that I am young and charming, so that this sweet reflection may encourage you to answer me.

Methinks that if I were a man, I shouldn't care to have any truck, not even by letter, with an old slob of an Englishwoman, whatever might be thought by—.

Miss Hastings
(c/o the Madeleine Post Office.)

Maupassant replies from Cannes

Madame,—My letter assuredly will not be what you expect. I wish at the outset to thank you for your kindness to me and for your compliments. Now let us talk like reasonable people.

You ask to become my confidante ? By what right ? I do not know you at all. Why should I say to you— an unknown person, whose mind, inclinations, and so on, may not accord with my intellectual temper— what I would perhaps say verbally and familiarly to the women who are my friends ? Would that not be the act of an imbecile, of an inconstant friend ?

What charm can mysterious letters add to the intercourse ? Does not all the sweetness of affection between man and woman (I mean chaste affection) arise principally from the joy of meeting, of talking face to face, and of calling to mind, in writing to one's *amie*, the vision of her face outlined between one's eyes and the paper ?

How could one even put to paper those intimacies of one's inmost self and address them to a being whose physical shape, the colour of whose hair, her smile and look, one is not familiar with ?

And then in a second letter, probably piqued at her reproach in one of her letters at his having used a threadbare theme :

Yes, madame, a second letter ! It surprises me. I feel, perhaps, an undefined desire to utter impertinences. That is legitimate, since I do not know you ; and it is just as well that I do not. I write to you, because I am abominably bored.

You reproach me for having used a commonplace theme with regard to the old woman and the Prussians. But everything is a commonplace ; I do nothing else ; I hear nothing else ; all the ideas, all the phrases, all the discussions, all the creeds are worn out. Is it not a commonplace in the extreme, not to say childish, to write to an unknown person ?

In brief, at heart I am a simpleton. You understand me more or less. You know what you are about, and with whom you have to do ; you have been told this or that about me, good or bad ; it matters little. . . . Even if you have not met any of my relatives, who are numerous, you have read articles of mine in the papers—physical and intellectual portraits ; in short, you are doing it on purpose to pass the time. But I ? You may be, it is true, a young and charming woman whose hands I shall be happy one day to kiss. But you may also be an old housekeeper battening on the novels of Eugène Sue. You may be a young woman of literary attainments, as hard and dried up as a mattress. By the way, are you slender ? Only middling so, eh ? It would distress me to have a skinny correspondent. I have come to be very cautious about jumping in the dark.

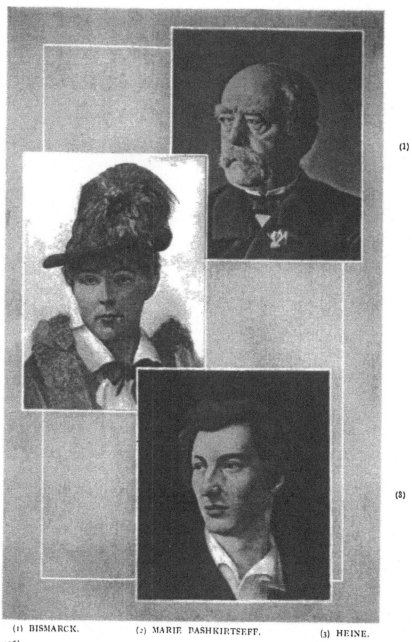

(1) BISMARCK.   (2) MARIE BASHKIRTSEFF.   (3) HEINE.

I have been caught in ridiculous traps. A young girls' boarding-school carried on a correspondence with me through the pen of an assistant mistress; my replies passed from hand to hand in the class. The trick was droll, and made me laugh when I heard of it—from the mistress herself.

Are you worldly? or sentimental? or merely romantic? or maybe only a bored woman seeking distraction? I, look you, am not the man you seek.

I have not a ha'porth of poetry in my composition. I take everything as it comes, and I pass two-thirds of my time in profound boredom.

The third-third I employ in writing words which I sell as expensively as I can, while deploring that I am obliged to ply this abominable trade, though it has brought me the honour of being distinguished—morally—by you. Here are confidences! What do you say to them, madame? You must find me very unceremonious. Forgive me.

In writing to you, I seem to be walking in subterranean gloom, afraid of pitfalls in front of my footsteps; and I strike my stick on the ground at hazard to feel if it is safe.

What scent do you use? Are you a gourmande? What is the shape of your ears? The colour of your eyes? A musician?

I do not want to know if you are married. If you are, you will reply " No "; if you are not, you will reply " Yes."

I kiss your hands, madame,

GUY DE MAUPASSANT.

Marie Bashkirtseff to Guy de Maupassant (in reply to his second letter)

You are bored to death! Oh, you horrid man! You say that to deprive me of the illusion as to the motive of your esteemed letter of the ——, which, by the way, arrived at a propitious moment, and delighted me.

Quite true, I'm having lots of fun. But it isn't true that I know you as well as you say I do. On my oath, I don't know whether you are fair or dark, fat or thin; whilst, as an individual, I only get a glimpse of you by the lines you devote to me, through the dust of much intentional malice and affectation.

However, for an authority of the Naturalistic school, you are no fool, and my reply would assume untold proportions were I not handicapped by overweening self-esteem. I must not let you run away with the idea that you captivate all my vital fluid.

First with your permission, let us dispose of our argument *re* the Commonplace. That will take up quite a while, for you bombard me with reasons, and no mistake. On the whole, I agree with you.

But the real function of art is to gild the commonplace, by making it perpetually fascinating, just as Nature does by her eternal sunlight, her hoary old earth, her men and women, all fashioned on the same plan, and animated by the same spirit; but—there are musicians whose range is limited to a few notes, and painters who only employ a few colours. Of course, you know this better than I do, and are merely trying to take a rise out of me. Why, certainly go ahead, I like it.

Commonplaces, we said, didn't we? the mother and the Prussians[1] in literature, and Joan of Arc in painting. Are you so sure that a shrewd fellow (un malin—that's the term, isn't it?) might not discover a new and touching aspect? As subject-matter for your weekly article, it evidently serves its purpose well enough, and so do my remarks. And those other commonplaces about the hardships of your profession. You take me for a shopkeeper who takes you for a poet and you wish to enlighten my ignorance. George Sand gloried in the fact that she wrote for money, and Flaubert, most laborious of men, made a fuss

[1] De Maupassant had written a good many short stories on the brutality of the Prussians to women during the Franco-Prussian war.

about the magnitude of his toil. Rubbish! one soon noticed when his work was laboured.

Balzac never grumbled at work; he was always enthusiastic about whatever he had in hand. As for Montesquieu, if I may make so bold, his passion for study was so intense that, if it was the source of his glory, so it was that of his happiness, as the assistant mistress of your fabulous girls'-school would have remarked.

Your claim to sell your wares at a good price is perfectly just, for there never has been any really lasting glory without gold. Thus spake the Jew Baahrou [Baruch ?—ED.], contemporary of Job (fragm. preserved by the learned Spitzbube, of Berlin).

Besides, everything is enhanced by an appropriate display, beauty, genius, and even faith. Did not the Lord deign to appear in person to His servant Moses to explain the ornaments of His ark, and instruct him to see that the cherubim on either side should be of gold and of *exquisite workmanship*. And now you are bored, are you, things leave you cold, and there isn't a ha'porth of poetry in your composition.

And you expect me to take that in ?

I can see you in my mind : too much little Mary, of course, inadequately protected by too short a waistcoat, of a nondescript hue, with the lowest button unfastened. Never mind, with all your faults, you have my sympathies. The only thing that I can't get over is how you can be bored. There are times when I, too, am in the dumps, downhearted, or in a temper, but bored—*jamais!*

You are not the man I am looking for !

The fact is, I'm not really on the look-out for men at all, monsieur ; in my opinion, to a woman who knows her own mind, they can only be a minor consideration, in any case.

Talk of withered old maids ! bad luck to them ! Here comes my housekeeper ! " Would you be kind enough to show me how this is done ? "

Well, now, it's high time to answer those questions

of yours without beating about the bush, for I should hate to take advantage of a simple-minded gentleman of genius who dozes after dinner over his cigar.

Am I slender ? Well, no, but neither am I stout. Worldly, sentimental, romantic. What meaning do you attach to those terms ? Methinks there ought to be room for one and all in the same person ; it all depends on the moment, the occasion, and the circumstances. I take things as they come, and am very prone to fall a prey to moral infections. For instance, my poetical feeling might evaporate because yours did. What scent do I use ? Virtue ! *vulgo—* none.

Yes, I am fond of food, or rather, I am fastidious. My ears are small, somewhat irregular in shape, but pretty. Yes, I am fond of music, but probably not so good a pianist as would be your assistant school-mistress.

Am I docile enough to suit you ? If you assent, undo another button, and think of me when the twilight falls. If not—I can't help it ; in any case, you've had all the change you are entitled to, out of your faked confessions.

Dare I ask, which are your favourite musicians and painters ? and supposing, after all, I turned out to be a man ?

[*Note.*—The letter was accompanied by a sketch, representing a rotund little man, asleep in an easy-chair under a palm-tree by the seashore ; a table by his side, upon which are a glass of beer and a cigar.]

Guy de Maupassant (in answer to Marie Bashkirtseff, No. 2)

April 3rd, 1884.

MADAME,—I have just spent a fortnight in Paris, and as I left in Cannes the cabalistic indications needed for my letters to reach you, I could not reply sooner.

And then, do you know, madame, you have quite frightened me. You quote, one on top of the other, without warning me, G. Sand, Flaubert, Balzac,

Montesquieu, the Jew Baahron, Job, the savant Spitzbube, of Berlin, and Moses.

Oh, now I know you, my pretty masquerader! You are a professor of the sixth form in the Louis-le-Grand Collège. I confess that I rather suspected it, your paper having a vague odour of snuff. Then I am going to cease to be gallant (was I so?), and I am going to treat you as of the University, that is, as an enemy. Ah, cunning old man, old usher, old mugger-up of Latin, you tried to pass yourself off for a pretty woman, did you? And you sent me your essay, a manuscript dealing with Art and Nature, to recommend it to some magazine, and to praise it in some article.

What luck that I did not give you notice of my visit to Paris! I should have seen you come in, one morning—a shabby old man who would have put his hat on the floor in order to pull out of his pocket a roll of paper tied up with string. And he would have said, " Monsieur, I am the lady who . . ."

Ah, well, sir Professor, I am nevertheless going to answer some of your questions. I begin by thanking you for the pleasant details that you give me of your physique and your tastes. I thank you equally for the portrait that you have drawn of myself. It is some likeness, God wot! I notice some errors, however.

1. Less paunch. 2. I never smoke. 3. I neither drink beer, nor wine, nor spirits. Nothing but water.

Then the beatitude before the " bock "[1] is not exactly my favourite posture. I more often squat in Eastern fashion on a divan. You ask me who is my painter? Among the moderns, Millet. My musicians? I have a horror of music.

In truth, I prefer a pretty woman to all the arts. I put a good dinner, a real dinner, the rare dinner, almost in the same rank with a pretty woman. There is my profession of faith, my dear old professor. I think that when one has a good passion, a capital

---

[1] A " bock " is a glass of beer.—ED.

passion, one must give it full swing, must sacrifice all the others to it. That is what I do. I had two passions. It was necessary to sacrifice one—I have to some extent sacrificed gluttony. I have become as sober as a camel, but dainty in no longer knowing what to eat.

Do you want yet another detail? I have a passion for violent exercise. I have won big stakes as a rower, a swimmer, and a walker. Now that I have unburdened myself of all these confessions, Sir Usher, tell me of yourself, of your wife, since you are married, of your children. Have you a daughter? If so, remember me, I beseech you.

I pray the divine Homer to call down upon you, from the God whom you adore, all the blessings of the earth.

Guy de Maupassant.

Marie Bashkirtseff to Guy de Maupassant

Unhappy Follower of Zola,—This is delightful. If the Heavens were just, you would think so too. It seems to me not only very amusing, but susceptible of more refined enjoyment leading to really valuable results, provided we were frankly sincere.

For indeed, where is the friend, man or woman, to whom one can speak without reserve? There is always something to hold back, whilst with people in the abstract . . . not to belong to any country, to any world, but simply to be true. One would reach the grandeur of expression of Shakespeare . . .

But a truce to playing the fool. Now that you have found me out, I will no longer hide anything from you. Yes, sir, I have the honour to be a schoolmaster, as you say; and I am going to prove it by eight pages of admonitions. Too cunning to bring you MSS. with unmistakable string, I will rub in my exhortations in graduated doses.

I have profited, sir, by the leisure of Holy Week to re-read your complete works. Undeniably you are hot stuff. I had never read you before *en bloc*, without a break. My impression is therefore still fresh, and that impression. . . . It is enough to debauch all my pupils and to play old Harry in all the convents of Christendom.

Even yours truly, who is not by way of being bashful, is dumbfounded—yes, sir, dumbfounded—by this all-engrossing absorption of yours upon the sentiment which M. Alexandre Dumas fils calls Love. It will develop into an obsession, and that would be regrettable, for you are richly gifted, and your peasant tales are well drawn. I know that you have done *Une Vie*, and that this book is permeated with many expressions of disgust, sadness, and discouragement. This attitude which induces one to forgive you for the other part, is evident, now and then, in your work and leads people to believe that you are a superior person who suffers from life. It is this that cuts me to the heart. But your lamentation is, I fear, only an echo of Flaubert.

The fact is that we are simple-minded fools, and you are a proper humbug [*farceur*] (you see the advantage of not being acquainted) with your solitude and creatures with long hair. Love, what a word it is to keep the whole world spellbound ! Oh, la ! la ! Gil Blas, where art thou ? It was after perusing one of your articles, that I read the *Attaque du Moulin*. It seems like entering a magnificent and fragrant forest where the birds sang. "Never did so large a peace fall upon a happier spot." This masterly phrase recalls a few famous phrases in the last act of the *Africaine*. But you abhor music. Is it credible ? You have been led astray by the music of the schools. Fortunately your book is not yet written, the book in which there will be a woman—yes, sir, an individual —and no strenuous exercises. To be first in a race, only makes you equal to a horse, which, however noble as an animal, is still an animal, young man. Permit an old Latinist to invite you to con the passage in which Sallust says, " omnes homines, qui sese student, prestari," etc. I shall set it to my daughter Anastasia to prepare as well. But there is no knowing, perhaps you will reform. The Table; Women! Oh, my young friend, do take care. That is the road to dubious talk, and my profession of schoolmaster forbids me to follow you upon such dangerous ground.

No music, no tobacco? Deuce and all! Millet is first-rate, but you cite Millet as the ignoramus would cite Rafael. Let me advise you to cast a glance at a young modern called Bastien-Lepage. Go to the Rue de Sèze.

What age are you really? Do you seriously pretend that you prefer pretty women to all the arts? You are chaffing me.

Forgive the incoherence of this thing of shreds and patches, and do not leave me long without a letter.

And now, great woman-eater, I wish you—and remain, in holy terror,

Your obedient servant,
SAVANTIN, JOSEPH.

Marie Bashkirtseff to Guy de Maupassant
Disenchantment

We quote this letter as a fitting conclusion to the battle of wits between two such brilliant but capricious people. Perhaps it may serve as a warning to other young girls of eighteen so prone to put their heroes on a pedestal, in spite of their feet of clay. Then, like to poor Marie Bashkirtseff, there comes the inevitable disenchantment! " The world is all hollow, my doll is stuffed full of bran and I want to go in a convent."

Now I am going to tell you something incredible, something you will never believe. It has no further significance, excepting as a record of what is past. I am getting as sick of the whole business as you are.

Your third.letter gave me the chills. We've overdone it!

Besides, I only want what I can't get. That ought to increase my eagerness in your direction, oughtn't it? Why did I write you? One awakens on a fine morning, and discovers that one is an exceptional being surrounded by idiots. One breaks one's heart over the waste of so many pearls on so many swine. Supposing I were to write to a great man, capable of understanding me? How charmingly romantic that would be, and who knows? After a certain number of letters, you might secure a friend under unusual circumstances; one puts the question: Who shall it be? and the choice falls on you.

A correspondence such as ours is only possible under two conditions.

The second is boundless admiration on the part of the incognita. And from this boundless admiration rises a current of sympathy, impelling her to confessions which cannot fail to touch and interest the great man.

None of these things has to come to pass. I chose you, hoping that the boundless admiration would gradually grow, for I was not far wrong in giving you credit for retaining, comparatively, much of your youthful spirit. So I sat down and working myself up in imagination, wrote those letters. And so it has come about that I have said things which were not polite and even rude, assuming that you have taken the trouble to notice them.

Seeing we have got so far, as you say, I may as well admit that your shameful letter upset me for the day. I am as annoyed as if you had really insulted me, which is absurd.

Goodbye, and thank you.

If you are still in possession of my autographs, please return them; as for yours, I disposed of them to America for a crazy price.

FRIEDRICH NIETZSCHE

(1844–1900)

Nietzsche, the superman, never had much inclination for the fair sex, too much engrossed as he was in himself and his nervous condition, which eventually led him to the madhouse. In his wandering life, he happened to meet with a pretty Dutch girl in Geneva, to whom he made an offer of marriage, after having made her acquaintance on a walk. Of course, she rejected him, without his being very much affected by her refusal, as, fundamentally he was opposed to marriage.

Friedrich Nietzsche to a young Dutch girl

GENEVA, *April 11th,* 1876.

MEIN FRAEULEIN,—You are writing this evening something for me; I will also write something for you. Summon all the courage of your heart, so as not to start back at the question, which I herewith address to you. "Will you be my wife?" I love you, and it seems to me that you already belong to me. Not a word about the suddenness of my inclination! At least there is no discredit attached to it; there is therefore nothing that needs excusing. But what I should like to know, is, whether you feel the same as I do—that we have not really been strangers to each other, not for a moment! Do you not also believe that in a union each of us will be freer and better than he would be singly, therefore excelsior? Will you risk it, to go with me together, as with one who longs very heartily for liberation and amelioration? Thus on all the paths of life and thought? Now, be frank and hold nothing back. About this letter and my proposal, nobody knows but our mutual friend, Herr v.S. I return to-morrow at eleven o'clock by the express to Basel. I have to go back; my address in Basel I enclose. If you can say "Yes!" to my question, I will immediately write to your Frau mother, for whose address I would then ask you. If you have the heart to make a quick decision, with "Yes," or "No"—a written word from you will find me till to-morrow at ten o'clock Hôtel Garni de la Poste. Wishing you everything of the best and blessedness for all time,

FRIEDRICH NIETZSCHE.

MULTATULI (EDUARD DOUWES DEKKER)
(1820–87)

The pseudonym of Multatuli ("Much I have borne") is practically unknown to English readers, and yet the author, Eduard Douwes Dekker, a Dutchman, wrote an epoch-making book *Havelear*, in language which burns with indignation, on the merciless rapacity of the Dutch colonial system and the unworthy treatment of the natives by the Dutch Government in Java. The following letter shows the author's independence and moral courage in broaching the subject of sexual enlightenment before marriage with his future wife. Even now a battle-royal is going on between educationists as to what information on sexual subjects should be given to the young, and at what age, if at all, it should begin. And who is to give the information—father, mother, schoolmaster, or doctor ? Dekker takes the bull by the horns, and discusses with his bride frankly their sexual relationship after marriage.

Multatuli (Eduard Douwes Dekker) to his Bride, Eva

PURWAKARTA, *Friday, October 24th,* 1845.

. . . But what I had to say about our "future" is not yet said entirely. You know what we call future : our children. Why should it not be permitted to speak about them ? May I not say to you, you who will become the mother of my children, that I hope for them and ask for them ? One avoids this generally, one does not speak as a rule to a girl on this chapter, and from a feeling (in my opinion) of false shame puts on one side as something indecent the supremest, most delicious part. Even if it were not suitable for other girls, my girl will forgive me if I speak to her as a woman, not as a child. Is that not so, my Everdine?

May we not have confidence in each other, we who have *one* goal, *one* interest, one future. In general, in my opinion there are certain things which are too closely veiled. One is right to keep children's imaginations pure, but this purity is not maintained by ignorance. I rather think that the concealment of anything from boys and girls leads them all the more to suspect the truth. They pry for things out of curiosity, which would if communicated to us simply, without any to-do, provoke little or no interest. If one could preserve this ignorance intact, I might be inclined to tolerate it, but that is impossible; the child comes into contact with other children, it comes across books, which make it perplexed; it is just that attitude of secrecy adopted by the parents towards matters that, in spite of them, are unwittingly understood, which augments the desire to know more; this desire, only satisfied in part, secretly inflames the heart and vitiates the imagination; the child has already sinned, while the parents still believe that it does not know what sin is!

Now you will realise what a high estimate I place upon your character in treating you as a woman. Would I not carefully avoid touching on such subjects with any other girl? I know that you will be startled, so to speak, at the subject, and that you will be astonished at my audacity. There must be nothing between us, no custom, no law, no shame; we must be free to tell each other everything. Not in every engagement would I approve of this, but, so God wills, you will be my wife soon, and I do not wish to realise that my wife was still a child the day before we were made one.

The marriage relation is a serious and elevated one,

and not subject to rules of propriety fortuitously
laid down. Do not think, however, that I despise
the proprieties themselves. I am only referring to
the conventional rules. I do not consider myself
indelicate, and am indeed more punctilious in many
ways than others. You may not believe it, but I do
not like to kiss before company. And further, that
when married, I should like my wife to have her
separate bedroom, into which she would not admit
me without knocking, and so forth. That would be
affectation, you think, and I too would distrust my
impulse, if I had been taught to behave like that.
However, that is not the case ; it is my instinct of
propriety which dictates this, and that is why I lay
stress on it. True, I cannot lay claim to being entirely
du monde, but what I do know of decent behaviour,
I believe, I have never been taught, for everything, I
consider, should come naturally. Write me frankly,
dearest, what you thought, when reading the last
page. All my correspondence aims at the one goal,
that we should become well acquainted with each other;
you can help me by not hiding behind that young
lady's fan of yours, when I speak to you on subjects
which nobody, at least no young man, has ever dis-
cussed with you. Consider, that nobody is as near
to you as I am. I look upon myself as your nearest ;
you are closer to me than brother or sister, nearer
than my mother. That we are not yet married is
a social and civic convention, but our relations are
already those of marriage. I know very well that a
girl should be reserved—it is so—too great a familiarity
in your speech might compromise you, in case the
affair were to be broken off, in case circumstances
prevented us from becoming man and wife, in case
I were treacherous enough to reward your love and
intimacy with ingratitude, and not to love you
any more. Just imagine, if I, who am young and
inclined towards love-affairs, did not love you, but
only looked for a few months' amusement in your
love. For such things do happen. Then you

would be unhappy, if you had confided in me too much.

And that is why I ask you to confide in me entirely. Hazard your peace, your future, on one throw, and say to yourself, " I should never trust another man, if *he* were to prove false."

Oh, your letters show that you love me; I should like to kiss the dear sentences in which you pour out the effusions of your loving heart. Don't you know that you are acting imprudently to lay bare your love so completely to an individual of whom you know nothing, except what it pleases him to tell you ? Have you enough knowledge of mankind, my little Eva, to be able to distinguish without fail sincerity from falsehood ? Are you not risking too much ? . . . Ah, but that is why I love you so much . . .

BJOERNSTJERNE BJOERNSON

(1832–1910)

Norwegian poet, dramatist, and novelist, Bjoernson was director of the theatre at Bergen in 1857-9, and has also had great influence on Norway's political development through his democratic eloquence. He belongs by the simplicity of his diction and the ruthless truth of dramas to the school of Ibsen. A muchly travelled man, he writes to his wife, Karoline, in the following letter from Dresden.

DRESDEN, *November 17th*, 1862, 8 *o'clock evening.*

MY DEAR KAROLINE,—I just come out of the theatre, where I could not stand more than two acts—they performed a drama, which the celebrated universal traveller Friedr. Gerstaecker has written. A young inn-proprietor is in love with the daughter of the gamekeeper, but cannot give up poaching, although he knows that he risks going to prison for it some day, and that he will lose her for ever. She believes in him and his innocence, and just as she has told him that and he has kissed her, he goes into the forest, poaches, and is caught, and then he kills the man who is about to arrest him.

Then I went home; after these happenings I had no further inclination to see his beloved again. But is it not abominable? . . . And I longed for you, and asked myself, Have I always been as faithful to her, in thoughts and deeds, as I should? Always? That I have not been, and thus something of that which I considered abominable in the man referred to applies to me too, even though I have committed no murder. But then again I said to myself: It is true I am easily kindled, but untrue I have never yet been. She is not only the first to me among many, she is also my only one. And even though this has not always been so, it has become so now. And never have I loved her as I do now; for now I know who she is, and particularly, what she is to me. I am changeable, I permit myself to be carried away, but not away from her, not away from her love; I can never love another beside her, God is my judge. So help me then, Almighty God, that I do not bring shame to her fidelity and my own resolves. You, who wipe out our sins, make me strong and create another man in me, and give me the happiness of a good conscience, which lightens the load of life to us; it is a necessity for me to be conscious of my power—I have much to accomplish. But here lies the root of my strength; if I am struck at this root, then I am in any case done for! For the sake of Jesus, listen to my prayer! . . .

Are you reading anything? I suppose you are busily occupied with Christmas preparations. You really should take the time to read something, and had better buy, what one can get for money—for no other person and no other thing can do your reading for you, anyhow. A woman does not need much; but a certain measure of intellectual material, taking her thoughts somewhat outside of her four walls, she really does need, and that you should acquire.

And then you must go to church. I realise from your inordinate praise of Maren that I ought to give her some kind of a Christmas present. Well, it will be hard, all this present-business, for me, poor tramping traveller, but I suppose I must bite in the sour apple. [i.e. take my medicine]. But you mustn't ask your relatives in Bergen for money, do you understand, and, if you get anything from my mother, you must inform me at once. . . . I hope that my letter may reach you in good time, and cheer you up mightily, you dear, dear, dear! Kiss the boy, and let him give you a kiss for me; kind regards to your relatives and friends from your

BJOERNSTJERNE.

HENRIK IBSEN

(1828–1906)

The genius of Ibsen, the greatest realistic playwright of our time, is too well known to need any exhaustive analysis here. But in the loneliness of the great solitary there shines a gleam of romance when he meets the young Viennese girl Emilie Bardach, one summer in Gossensass, and incorporates her as Hilde Wangel in *Solness*. But he is sixty-one years old, and he realises that she is not for him. Youth vindicates its claim to youth, as that other great dramatist, Molière, found to his cost.

Ibsen to Emilie Bardach

MUNICH, *December 6th*, 1889.

Two dear, dear letters I have received from you and have not answered until now. What must you think of me? But I cannot yet find the needful quiet, in order to write you something substantial and elaborate. This evening I have to go to the theatre, to be present at a performance of *The Enemy of the People*. It is really painful to me, only to think of it—for the present, then, I must waive my desire for your photograph. But it is better thus, better to wait, than not to get a satisfactory picture. And besides—how lively your charming, reverential appearance is still limned in my memory ! For I still believe in a mysterious princess, who is behind it all. But the riddle itself ?—Why, yes—one may dream all sorts of things about it, and imbue it with poetic beauty ; and I do that of course. That surely is a sort of compensation for the unobtainable and—unfathomable reality. In my fancy I always see you adorned with pearls. For I know you are very fond of pearls. There lies something deeper—something hidden in this inclination. But what is it really ? I often puzzle my head about it. And believe too, now and then, that I have found, discovered the hang of it. And then again, I have my doubts. Some of your questions I will perhaps try to answer next time. But I have myself to ask so many questions with regard to you. And I do it too—in my mind—ceaselessly.

Your devoted,

H. I.

COUNT LEO TOLSTOI

(1828–1910)

It has been a common Russian characteristic for men midway in a successful career to turn aside from it altogether, and seek consolation in the things which are not of this world. At the time he wrote the letters quoted to his wife, Tolstoi had turned to the management of his estate, which eventually brought out his socialistic tendencies, when in 1895 he voluntarily renounced his property in copyright, land, and money, though he was prevailed upon to make over his estate to his wife. But they are in continual conflict. He loves his wife and hates her because she refuses to associate herself with his apostolic abnegations, because of his conscientious conflicts on her behalf. It is doubtful if Tolstoi had much feeling for women ; he certainly was an iconoclast with regard to the marriage institution, as we see in *The Kreutzer Sonata*. In fact, the essence of his life is a magnificent intolerance and want of philosophic sanity in which he lived, not in the world, but in spite of the world.

October, 1881.

. . . I have something very difficult in view : I propose to occupy myself with running the estate, i.e. not really the business of it, but wish to associate with the people in the house. It is difficult not to allow oneself to be carried away and not to sacrifice one's relations with individuals to work ; but one must do that, if one wishes to run an estate. Every time the question crops up, what is one to prefer, personal advantages or one's relation to other people ? —one should choose the latter. I am so bad, that I feel my incapacity for doing this. But it has so happened that the necessity arises, so I cannot but try it. To-day I have been looking after the business end and then went out for a ride. The dogs are very attached to me. Agafa Michailowna said, without a lead, they would chase the animals, and sent Waska along. I wanted to test my passion for the chase, riding and stalking game according to my forty years' training—all very well. But when I had unearthed a hare, I wished him good luck. The most of the time I was ashamed of myself. . . . I cannot help it, my heart's love ; do not be angry, but I can attach no importance to these monetary affairs. Surely they are not important events, as for instance, sickness, marriage, birth, death, acquired knowledge, good or bad actions, pleasant or unpleasant habits of those dear and near to us, but they are our forms, arrangements, which we have arranged thus, but could have arranged in a thousand different ways. I know that what I am here saying is often unbearably tiresome to you and to the children (I believe that this is sufficiently well known), but I must always repeat, that all our happiness or unhappiness does not depend one's hair's breadth, whether we make money or spend it, but only on this, what we are ourselves. Let Kostja inherit a million—will he become thereby happier ? So that the matter may not become trivial, one must really look at life somewhat more freely and with less prejudice. As both of our lives are carried on with their grief and their joys, so in reality it will be with the lives of our children ; therefore we must help them to acquire that which has made us happy, and to deliver themselves from that which brought us misfortune. Languages, diplomas, the world, but in particular, money, have had no part in our happiness and unhappiness. Therefore the question as to how much we spend cannot interest me ; if one attaches particular importance to it, it pushes the chief thing out of sight.

GIOVANNI SEGANTINI

(1858–99)

An Italian painter, passionate lover of nature and a mystic, Segantini developed an individual style in technique based on the juxtaposition of colours for purity of effect. We choose this delightful little word-painting, tinged with melancholy, to indicate the charm of his feeling.

Giovanni Segantini to his Wife

1890.

DEAREST BICE,—Take, O dearest, these unpretentious flowers, these violets, as a symbol of the greatest love. I picked them solely with thoughts of you. If ever there should come a spring when I do not offer you such a gift, then I shall be no longer on this earth.

Then you will pick every spring these my beloved flowers and will proceed thither, where in the peace of the grave I shall await the familiar rustle of your dress, and you will cover the grave with these flowers.

The sparrows will twitter their accompanying song of love, which never dies, and I shall follow the song in my slumber as long as a trace of an atom of myself shall remain on this earth, and you will then think of him who brought you every year the first flowers.

BIBLIOGRAPHY

(*Editor's Note.*—For those readers whose zest for further love-letters has been stimulated by the present selection, I append a bibliography of works to be consulted. There are no representative collections in English of love-letters from all countries. Hence arose the present work, many of the letters herein appearing being translated into English for the first time. I give a short list of other existing selections, which have been occasionally referred to, although, wherever feasible, the copies and translations have been made directly from the originals.

A large number of the "correspondences" referred to, may be found by the polyglot reader at Mudie's, both in the original as well as in translations, which should never be consulted, excepting by those who are not conversant with foreign languages, as, especially in these unstudied outpourings of the heart, much of the charm and meaning is lost in translations: Traddutore—Tradditore, translator —traitor. But personally, I have enjoyed the invaluable assistance of the vast store of reference works at the London Library, to both of whose librarians, Dr. Wright and Mr. Cox, I herewith wish to express my thanks and gratitude for allowing me to draw on their unequalled fund of knowledge and individual information.

GENERAL SELECTIONS OF LOVE-LETTERS (WORKS ON)

ENGLISH

Epistles, Elegant, Familiar, and Instructive. Selected from the best writers. (London, 1791)

J. T. Merydew: Love-letters of Famous Men and Women.

FRENCH

Annie de Pène: Les plus jolies lettres d'amour.

Crépet, Eugène: Le trésor épistolaire de la France.

GERMAN

Steinhausen, George: Geschichte des Deutschen Briefes.

Zeitler, Julius: Deutsche Liebesbriefe aus acht Jahrhunderten.

ITALIAN

See individual letters.

LIST OF WORKS TO CONSULT

Alfieri, Vittorio: Own Memoirs. (English translation, 1810.)

Balzac, Honoré de: Letters: Balzac et ses amies, G. Ferry.

Barri, Countess du: Original letters: Mémoires, Madame Dubarry.

Bashkirtseff, Marie: Correspondance avec Guy de Maupassant.

Benedek, Field-Marshal Ludwig von: Nachgelassene Papiere.

Barrett-Browning, Elizabeth: Robert Browning and Elizabeth Barrett; Letters.

Bismarck, Fuerst Otto von: Briefe an seine Braut und Gattin (Cotta.)

Bjoernson, Bjoernsterne: Letters, published by Halvdan Koht; Georg Brandes, Bjoernson og Ibsen.

Beethoven, Ludwig von: Briefe.

Béranger, Pierre de: Les plus jolies lettres d'amour, A. de Pène.

Bluecher, Feldmarschall, Gebhardt Leberecht von: Briefe an seine Frau.

Bonaparte, Lucien: Mémoires.

Browning, Robert. See Barrett.

Brummell, Beau: Love-letters of Famous Men and Women, J. T. Merydew.

Burns, Robert: Correspondence.

Byron, Lord: Works, Letters, and Journals, R. E. Prothero.

Carlyle, Thomas, and Jane Welsh, Love-letters.

Carpenter, Charlotte. See Sir Walter Scott.

Catherine the Great of Russia: Les plus jolies lettres d'amour, A. de Pène.

Chateaubriand, Vicomte René de: Correspondance.

Congreve, William: Love-letters of Famous Men and Women, J. T. Meridew.

Constant, Benjamin: Lettres à Madame Récamier.

Du Deffand, Marquise: Lettres à Horace Walpole.

Desmoulins, Camille, et Lucile Desmoulins, par J. Claretie.

Dickens, Charles: Letters.

Diderot, Denis: Lettres à Sophie Voland.

Doenniges, Helene von. See Lassalle.

Dubarry, Countess. See Barri, Countess du.

Fitzherbert, Mrs. See George IV.

Flaubert, Gustave: Correspondence.

Foscolo, Ugo: Epistolario raccolto. (Orlandini e Mayer, Florence.)

Gambetta, Léon: Le cœur de Gambetta, Francis Laur.

Garibaldi, Giuseppe: Epistolario di Giuseppe Garibaldi (Milan).

George IV: Love-letters of Famous Men and Women, J. T. Merydew.

Goethe, Johann Wolfgang von: Briefe aus der ersten und der zweiten Haelfte seines Lebens (Duesseldorf); Briefe an Charlotte von Stein.

Gottsched. See Kulmus.

Hazlitt, William. See J. T. Merydew (as above).

Heine, Heinrich: Briefe, Hans Deffis.

Hogg, James. *See* Merydew.

Hood, Thomas. *See* Merydew.

Howard, Mrs. *See* Merydew.

Hugo, Victor, intime par Mme. Lesclide.

Hunt, Leigh, *See* Merydew.

Ibsen, Henrik: Seine Briefe an eine Freundin, and Georg Brandes, Bjoernson og Ibsen.

Johnson, Samuel: Letters; also Mrs. Piozzi's Anecdotes of Johnson.

Joséphine, Empress. (*See* Napoleon, Lettres à Joséphine.)

Kulmus, Luise Adelgunde Victorie: Gottsched, geb. Kulmus, Briefe.

Keats, John: Letters, edited by Buxton Forman.

Kleist, Heinrich von: Briefe an seine Braut.

Lassalle, Ferdinand: Tagebuch von Paul Lindau.

Lenau, Nicolas, und Sophie Loewenthal, by L. A. Frankl.

L'Enclos, Ninon de: A. de Pène (as above).

L'Espinasse, Mlle. de: Lettres inédites.

Lessing, Gotthold Ephraim: Briefwechsel mit Eva Koenig.

Ludwig I of Bavaria: A. de Pène (as above).

Luise, Koenigin von Preussen; 25 auserwaehlte Briefe.

Maupassant, Guy de. *See* Bashkirtseff.

Marlborough, Duke of: Merydew (as above).

Metternich, Prince de: Lettres à la Comtesse de Lieven.

Miller, Hugh: Merydew (as above).

Mirabeau, Count Gabriel de: Lettres d'amour à Sophie.

Moltke, Feldmarschall Helmuth von: Graf Helmuth von Moltke, Briefe an seine Braut und Frau.

Montagu, Lady Mary Wortley: Merydew (as above).

Montez, Lola. *See* Ludwig I of Bavaria.

Mozart, Wolfgang Amadeus: Briefe.

Multatuli (Eduard Douwes Dekker): Briefe.

Musset, Alfred de. *See* George Sand.

Napoleon I: Lettres à Joséphine, lettres inédites par F. Décori.

Napoleon II. *See* Reichstadt, Duc de.

Napoleon III. *See* A. de Pène (as above).

Nelson, Horatio, Lord; Letters to Lady Hamilton.

Nietzsche, Friedrich, von E. Foerster-Nietzsche.

Peterborough, Lord. Merydew (as above).

Pestalozzi, Johann Heinrich, und Anna Schultess. (Pestalozzis sämtliche Werke).

Pope, Alexander: Epistles, Elegant, Familiar, and Instructive. (1791.)

Pueckler-Muskau, Hermann Fuerst von: Aus Schriften und Briefen.

Puschkin, Alexander: Biography with letters, edited by Mozosow.

Récamier, Madame: Souvenirs et correspondance.

Reichstadt, Duc de: A. de Pène (as above).

Roland, Madame: Lettres.

Rousseau, Jean Jacques: Lettres.

Sand, George : George Sand et Alfred de Musset, Correspondance par F. Décori).

Schiller, Fr. von : Friedrich und Lotte, ein Brief Wechsel.

Schumann, Robert : Dichtungen und Briefe (der junge Schumann).

Scott, Sir Walter : Merydew (as above).

Segantini, Giovanni : Lettres.

Shelley, Percy Bysshe : Essays and Letters.

Southey, Robert : Merydew (as above).

Staël, Madame de, et Benjamin Constant.

Steele, Richard : Epistles Elegant (as above).

Stein, Frau von. *See* Goethe.

Stendhal (Marie Henri Boyle) : Lettres.

Sterne, Laurence : Epistles Elegant (as above).

Swift, Jonathan : Epistles Elegant (as above).

Tolstoi, Count Leo : Letters.

Voltaire, François Marie Arouet de : Lettres.

Wagner, Richard : an Mathilde Wesendonk ; Briefe.

Walpole, Horace : Merydew (as above).

Weber, Carl Maria von : Reise-Briefe an seine Gattin Caroline.

Welsh, Jane. *See* Carlyle.

INDEX

Printed in Great Britain by Hazell, Watson & Viney, Ld.,
London and Aylesbury.

Printed in October 2021
by Rotomail Italia S.p.A., Vignate (MI) - Italy